W9-CJB-421

Dear Mr. President

ABOVE: *Rough Rider and man of action, Teddy Roosevelt takes time out to read a letter.*
FOLLOWING PAGES: *His desk piled high, Franklin Roosevelt shows his mother, Sarah, some of his correspondence.*

Dear Mr. President

Letters to the Oval Office from the Files of the National Archives

Introduction by Brian Williams
Text by Dwight Young

Washington, D.C.

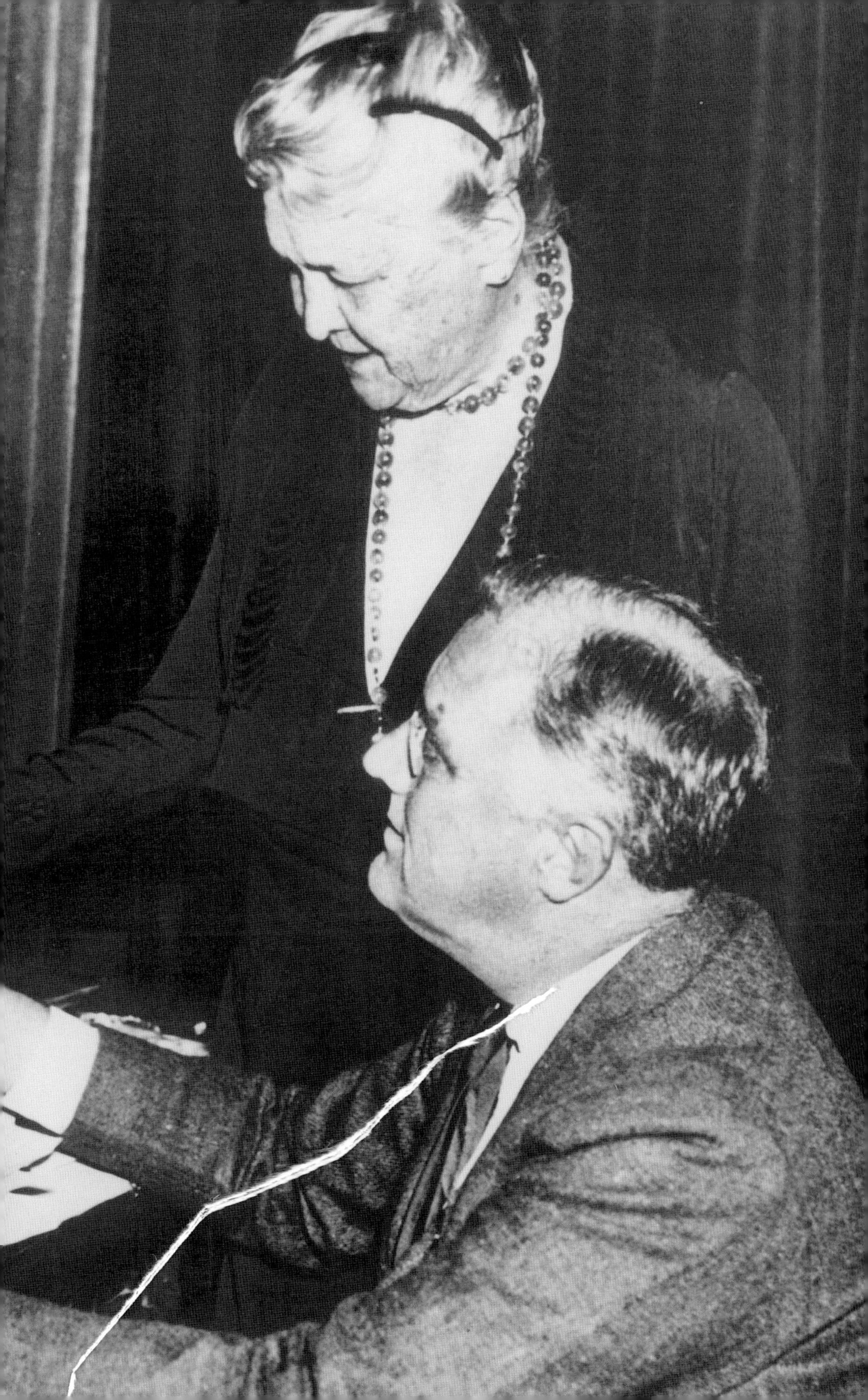

TABLE OF CONTENTS

WITH RIGHTS COME RESPONSIBILITIES: The Presidential Records and Freedom of Information Acts guarantee public access to recent Presidential papers, but only after suitable periods of time have elapsed—a minimum of five years after the administration has concluded, with a maximum of twelve or more years when issues such as national security are involved. Thus, the correspondence of the latest former President, Bill Clinton, remains largely restricted; the email published in this book is one of the few in the public domain.

The sitting President's correspondence currently belongs to his administration, and is inaccessible. How many letters does President Bush receive? Between 40,000 and 100,000 a week, depending on national and world events—though, of course, not all correspondence arrives in letter form. The modern-day White House receives faxes, cables, and emails in addition to traditional letters; all are read, though not necessarily by the occupant of the Oval Office. While the President does not have a personal email account, many electronic missives sent to the White House bear the salutation "Dear Mr. President."

OPPOSITE: *Lyndon Johnson reads some rare good news about Vietnam in 1968.*

B U L L E T I N
DRV PROPOSAL
FOR YOUR INFORMATION

FOREWORD BY ALLEN WEINSTEIN

Archivist of the United States

EACH WORKING DAY, THE NATIONAL ARCHIVES and Records Administration (NARA) provides access to millions of documents of interest to the American people. Perhaps this mission is most evident in the thousands of people who daily stand in orderly lines just to see the Charters of Freedom—the Declaration of Independence, the Constitution of the United States, and the Bill of Rights.

Few of the records preserved by NARA are quite as grand as the Charters of Freedom, but one type of document is both common and special at the same time—letters. Letters may be mundane, or memorable, personal accounts of our lives at a moment in time. They become noteworthy in a different way when written to public figures, especially Presidents of the United States. Without question, it requires special motivation to sit down and write: "Dear Mr. President." This salutation means we have something important to say, and we expect the most powerful person on earth to pay attention to our concerns.

The letters in this volume have been drawn from the rich holdings of the National Archives, most notably from the National Archives' Presidential Libraries. To be sure, the Library of Congress has many such letters to the Presidents from George Washington to Calvin Coolidge. But NARA's Presidential Libraries can collectively claim to be the single major source of Presidential letters, not only on the basis of sheer volume, but most importantly on the rich variety and the substantive content of the documents.

The letters collected here are just a sample of the many thousands in NARA's holdings. In this book you will find letters of grave importance such as the personal appeal of Albert Einstein to President Roosevelt urging him to take action on the construction of an atomic bomb. It was Einstein's simple letter that heralded the now famous Manhattan Project and the beginning of the nuclear age.

Other letters were matters of conscience. In May 1958, baseball great Jackie Robinson wrote to President Eisenhower chastising him for the slow pace of progress on civil rights. "17 million Negroes cannot do as you suggest and wait for the hearts of men to change," Robinson wrote. "We want to enjoy now the rights that we feel we are entitled to as Americans. This we cannot do unless we pursue aggressively goals which all other Americans achieved over 150 years ago."

Some letters provided comfort to the Presidents. I was moved by the simple telegram from J.B. Manual of Bridgeport, Connecticut, to President Roosevelt regarding a radio address. "Just heard your speech," he wrote. "It cheered me up. Received notice today that my son was killed in service of the United States at Pearl Harbor December 7th." Simple words that send a chill up your spine.

A letter that may surprise some readers is the apology from Tom and Dick Smothers. Known for their vicious attacks on President Johnson on their television program, the Smothers Brothers wrote to the president shortly before the election of 1968: "We frequently disregarded the many, many good works and the progress the country has made under your administration," the comedians observed. "If the opportunity arose in this coming election to vote for you, we would."

Presidents also wrote to each other. This isn't new; in fact, this form of communication has been going on since the days of

John Adams and Thomas Jefferson. What I found interesting, however, was the compassion and friendship of very different men who shared a common office. One only need read the exchange of letters between Harry S. Truman and Herbert Hoover to get a sense of mutual admiration that Presidents have for one another.

Finally, no volume of Presidential letters would be complete without letters from children. One of my personal favorites is the letter from Andy Smith to President Reagan. "Today my mother declared my bedroom a disaster area," Andy wrote. "I would like to request federal funds to hire a crew to clean up my room." The President wrote back telling Andy that he was in "an excellent position to launch another volunteer program to go along with the...3000 already underway in our nation."

These letters and much more await you at the National Archives in Washington and the eleven Presidential Libraries around the country. I encourage you to visit one of these institutions for personal insight into the nation's record and the Office of the Presidency. Until you can visit us in person, please visit us online at *www.archives.gov* for additional information about the National Archives and the Presidential Libraries.

It has often been said that the Smithsonian Institution is "The Nation's Attic." If that is the case, then the National Archives and Records Administration is "The Nation's Rolltop Desk." The 87 letters contained in this wonderful volume are but a few examples of the tens of thousands of such letters that have crossed Presidents' desks since 1789. I hope you enjoy them as much as I did. And I hope that these letters inspire you to sit down and write to 1600 Pennsylvania Avenue and tell the President what's on your mind.

ABOVE: *The National Archives sits in stately Neoclassical splendor in Washington, D.C.*
PRECEDING PAGES: *Richard Nixon's turbulent Presidency generated plenty of mail.*

REC'D DEC 1 66

Fri, November 25, 1966

Dear Mr. President -

I hope that the men in Vait Nam are doing well! Do thay do this each day? How are you felling? I hope you are felling good! I'am 7 and ½ years old! And I like you! I have not ben in the White house befor. but I will some time. I live in new york stat in Elmira! I want to visit you!

One of you'r young Democrets Brian Williams
927 W. Church St.
Elmra N.Y., 14905

look at this!
↓ ↓ ↓ ↓ ↓

INTRODUCTION BY BRIAN WILLIAMS

Anchor and Managing Editor, NBC Nightly News

As a child, I was not allowed to eat supper until the network evening news was over. While such a biographical detail, when repeated today, carries with it the slight whiff of suburban barbarism, it was actually one of the best things my parents ever did for me. Our evening ritual, and the knowledge I gained from it, may have had more to do with my current occupation and with the direction of my life than any other single act of parenting.

Sitting in front of the television at 6:30 p.m. in the den of our three-bedroom beige suburban ranch home in Elmira, New York, I watched the Cold War unfold and saw the moving pictures of the Vietnam War at its height. Our first color television set arrived in 1968—perversely timed to coincide with the start of the Tet Offensive, an often misreported but bloody affair covered in great detail by the networks at the time. During later evenings, I counted down with Cronkite during the lunar landing, and cried when he did. I was watching television the night Martin Luther King, Jr. was killed, and again on the night Bobby Kennedy was killed. I feared for our nation, I dreamed of the world outside Elmira, and I hatched an outlandish and lofty dream of my own that I could never share with anyone until adulthood: I wanted to be one of those journalists I saw on television. Preferably, I wanted to be one of the three men who each evening were invited into people's homes to tell them what had happened that day. I wanted to go places and cover great people and events and report my findings to an eager American viewing audience. I was confident that I had seen how the job should be done.

So I thought it was only natural to sit down at the dining room table with a ballpoint pen and a piece of lined paper and write to the President. By November 25, 1966, Lyndon Johnson was the only President I felt I really knew. Naturally, I regarded him as the archetype: All Presidents, my theory went, should be tall, have a commanding presence, big hands and big ears. Through my electronic window I felt I could read this man. In magazines like *Time, Life,* and *Look,* I read about his troubles. I recall seeing a particular photo of the President seemingly in distress, slumped over a table and looking distraught. I later learned he was listening to a reel-to-reel tape recording from his future son-in-law, Marine Corps Lt. Charles Robb. The young marine sent tapes home to Lynda Bird Johnson and her father, in effect narrating the Vietnam War as he saw it. The detail

OPPOSITE: *Brian Williams wrote to President Johnson in reaction to seeing his photo, next page.*
ABOVE: *Williams exudes confidence as a nattily dressed 7-year-old.*

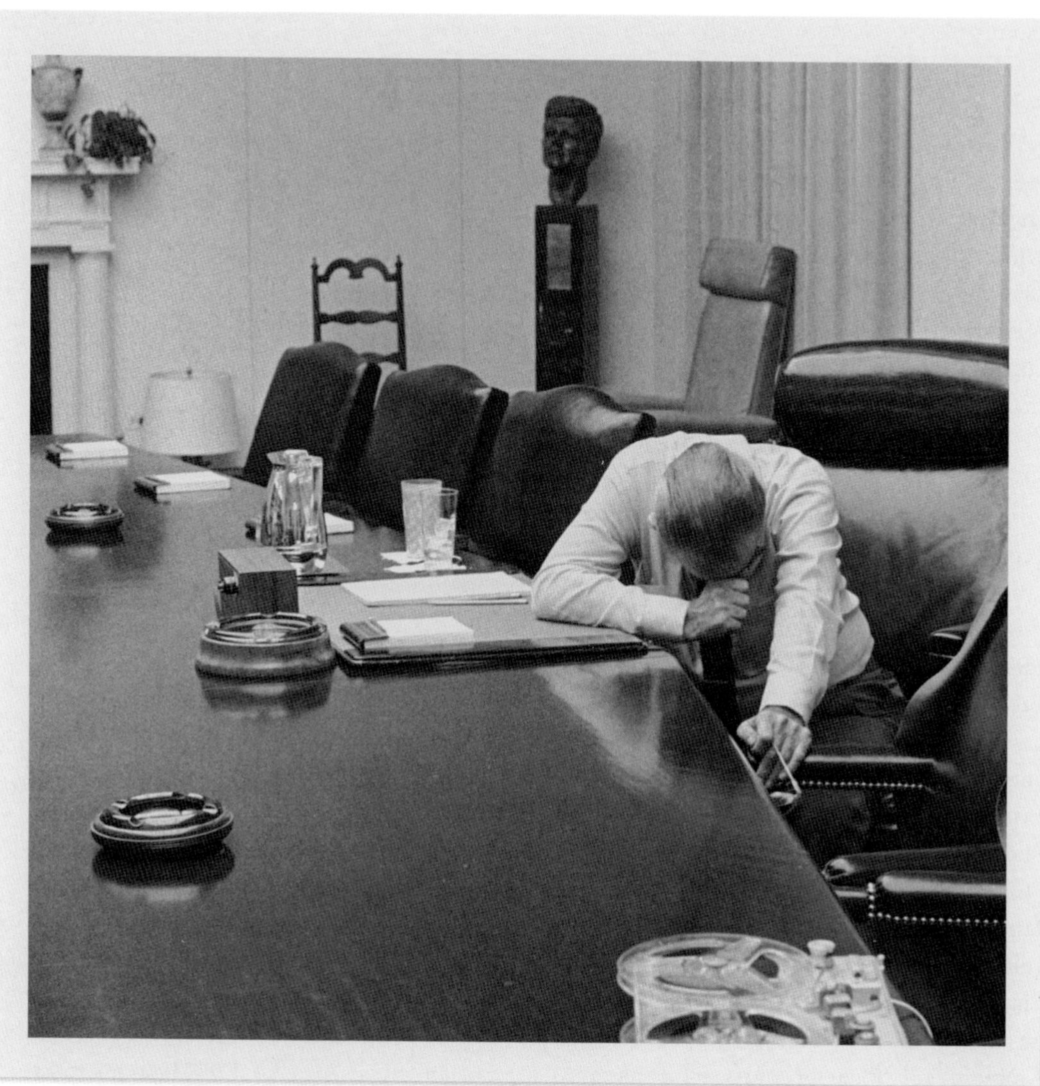

was lost on me then...I just knew I needed to write.

How I wish today my letter was among the more profound works to be found in the pages of this fine volume. Instead, I'm afraid it's the work of an archetypal seven-year-old. I attached with tape a photo of a young American soldier in combat, which was in hindsight perhaps not the most cheering image to pass along to the beleaguered wartime President. In the text, I all but invited myself to the White House, and I declared my membership in a party of "Democrets" which apparently hasn't been heard from since (and which would later become something of an embarrassment for a journalist who is an avowed and registered Independent).

In return I received a letter from the President, as obvious a form letter as was ever written, though my parents had the good sense to pretend LBJ had slaved over the text himself. He nicely included a booklet entitled "Lyndon Johnson Speaks to Young Americans." While I cherished both at the time, they were long ago placed in a cardboard box and lost—

ABOVE: *The weight of Vietnam burdened Lyndon Johnson's Presidency in the 1960s.*

somewhere—in the series of moves required by adult life and a nomadic career.

Fast-forward through a middle-class life in America: a move to New Jersey, high school, some college. Owing to combined precociousness and good fortune, I was able to land an internship at the White House in 1979. I was assigned to the Office of Presidential Correspondence. During my first day on the job, opening letters from seven-year-old boys and 70-year-old women, a moment arrived when I thought life had come full circle and the American Dream had been realized: I was now on the other end. I was opening someone's precious letter to the President. Some sent along pictures. Some expressed their dreams, some spewed their anger...all of them wrote to the President empowered by a sacred right of citizenship as old as the Republic itself.

Fast-forward again through the continuation of a life: more college, a few years as a volunteer firefighter and then, after several false starts, a successful career in journalism. One night while my wife and children slept upstairs, I watched an interview with the historian Michael Beschloss on C-SPAN. He told a fantastic story of writing President Johnson as a boy growing up in Illinois. Michael's life had come full circle, too: He was now the author of two books on the Johnson Presidency. He told the interviewer of having casually mentioned to a researcher at the LBJ library that he had written a letter to President Johnson. It turned out Michael's letter had been saved in the files, as it apparently was one of several set aside each day as part of a representative sample for the President to see. The library found Michael's letter. I called Michael and asked if the same search could be launched for my letter, which to my amazement was also found. Today both letters, from two boys who shared the American experience, sit side by side in a display case in the LBJ Presidential Library and Museum in Austin, Texas.

It turns out I had been premature in declaring the American Dream fully achieved, way back on that first day at work as a White House intern. It gets even better. My outlandish and lofty childhood dream, hatched while I was sitting in front of a television set in Elmira, New York, and shared with no one until I met my wife, came true on December 2, 2004, when I was appointed as one of the three journalists who are invited into millions of homes each evening. Life has indeed come full circle, and it may once more: It is made even richer by my absolute conviction that somewhere, at this very moment, a young child is taking out a piece of lined paper to write to the President about something he or she saw on the evening news.

Dear Mr. President:

I hope that the men in Vait Nam are doing well! Do they do this ever day? How are you felling? I hope your are felling good! I'am 7 and 1/2 years old!

And I like you! I have not ben in the White house before but I will some time. I live in new york stat in Elmira! I want to visit you!

One of your young Democrets Brian Williams

Copy

New York, 6th April, 1789.

Sir,

I have the honor to transmit to your Excellency the information of your unanimous election to the office of President of the United States of America. Suffer me, Sir, to indulge the hope, that so auspicious a mark of public confidence will meet your approbation, and be considered as a sure pledge of the affection and support you are to expect from a free and an enlightened People.

I am, Sir, with
sentiments of respect,
Yr. Ob. hb. Servt.
J L

His Excellency
George Washington, Esqr.

JOHN LANGDON TO GEORGE WASHINGTON

New York, NY ★ April 6, 1789

THE LONG EPISTOLARY AFFAIR BETWEEN Americans and their Chief Executive begins here, with what is arguably the first letter ever received by a President of the United States.

In a single paragraph of fewer than a hundred words, John Langdon, president of the Senate, employs the graceful penmanship and elegant rhetorical flouishes expected of a cultured eighteenth-century gentleman to inform George Washington that he has been elevated to the highest office created by the newly written Constitution of the newly established republic.

The news was not unexpected, since it was inconceivable that the title of President should be bestowed on anyone but Washington. Still, the citizens who adored him didn't get to vote for him. Worried that the people might not always choose their leaders wisely, the framers of the Constitution created a system whereby each state would select several Presidential electors. Each elector was to vote for two candidates; the one receiving the most votes would be named President, while the runner-up would serve as Vice President.

On February 4, all 69 electors cast their votes for Washington. Two months later, when the new Congress finally mustered a quorum, the votes were counted and Langdon wrote his letter.

Putting aside his reluctance—he once wrote that the prospect of the Presidency filled him with feelings "not unlike those of a culprit who is going to the place of his execution"—Washington embarked on a triumphal progress northward from Mount Vernon. He crossed New York Harbor in a ceremonial barge with thirteen oarsmen (an optimistic number, since only eleven states had ratified the Constitution) and on April 30, John Langdon, the same New Hampshire merchant-soldier-legislator who had notified Washington of his election, administered the oath of office on the balcony of Federal Hall.

Sir,

I have the honor to transmit to your Excellency the information of your unanimous election to the office of the President of the United States of America. Suffer me, Sir, to indulge the hope, that so auspicious a mark of public confidence will meet your approbation, and be considered as a formal pledge of the affection and support you are to expect from a free and an enlightened people.

I am, Sir, with sentiments of respect,
(illegible)

J. L.

His Excellency
George Washington, Esq.

OPPOSITE: *Possibly the first letter ever written to a president, this one is practically illegible.*

พระราชสาส์น

KING MONGKUT OF SIAM TO ABRAHAM LINCOLN

Siam ★ February 14, 1861

TO MOST AMERICANS, MONGKUT IS THE swaggering, imperious monarch portrayed so memorably in the Rodgers and Hammerstein musical *The King and I.* Caught up in the theatrical intensity of Yul Brynner's performance (not to mention the tuneful antics of an English governess and a palace full of wives and children), we can easily forget that Mongkut was a real person, a onetime monk who became a strong and enlightened ruler and whose memory is still revered in Thailand.

Mongkut's intelligence and thoughtfulness shine from every page of this letter he sent to Abraham Lincoln in 1861. By then, the king was in his eleventh year on the throne and well into a wide-ranging campaign to modernize Siam, as Thailand was then known. Having introduced several Western innovations into his own kingdom, he sought to return the favor by sending the American President some elephants.

Having recently learned that America is sadly pachyderm-free, Mongkut suggests that pairs of male and female elephants "turned loose in forests" of the United States will surely "increase till there be large herds"—and eventually, Americans will be able to "catch them and tame and use them as beasts of burden." He assures Lincoln that he is ready to procure the elephants and "forward them one or two pairs at a time" if the U.S. will provide a suitably fitted-out ship. In the meantime, he sends some presents: a daguerreotype of himself and one of his daughters (he had 82 children), a sword, and a pair of huge elephant tusks.

In his gracious response several weeks later, Lincoln thanked his "Great and Good Friend" Mongkut for the gifts, which were to be "placed among the archives of the Government" as required by law. As for the proffered elephants, however, Lincoln thought they weren't such a good idea. He noted America's preference for steam as "our best and most efficient agent of transportation"—and in any case, he wrote, the territory of the United States "does not reach a latitude so low as to favor the multiplication of the elephant."

It's a pity, really. Herds of elephants lumbering through the dappled glades of an American forest—that would have been quite a sight.

OPPOSITE: *The King of Siam's elephant seal depicts the animal his majesty wished to give Abraham Lincoln.*
ABOVE: *For all his democratic ideals, King Mongkut sits alone in regal splendor on his throne.*

Respected and Distinguished Sir,

At this time we are very glad in having embraced an excellent opportunity to forward our Royal letter under separate envelope together with complimentary presents Viz

A sword with a photographic likeness of ourselves accompanying herewith, directly to Washington as being a much better way of forwarding it than the way we had intended, by delivering it to the Consul of the United States of America here to be forwarded on, sometimes by a steamer, sometimes by a sailing vessel from one port to another till It should reach Washington. This sending where there are many changes from one vessel to another is not a trustworthy way. There is danger of delay and indeed that the articles may be damaged and never reach their destination. . . .

We are assured that Captain Berrien will deliver them in safety to you who are President of the United States when our letter would reach Washington. During the interview in reply from Captain Berrien to our enquiries of various particulars relating to America he stated that on that continent there are no elephants. Elephants are regarded as the most remarkable of the large quadripeds by the Americans so that if any one has an elephant's tusk of large size, and will deposit it in any public place, people come by thousands crowding to see it, saying it is a wonderful thing. Also, though formerly there were no camels on the continent the Americans have sought for and purchased (illegible) some from Arabia, some from Europe and now camels propagate their race and are serviceable and of benefit to the country, and are already numerous in America.

Having heard this it has occurred to us that, if on the continent of America there should be several pairs of young male and female elephants turned loose in forests where there was abundance of water and grass in any region under the sun's declination both North and South, call by the English, the Torrid Zone, and all were forbidden to molest them, to attempt to raise them would be well and if the climate there should prove favorable to elephants, we are of opinion that after a while they will increase till there be large herds as there are here on the continent of Asia until the inhabitants of America will be able to catch them and tame and use them as beasts of burden making them of benefit to the country. Since elephants being animals of great size and strength can bear burdens and travel through uncleared woods and matted jungles where no carriage and cart roads have yet been made. . . . we are as yet uninformed what forests and what regions of that country are suitable for elephants to thrive and prosper. Besides we have no means nor are we able to convey elephants to America, the distance being too great. . . .

In reference to this opinion of ours if the President of the United States and Congress who conjointly with him rule the country see fit to approve let them provide a large vessel loaded with hay and other food suitable for elephants on the voyage, with tanks holding a sufficiency of fresh water and arranged with stalls so that the elephant can both stand & lie down on the ship and send it to receive them.

We on our part will procure young male and female elephants and forward them one or two pairs at a time. . . . When elephants are on board, the ship let a steamer take it in tow that it may reach America as rapidly as possible before they become wasted and diseased by the voyage. . . .

OPPOSITE: *Much of the King of Siam's original letter was written in his native Thai script.*

ช้างน้อย ๆ ไปปล่อยไว้ในป่า ที่มีในเกาะสุมาตราแลเกาะเบฤเนียว เพราะฉนั้นบัดนี้
ช้างในเกาะทั้งสองนั้นก็มีชุกชุม ด้วยเหตุนี้เกล้าพระเจ้ากรุงสยามมีความปรารถนา จะใคร่
หาช้างส่งออกไป ปล่อยไว้ให้สืบพืชพันธุ์ในทวีปอเมริกา แต่ยังไม่ทราบว่าป่าตำบลใด
ที่ใดจะเปนดี ควรที่ช้างจะอยู่เปนศุขสืบไปได้

อนึ่งไม่มีพาหนะแลกำลังเลย ที่จะคิดได้จนเอาช้างออกไปส่งถึงทวีปอเมริกา
เปนทางไกลได้ ก็ทวีปแลเกาะทวีปสมาตราทวีปเบอเนียนั้นอยู่ใกล้กับทวีปเอเชียนี้
ผู้ที่คิดค้าขายการแต่ก่อนก็รับเอาช้างไปได้โดยง่ายไม่ยากนัก ก็การความคิดของเกล้า
พระเจ้ากรุงสยามดังนี้ ถ้าท่านปริไสเดนต์ของยุไนติศเตศอเมริกากับเสเนตทั้งปวง
ผู้พร้อมเพรียงกันครอบครองบ้านเมืองจะเห็นชอบด้วยแล้ว ขอให้คิดอ่านให้มีเรือ
กำปั่นใหญ่ บันทุกเคยไปด้วยหญ้าแห้งแลสิ่งของซึ่งจะเปนอาหารแก่ช้าง
ในกลางทางได้ ทั้งถังใหญ่ที่ใส่น้ำจืดให้ช้างกิน แลมีที่ให้ช้างยืนแลนอนไปได้
ในเรือแล้วส่งมารับ ผู้ครองฝ่ายสยามจะจัดช้าง พลาย พัง น้อย ๆ ส่งไปให้
คราวละคู่สองคู่ เมื่อช้างบันทุกในเรือใหญ่แล้ว ขอให้มีเรือกลไฟชักลากไป
ให้ถึงทวีปอเมริกาโดยเร็ว อย่าให้ท่านช้างอิดโรยเปนอันตรายเสียกลางทางได้
เมื่อไปถึงที่นั้นแล้ว อย่าพาช้างไปไว้ในเมืองหนาว พ้นจากที่ใกล้สุริยายน
ที่เรียกว่าตอเรียดโซนไป รีบปล่อยในป่าที่สมควรแห่งหนึ่งแห่งใดโดยเร็ว
อย่าขังอย่าผูกไว้ให้ช้าง ถ้าได้ดังนี้เกล้าพระเจ้ากรุงสยามแน่ใจว่า ช้างจะสืบ
พืชพันธุ์ทวีไปภายหน้าในทวีปอเมริกา การที่หาฤามานี้ท่านปริไสเดนต์
ของยุไนติศเตศอเมริกา แลเสเนตทั้งปวงจะเห็นชอบเห็นควรประการใด
ขอจงให้ทราบไปโดยเร็ว

ในกรุงเทพมหานครนี้ การจับช้างออกจากป่าจากโขลงในป่า
ย่อมมีในเดือนผคุณแลเดือนเจตร ซึ่งเปนเดือนสี่เดือนห้า ที่ตรงกัน
กับเดือนมาร์ชแลเดือนเอเปรียล ถ้าปริไสเดนต์แลเสเนตจะเห็นชอบด้วย
ในการอันนี้แล้ว จะแต่งเรือให้มารับช้าง ถ้าเรือนั้นจะมาถึงเมืองสยาม
ในเดือนทั้งหลายซึ่งเปนภายหลังแต่เดือนสี่เดือนห้า คือเดือนมาร์ชแลเดือน
เอเปรียลของปีใด ขอจงได้ให้ทราบข่าวเสียก่อนแต่เดือนสี่เดือนห้า

Camp of 54th Mass Colored Regt

Morris Island. Dept of the South. Sept 28th 1863.

Your Excelency: Abraham Lincoln:

Your Excelency will pardon the presumtion of an humble individual like myself, in addressing You. but the earnest Solicitation of my Comrades in Arms, besides the genuine interest felt by myself in the matter is my excuse, for placing before the Executive head of the Nation our Common Grievance: On the 6th of the last Month, the Paymaster of the department, informed us, that if we would decide to recieve the sum of $10 (ten dollars) per month, he would come and pay us that sum, but, that, on the sitting of Congress, the Regt would, in his opinion, be <u>allowed</u> the other 3 (three.) He did not give us any guarantee that this would be, as he hoped, certainly <u>he</u> had no authority for making any such guarantee, and we can not supose him acting in any way interested. Now the main question is. Are we <u>Soldiers</u>, or are we <u>Labourers</u>. We are fully armed, and equipped, have done all the various Duties, pertaining to a Soldiers life, have conducted ourselves, to the complete satisfaction of General Officers, who, were if any, prejudiced <u>against</u> us, but who now accord us all the encouragement, and honour due us: have shared the perils, and Labour, of Reducing the first stronghold, that flaunted a Traitor Flag: and more, Mr President. Today, the Anglo Saxon Mother, Wife, or Sister, are not alone, in tears for

James H. Gooding to Abraham Lincoln

Camp of 54th Mass. Volunteer Infantry, SC ★ September 28, 1863

As President during the worst crisis in the nation's history, Lincoln had to deal with an array of calamities. Secession, the firing on Fort Sumter, the parade of inept military commanders and the battlefield disasters for which they were responsible, the slaughter of thousands of young American soldiers—letters and reports detailing all of them came flying into Lincoln's office and landed, blood-spattered, on his desk and in his mind.

In that context, a soldier's complaint about his pay seems relatively mundane—but the author of this letter was no ordinary blue-jacketed Billy Yank.

James Henry Gooding was a young corporal in the 54th Massachusetts Volunteer Infantry, the famed black regiment organized by Robert Gould Shaw of Boston. After some months of training, the 54th Massachusetts was shipped to South Carolina, where it distinguished itself in a doomed assault on Fort Wagner, near Charleston, on the evening of July 18, 1863. Before the battle, Shaw had told his men, "The eyes of thousands will look on what you do tonight"—and he was right. The bravery of the regiment, which suffered 256 casualties among its 600 men, was a major factor in dispelling the widely held notion that African Americans made poor soldiers.

Corporal Gooding wrote this letter to President Lincoln a few weeks after the battle. In response to his own rhetorical question about how black men have conducted themselves in the war, he summons images of the carnage at Fort Wagner: "Let the rich mould around Wagners parapet be upturned, and there will be found an Eloquent answer."

But Gooding is seeking fairness, not praise. Specifically, he wants to be paid the same as a white soldier: \$13 per month, \$7 more (including a \$3 monthly deduction for clothing) than he is currently receiving. His summation could hardly be simpler—or more compelling: The men of the regiment want their government to pay them "as american SOLDIERS, not as menial hierlings."

The 54th Massachusetts, or what was left of it, was later transported to Florida and took part in the bloody Battle of Olustee, where it was reported that "the colored troops…fought like devils." Wounded in the thigh, Corporal Gooding was captured and taken to the notorious Andersonville prison, where he died on July 19. Just a month earlier, Congress had finally authorized equal pay for black soldiers.

Your Excelency will pardon the presumtion of an humble individual like myself, in addressing you. . . . On the 6th of the last month, the Paymaster of the department informed us that if we would decide to receive the sum of \$10 (ten dollars) per month, he would come and pay us that sum, but, that on the sitting of Congress, the Regt would, in his opinion, be allowed the other 3 (three.) . . .

Are we Soldiers or are we Labourers. We are fully armed, and equipped, have done all the various Duties, pertaining to a Soldiers life, have conducted ourselves, to the complete satisfaction of General Officers, who, were if any, prejudiced against us, but who now accord us all the encouragement, and honour due us: have shared the perils, and Labour, of Reducing the first stronghold, that flaunted a Traitor Flag: and more. Mr President. Today, the Anglo Saxon Mother, Wife, or Sister, are not alone in tears for departed Sons, Husbands, and Brothers.

OPPOSITE: *Evenly flowing penmanship bespeaks James Gooding's quiet dignity.*

Belair Aug 25th/1864

Mr president

It is my Desire to be free. to go to see my people on the eastern shore. my mistress wont let me you will please let me know if we are free. and what i can do. I write to you for advice. please send me word this week. or as soon as possible and oblidge.

Annie Davis
Belair Harford
County. M D.

Belair Harford
Co

Annie Davis to Abraham Lincoln

Belair, MD ★ August 28, 1864

People write to the President with questions on every subject and at all levels of complexity: When will this war be over? What's your favorite ice-cream flavor? Why did I lose my job? What gives you the idea that you're fit to be President?

Annie Davis's question is deceptively simple—but, unlike the responses to the playful or rhetorical queries posed by other writers, the answer she received would determine the future course of her life. Annie Davis asks Abraham Lincoln: Am I a free woman or a slave?

She had doubtless heard about the Emancipation Proclamation Lincoln had issued almost two years before, close on the heels of the Union victory at Antietam. It declared that on January 1, 1863, slaves would be "then, thenceforward, and forever free" in areas "in rebellion against the United States." In practical terms, this meant that slavery was abolished in areas where the federal government had no authority to enforce emancipation. Slavery remained untouched in areas under Union control, including the so-called border states—Maryland, Delaware, Kentucky and Missouri—which had large numbers of slaves (Maryland had just over 87,000 in 1860) but had never officially seceded.

So Lincoln's proclamation didn't free Annie Davis. It wasn't until a new state constitution took effect on November 1, 1864—slightly more than two months after this letter was written—that slavery was outlawed in Maryland. Another year later, in December 1865, ratification of the Thirteenth Amendment put an end to the "peculiar institution" of slavery in every U.S. state and territory.

Annie Davis's visit to her family on the Eastern Shore, as well as the fulfillment of her "desire to be free," would have to wait a bit longer.

Mr. President

It is my Desire to be free. to go to see my people on the eastern shore. My mistress wont let me you will please let me know if we are free. and what i can do. I write to you for advice. please send me word this week or as soon as possible and oblidge.

Annie Davis, Belair Harford County, MD.

OPPOSITE: *Short and to the point, Annie Davis asks Lincoln the most basic question: Am I free?*
ABOVE: *Lincoln strikes a characteristically stoic pose on the Antietam battlefield in 1862.*

Washington City D.C.
April 15, 1865.—

Sir:

Abraham Lincoln, President of the United States, was shot by an assassin ~~this~~ last evening, at Ford's Theater in this City and died at the hour of 22 minutes after seven o'clock.

About the same time at which the President was shot, an assassin entered the sick chamber of the Hon. Wm. H. Seward, Secretary of State, and stabbed him in several places, in the throat, neck, and face, ~~[illegible]~~ severely if not mortally wounding him. Other members of the Secretary's family were dangerously wounded by the assassin while making his escape. By the death of President Lincoln, the office of President has devolved under the constitution upon You. The emergency of the government demands that you should immediately qualify, according to the requirements of the Constitution, and enter upon the duties of ~~the~~ President of the United States. If you will please make known your pleasure, such

Lincoln's Cabinet to Andrew Johnson

Washington, D.C. ★ April 15, 1865

When the endless night was finally over, when Abraham Lincoln had taken his last rattling breath and a sense of dreadful finality had settled over the tiny bedroom in Petersen's Boarding House across the street from Ford's Theatre, members of the martyred President's Cabinet had an important job to do: Andrew Johnson had to be officially notified that he was President of the United States.

None of the Cabinet liked Johnson very much. He was bad tempered and stubborn, an ardent advocate of states' rights, a racist and former slave owner, and a heavy drinker. Most damning of all, he wasn't Lincoln. Writing this letter must have been a thoroughly distasteful task, so they kept it brief—almost as brief as John Langdon's letter to George Washington 76 years earlier.

In plain language befitting the occasion, they summarize the terrible events of April 14 and inform the Tennesseean that "the emergency of the government" makes it imperative that he quickly "enter upon the duties" of the office that has been thrust upon him by a bullet fired from an actor's gun.

On that same Good Friday evening, the man who was supposed to kill Vice President Johnson had lost his nerve, but Secretary of State William H. Seward had been gravely wounded by would-be assassin Lewis Paine. Seward's signature is missing from this letter, but all the other names are in a neat column: McCulloch, Stanton, Welles, Dennison, Usher, Speed.

It's a short list—by 21st-century standards, Lincoln's wartime Cabinet was a shockingly small group—and it would be even shorter if Secretary of the Treasury Hugh McCulloch hadn't signed twice. Was it nerves, or fatigue? Or was he, as much of the nation would be in the weeks to come, blinded by grief?

Sir,

Abraham Lincoln, President of the United States, was shot by an assassin this evening at Ford's Theater in this city and died at the hour of 22 minutes after seven o'clock.

About the same time at which the President was shot, an assassin entered the sick chamber of the Hon. Wm. H. Seward, Secretary of State, and stabbed him in several places, in the throat, neck and face, severely if not mortally wounding him. Other members of the Secretary's family were dangerously wounded by the assassin while making his escape. By the death of President Lincoln, the office of President has devolved under the Constitution upon you. The emergency of the government demands that you should immediately qualify according to the requirements of the Constitution and enter upon the duties of the President of the United States. If you will please make known your pleasure, such arrangements as you deem proper will be made.

Your Obedient Servants
Hugh McCulloch, Secretary of the Treasury
Edwin M. Stanton, Secretary of War
Gideon Welles, Secretary of Navy
W. Dennison, Postmaster General
J.P. Usher, Secretary of the Interior
James Speed, Attorney General
Hugh McCulloch, Secretary of the Treasury

OPPOSITE: *Shock and grief betray themselves in the letter Lincoln's Cabinet sent the slain leader's successor.*

"Washington great Father
President Garfield
Issued every thing
you mine will sell Wagon many $.
I did not like No $ great Father
I Will sell I can not Wagon great Father
President Garfield him talk. I hear.
Wagon sell think I did not like No. $
President Garfield. you tell. G Kauffman
all Wagon 80$. hear and Glad I think
tell me. Major Kauffman I hears
President Garfield G Kauffman. two will
sell like, all President Garfield talk
Major Kauffman issue Wagon sell I cannot.
Great Father you talk I hear I like. [illegible] cannot
you paper I did not recive I did not like
White man talk half I know and I Write half
I can and you paper. recive I like I am sure
President Garfield Issued. sell I cannot
and I tell you see Examine Good —.
Now great Father talk all I hear Good
all. and I am glad Gros Ventres all and
Gros Ventres all to be White man I think
great Father talk I hear I like.
you paper recive can not —
Washington great Father
White man Good all [illegible] skirer and
Examine all Issue, sell. I did not like
Fort Berthold. I Write paper Me Wolf Chief

WOLF CHIEF TO JAMES GARFIELD
GOV. EDMUND ROSS TO GROVER CLEVELAND

Fort Berthold, ND ★ December, 1881 ★★★ Santa Fe, NM ★ August, 1886

THE LONG-RUNNING, TRAGIC COLLISION between Native Americans and European Americans forms one of the dominant themes of our national history. By the end of the 19th century, the outcome was no longer in doubt: The continuing inrush of white settlers had pushed the Indians steadily westward, and by the time historian Frederick Jackson Turner famously proclaimed the "closing of the frontier" in 1893, most tribes that had not disappeared had been confined on reservations.

These letters, written five years apart in the 1880s, show two faces of the final phase of the struggle between Anglo and Indian cultures.

The first is from Wolf Chief, a member of the Hidatsa tribe (sometimes called the Gros Ventres) of the Upper Missouri River Valley. After a smallpox epidemic killed many members of the tribe in 1837, the survivors moved to a reservation at the trading post of Fort Berthold in what is now North Dakota. It was there that the young Wolf Chief decided that the only way to survive was to adapt himself to the white man's ways. He learned En-glish, converted to Christianity, and opened a small store. And he started writing letters to the "Great Father" in a far-off place called Washington.

In this early letter to President Garfield, Wolf Chief's fractured English conveys an almost desperate eagerness to ingratiate himself ("Great Father you talk...I hear I like") and to fit into the new realities that had reshaped his world. "I like White man ways," he says. He wrote dozens of letters to a succession of Presidents—sometimes signing himself "Mr. Wolf C. Chief"—well into the 1930s. By then, only about 600 Hidatsa remained.

The second letter, signed by several irate residents of the Territory of New Mexico, deals with some Indians who, unlike Wolf Chief, do not "like White man ways." A few months earlier, the warrior-leader known as Geronimo had escaped from the Apache reservation, sending the countryside into a panic. Led by Governor Edmund Ross (who, as a U.S. senator from Kansas, had cast the deciding vote against conviction in President Andrew Johnson's 1868 impeachment trial), the gentlemen from New Mexico insist that the Apaches must be "removed to distant and isolated localities." If not, "nothing short of extermination" will bring an end to "our Indian troubles."

A few weeks later, Geronimo finally surrendered and was sent to Fort Marion in Florida. After eight years in captivity, he settled in Oklahoma, spent a year with a Wild West show, and even rode in Theodore Roosevelt's 1905 inaugural parade. He was never allowed to set foot in Arizona again.

OPPOSITE: *Wolf Chief wrote to many "Great Fathers" in Washington, though they had only passing interest in Native American concerns.* ABOVE: *Like most Victorian-era gentlemen, Edmund Ross believed that Native Americans had little if any claim to their land.*

Washington Great Father
President Garfield

Issued every thing you mine will sell wagon many $. I did not like No $ great Father I will sell I can not wagon great Father President Garfield him talk. I hear wagon sell think. I did not like No. $ President Garfield. You tell. G Kauffman all wagon 80$. I hear and (illegible) I think tell me. Major Kauffman. I hears President Garfield G. Kauffman. Two will sell like. All President Garfield talk Major Kauffman issue wgon sell I can not. Great father you talk I hear I like. (illegible) cannot you paper I did not recive I did not like whiteman talk hatf I know and I write hatf I can and you paper. recive I like I am sure President Garfield Issued. sell I cannot and I tell you see Examine good Now great father talk all I hear good all. and I am glad Gros Ventrer all and Gros Ventrer all to be white man I think great Father talk I hear I like. You paper recive can not

Washington great Father Whiteman good all look (illegible) and Examine all issue. sell. I did not like Fort Berthold. Write paper (illegible) Wolf Chief Great Father talk all good Now all I know and I like Whiteman ways I like all talk I hear.

Good man a me Wolf Chief.

★★★

. . . Generations of hostility show them to be implacable, and that nothing short of extermination will stop their raids so long as they remain here in proximity to their traditional enemies. So long as they are here, that process of extermination will go on, but at a fearful cost of life and property to our people and of treasure to the government. For every warrior killed some boy is now growing up to take his place.

The boys of today are the outlaws and bandits--the Jus, the Nanes and the Geronimos--of tomorrow. It has been so for generations and will continue so, if they remain here, till they are exterminated; all the interests of these territories, in the meantime languishing and their development paralyzed, by the presence of an element that momentarily threatens destruction to our most important industries.

. . . Gen. Miles has so far since he has been placed in command here, by the wisdom of his plans and the vigor of their execution, kept the actively hostile portion of these bands out of New Mexico and finally driven them out of Arizona. They are practically conquered and are understood as being desirous to return to the reservation. To permit them to do so would be simply to tempt fate, and a repetition of the folly of two years ago--another drunken debauch and a murder of some of their number at the first opportunity, and a return to the warpath of pillage and murder to escape punishment. That will be the inevitable result if they are permitted to return. Of this we repeat that we are firmly convinced, and that no permanent peace can come to New Mexico or Arizona till these bands are removed to distant and isolated localities.

Governor E. G. Ross Et al

OPPOSITE: *In this complaint about hostile Apaches, Governor Ross misses the irony in his statement "Many of us have resided here for years. …"*

War

Santa Fe N. M. August 14 1886.

Hon. Grover Cleveland,

President,

Sir,-

We are much surprised to learn that opposition is being made to the proposition of Gen. Miles to remove portions of the Apache Indians from their present reservation in Arizona.

It does not seem possible that such opposition could originate with persons who comprehend the situation here and the need of radical measures for the pacification of our Indian troubles, or that it could be inspired by a desire to promote the civilization and welfare of these Indians, or the peace and successful developement of these territories.

Many of us have resided here for years, have seen this country the victim of Indian raids year after year, and have a right to be credited with intelligent and practical views on this subject. We are firmly convinced that no permanent cessation of these raids, or enduring safety to the isolated camps of miners and ranchmen, can be secured so long as the Chiricahua and Warm Springs bands of these Apaches are permitted to remain in any part of these territories. For two hundred years they have been traditional enemies and at constant war with the white race. It is true there are but few of them, less than five hundred all told, but there are enough, owing to the generally rugged and inaccessible character of the country they infest and raid, and the isolated nature of the settlements, to keep a very large scope of country in a state of ferment, and thereby to retard the developement of valua-

A SUCCESS IN ALL COUNTRIES.

ANNIE OAKLEY

America's Representative Lady Shot.

acd 4/5/98

For eleven years next to BUFFALO BILL the attraction with the Wild West. The wonder and talk of the American Exhibitions London '87, Paris Exhibition, '89, Horticultural Exhibition London '92, World's Fair, Chicago, '93

Miss Oakley, has appeared before all the Royalty and Nobility of Europe, including their R. H. the Prince and Princess of Wales before whom she has given fine exhibitions.

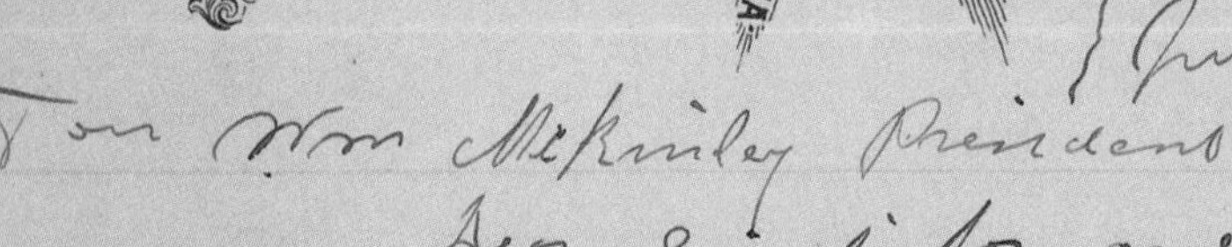

Nutley N J ap 5th

Hon Wm McKinley President

Dear Sir I for one feel Confident that your good Judgment will Carry America safely through without War—
But in Case of such an Event I am ready to place a Company of fifty Lady Sharpshooters at your disposal. Every one of them will be an American and as they will furnish their own Arms and Ammunition will be little if any Expense to the government.

Very truly Annie Oakley

ANNIE OAKLEY TO WILLIAM MCKINLEY

Address Unknown ★ April 5, 1898

SHE WAS BORN PHOEBE ANN MOSES, BUT no-body ever called her Phoebe. After her father died, little Annie helped keep food on the table by hunting in the woods around her family's home in Darke County, Ohio, and before long she became a crack shot. When a traveling shooting act came to Cincinnati, Annie entered a match against the star of the show, Frank Butler. She beat him—and a year later, she married him and joined his act, choosing "Oakley" as her stage name. The newlyweds traveled around the country, performing in small theaters and outdoor arenas, and Annie was such a hit that Buffalo Bill Cody hired her for his famous Wild West show.

Over the next few years, Annie's sharpshooting made her the most famous woman in America. Standing still or riding a horse or a bicycle, she blazed away with shotguns, rifles, and handguns at targets of all types and sizes, and almost never missed. Sitting Bull, who traveled with the Wild West show for a while, was so impressed that he gave her a Sioux name meaning "Little Sure Shot." She performed for Queen Victoria, shot a cigarette out of Kaiser Wilhelm II's mouth (she later said that she wished she'd missed that particular shot), and became the first movie cowgirl when Edison filmed her act with his new moving-picture machine. She finally retired in 1913 and died—back home in Ohio—thirteen years later.

Annie was still near the pinnacle of her fame when she wrote this letter to President William McKinley in the spring of 1898. The battleship *Maine* had sunk mysteriously in Havana harbor a few weeks earlier, and war with Spain seemed likely.

Eager to serve her country, Annie makes one of the most intriguing offers any President ever received: She is "ready to place a company of fifty lady sharpshooters" at McKinley's disposal, sweetening the deal by assuring him that this all-American troupe will "furnish their own Arms and Ammunition."

If her offer had been accepted, Annie's "lady sharpshooters" surely would have given Teddy Roosevelt's Rough Riders a run for their money as the most famous fighting outfit in the Spanish-American War—but McKinley, displaying a grave lack of imagination, turned Annie down.

There is much to admire about Annie Oakley—not only her legendary marksmanship skills and show-business acumen but also her grit and patriotism and generosity. And here's one more thing: She had a great-looking letterhead.

---

the Hon. Wm McKinley President:

Dear Sir

I for one feel Confident that your good judgment will carry America safely through without war.

But in case of such an event I am ready to place a company of fifty lady sharpshooters at your disposal. Every one of them will be an American and as they will furnish their own Arms and Ammunition will be little if any expense to the government.

very truly Annie Oakley

OPPOSITE: *Annie Oakley's stationery asserts her shooting prowess; her letter offers to put it to patriotic use.*

The Jungle Publishing Co.

"The Jungle," a Story of Packingtown.
The "Uncle Tom's Cabin" of wage slavery.—Jack London.
The greatest novel written in America in fifty years.
—David Graham Phillips

Publishers of the books of Upton Sinclair.
P. O. Box 2064, New York City.
(Letters intended for Upton Sinclair personally should be addressed to Princeton, N. J.)

King Midas: A Romance.
The Journal of Arthur Stirling.
Prince Hagen: A Phantasy.
Manassas: A Novel of the War.

March 10, 1906.

President Theodore Roosevelt,
Washington, D. C.

My dear President Roosevelt:

I have just returned from some exploring in the Jersey glass factories and find your kind note. I am glad to learn that the Department of Agriculture has taken up the matter of inspection, or lack of it, but I am exceedingly dubious as to what they will discover. I have seen so many people go out there and be put off with smooth pretences. A man has to be something of a detective, or else intimate with the workingmen, as I was, before he can really see what is going on. And it is becoming a great deal more difficult since the publication of "The Jungle." I have received to-day a letter from an employe of Armour & Company, in response to my request to him to take Ray Stannard Baker in hand and show him what he showed me a year and a half ago. He says: "He will have to be well disguised, for 'the lid is on' in Packingtown; he will find two detectives in places where before there was only one." You must understand that the thing which I have called the "condemned meat industry," is a matter of hundreds of thousands of dollars a month. I see in to-day's "Saturday Evening Post" that Mr. Armour declares in his article (which I happen to know is written by George Horace Lorimer) that "In Armour and Company's business not one atom of any

UPTON SINCLAIR TO THEODORE ROOSEVELT

New York, NY ★ March 10, 1906

THE FIRST DECADES OF THE TWENTIETH century were a golden age for investigative journalism. Scathing indictments of unsafe practices and corruption in business and politics appeared regularly in magazines that reached—and outraged—millions of readers. The resulting public outcry led to the adoption of long-overdue reforms in fields ranging from child labor laws to food and drug laws to forest conservation practices.

Among the writers who built a reputation for hard-hitting investigative reporting—a group that included such famous names as Jacob Riis, Frank Norris, Ida Tarbell, and Lincoln Steffens—few were better known than Upton Sinclair, whose 1906 novel *The Jungle* shocked readers with its stomach-churning depiction of conditions in the meatpacking industry. Now considered a classic of its kind, the book is credited as a major factor in the passage of the Pure Food and Drug Act and the Meat Inspection Act.

This letter to President Theodore Roosevelt was written soon after *The Jungle* was published. Appalled by Sinclair's revelations and eager to confirm their accuracy, Roosevelt had decided to send federal inspectors to the packing plants. In his letter, Sinclair applauds the decision, but adds that he is "exceedingly dubious as to what they will discover." He suggests that the President "find a man concerning whose intelligence and integrity you are absolutely sure" and send him to Packingtown disguised as a laborer so that he can "live with the men, get a job in the yards, and use his eyes and ears...."

The crusading zeal of Sinclair and his colleagues touched a responsive chord in Roosevelt. However, his enthusiastic support for their work cooled somewhat when one of them wrote a series of articles that included harsh criticism of some of the President's allies in the U.S. Senate. In a speech soon after the articles appeared, Roosevelt said that investigative journalists reminded him of the man in *Pilgrim's Progress* "who could look no way but downward with the muck-rake in his hands; who would neither look up nor regard the crown he was offered, but continued to rake to himself the filth on the floor."

Most of the journalists didn't like being called muckrakers, but the name stuck.

. . . I saw with my own eyes hams, which had spoiled in pickle, being pumped full of chemicals to destroy the odor. I saw waste ends of smoked beef stored in barrels in a cellar, in a condition of filth which I could not describe in a letter. I saw rooms in which sausage meat was stored with poisoned rats lying about, and the dung of rats covering them. I saw hogs which had died of cholera in shipment, being loaded into box cars to be taken to a place called Globe, in Indiana, to be rendered into lard. . . . There are a hundred streets and avenues by which diseased meat can enter the city and be put on sale in the markets. The public has made no effort to find out and it is left to the men who deal in this merchandise to dump what they please into the stomachs of the blissfully ignorant public. Neither do any of us know how much disease and suffering this food causes. The diagnosis of the best physicians is so often turned down at the post mortem table that the actual results of diseased food are difficult to ascertain.

OPPOSITE: *Upton Sinclair gives Teddy Rosevelt tips on undercover inspections in meatpacking plants.*

198589

OFFICES AND SALESROOMS
1444 ~ 1450 St. Clair Avenue
CLEVELAND OHIO

June 24th, 1924.

Honorable Calvin Coolidge,
President of the United States,
Washington, D. C.

My Dear Mr. President:

I have been a staunch Republican for many years, casting my first vote for James A. Garfield.

I have twenty-three Department Stores located throughout the different towns and cities of Ohio. In some of these towns and cities the Ku Klux Klan organization has placed a boycott on several of my stores, on account of me being fortunate enough to be born a Hebrew, and just as soon as the present leases expire I will be compelled to move from these sections.

In the town of Ashland, Ohio, where one of my stores is located, there was held a meeting in the Public Square, and in front of thousands of spectators who had gathered to hear the speakers, the Ku Klux Klan openly told the audience they should not patronize any Jewish merchant. I think this is just plain boycott and very unfair to an American citizen or even a Non-American citizen.

I have read your platform and taken special notice to the paragraph in which you state that you demand "law and order" and "the protection of all citizens."

All I am asking for is your protection in this matter. If you have promised it for the next four years there is no reason why you cannot give it to us now, as you are The President now, of this glorious country, the same as I hope you will be for the next four years.

I await your kind reply for which I thank you in advance.

Very sincerely,

Chas D. Levy

Ansd 7/7/24

198589-59

CDL/N

Charles D. Levy to Calvin Coolidge

Cleveland, OH ★ June 24, 1924

It is difficult now to comprehend the power once exercised by the Ku Klux Klan. Formed in the South after the Civil War, the Klan died out with the end of Reconstruction. Reborn in 1915 (partly because of its heroic portrayal in D.W. Griffith's epic film *The Birth of a Nation*), the Klan soon became a major political force in the North and Midwest. By the 1920s, some two million people had joined the "Invisible Empire," and the number continued to grow throughout the decade. In several states, Klan members were elected to the legislature and the governorship. Massed phalanxes of white-robed, hooded Klansmen paraded in force down the grand avenues of Washington, D.C., and the Broadways and Main Streets of dozens of other towns.

In a world of increasing—and increasingly perplexing—complexity, the Klan offered simple truths: The world was debauched and decadent; America must keep itself aloof and maintain its purity. "Hyphenated" Americans were bound to have divided loyalties, while a "true" American was, as Teddy Roosevelt proclaimed in 1916, "pro-America, first, last, and all the time, and not pro-anything else at all." National survival hinged on victory in the life-or-death struggle between "us" (upstanding, God-fearing, native-born white Protestant Americans) and "them" (everyone else, but especially those—Negroes and Jews and foreigners, for example—who were bent on the "mongrelization" of America).

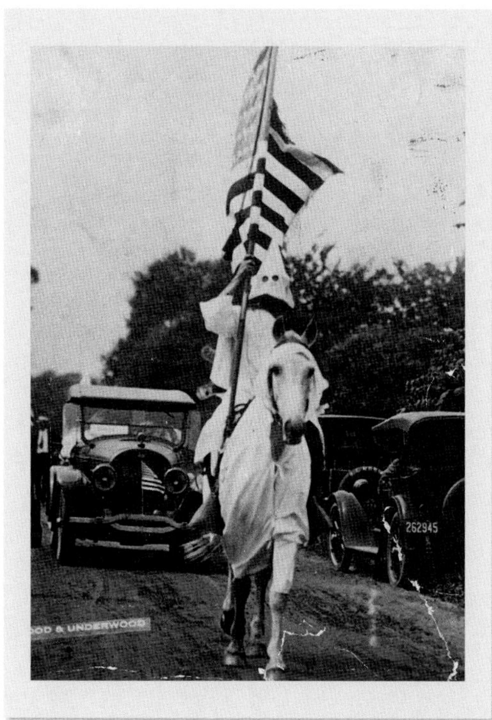

Against this background, Ohio businessman Charles D. Levy pens a letter to President Calvin Coolidge that fairly crackles with anger and frustration. He reports that the Klan has called for a boycott of his stores "on account of me being fortunate enough to be born a Hebrew," and the resulting economic hardship is forcing him out of business in some communities. Calling his treatment "unfair" (a remarkable understatement), he asks the President to give him the protection he deserves as a citizen.

The lack of a forceful response from Coolidge is hardly surprising. At the Republican Convention that had ended just a few days before Levy wrote his letter, some delegates had tried to insert a plank in the party platform condemning "any organization based on prejudice or discrimination against any citizens for reasons of race, color or creed." The convention, however, squashed the anti-Klan plank—and Coolidge, correctly gauging the political wind, apparently did nothing to curb the Klan's actions against Charles D. Levy.

OPPOSITE: *As Mr. Levy points out, the Ku Klux Klan relentlessly persecuted those it perceived as different.*
ABOVE: *Hiding behind their hoods and robes, the KKK used fear and hate as weapons.*

Alliance, Ohio, May #5,1924.

President Calvin Coolidge,
Washington, D.C.

Honored Sir,-

We, the Women of the Ku Klux Klan of Alliance, Ohio, do so heartily approve the Johnson Immigration Bill so overwhelmingly passed by House and Senate, and we earnestly request that you, the President of this United States, give your support and affix your signature to this bill.

We shall ever be devoted to the sublime principals of a pure Americanism, and valiant in the defense of its' ideals and institutions.

It is our earnest desire to promote real patriotism toward our civil government, honorable peace among men and nations, and protection for and happiness in the homes of our people.

Sincerely,
Alliance Klan # 1,
Women of the Ku Klux Klan.

Women of the Ku Klux Klan to Calvin Coolidge

Alliance, OH ★ May 15, 1924

Toward the end of the nineteenth century, some people felt it was time to close the fabled "Golden Door" through which immigrants were flooding into the U.S. and transforming the ethnic makeup of American society.

In 1882, immigration by Chinese laborers was suspended; a permanent ban was enacted in 1902. In 1891, several classes of would-be immigrants—including polygamists, persons suffering from "a loathsome disease," and anyone who had been convicted of a crime "involving moral turpitude"—were banned. In 1917, most of Asia was designated a "barred zone" from which immigration was prohibited. And in 1921, the first national-origin quota system was adopted, heavily favoring immigrants from northern and western Europe over those from anywhere else.

Even more restrictive was the 1924 Johnson-Reed Act, which limited immigration to 165,000 people annually. More than 85 percent of this quota was set aside for northwest Europe and Scandinavia, with far lower totals for the rest of the world. Germany's quota was pegged at 51,000, for example, while Italy's was less than 4,000 and Egypt's was 100.

Predictably, the Ku Klux Klan was among the Act's most vociferous supporters. The Klan's position was echoed by Women of the Ku Klux Klan, which was founded in 1923, grew to a nationwide membership approaching half a million, and eventually spawned the Tri-K-Klub for girls. Besides declaring that "the perpetuity of our nation rests upon the solidarity and purity of our native-born, white, Gentile, Protestant men and women," the "Creed of Klanswomen" also extolled the sanctity of the home, female emancipation, full equality of men and women, and other tenets of the suffrage and temperance movements.

Inspired by those noble sentiments, the women of Alliance Klan #1 sent this letter to President Calvin Coolidge. Their appeal is brief, but a tone of crusading zeal and militant patriotism thunders from every paragraph.

As he signed the Johnson-Reed Act into law, Coolidge declared "America must be kept American." His words doubtless sparked rejoicing among the Klanswomen of Alliance, Ohio—but by 1930, Women of the Ku Klux Klan had virtually disappeared.

OPPOSITE: *Ornate letterhead and lofty-sounding goals mask the xenophobia of the KKK.*
ABOVE: *As he did for the Johnson-Reed Act, President Coolidge signs a bill into law.*

National Cigarette Law Enforcement League Inc.

EXECUTIVE COMMITTEE
Dr. Dean C. Dutton, Pres.
Norman, Okla.
Dr. Wm. Forney Hovis, 1st Vice-Pres.
Oklahoma City, Okla.
Prof. J. R. Barton, 2nd Vice-Pres.
Oklahoma City, Okla.
Judge Jas. I. Phelps, 3rd Vice-Pres.
Oklahoma City, Okla.
Prof. Earl P. Weston, 4th Vice Pres.
Comanche, Okla.
Rev. Alva P. Jones, Supt.
Oklahoma City, Okla.
Mr. L. A. Coppage, Treas.
Oklahoma City, Okla.
Mr. D. N. Downing, Secy.
Oklahoma City, Okla.
Prof. Festus C. Snow, Auditor
Comanche, Okla.
Gov. Wm. J. Holloway, Council.
Hugo, Okla.

125 W. 17th St. Phone 4-9226

Other Director
Dr. Fred Mesch
Stillwater, Okla.
Mr. Ed L. Klein
Oklahoma City, Okla.
Cong. Jed Johnson
Anadarko, Okla.
Rev. L. H. La Grone
Blackwell, Okla.
Prof. C. W. Gethman
Oklahoma City, Okla.
Mrs. Alice M. David
Oklahoma, Okla.
Prof. Jno. S. Voughn
Durant, Okla.
Mr. U. M. Baughman
Oklahoma City, Okla.
Mr. Jno. A. Simpson
Oklahoma City, Okla.
Mr. Jno. W. Heidbrink
Oklahoma City, Okla.

THE WHITE HOUSE
MAY 31 1929
RECEIVED

Natl. Comm. on Law Observance and Enforcement

Ack. 5-31-29

Oklahoma City, Okla., May 25, 1929

RESPECTFULLY REFERRED FOR CONSIDERATION
Secretary to the President

To The Honorable Herbert Hoover, President,
United States of America,
Washington, D. C.

Dear Mr. President:

I understand that while you were Secretary of the Interior you gave out a statement saying, "There is no agency in the world today that is so seriously affecting the health, education, efficiency and character of boys and girls as the cigarette habit. Nearly every delinquent is a cigarette smoker."

Dr. C. L. Barber, former President of the Medico-Physical Research Association of America said, "This great wave of crime is due to the use of cigarettes and nothing else. The indiscriminate use of hooch, poison liquor, wine, Jamaica ginger and any other product that has a kick, is due to the use of cigarettes and nothing else." That, "You may legislate all the Volstead Acts, or any other acts you have a mind to, but you never will stop this wave of crime and demoralization until you stop the manufacture and sale of cigarettes."

Concerning "Acrolein," one of the 20 different poisons in the smoke of a cigarette, Mr. Edison says, "Ireally believe acrolein often makes boys insane." And Dr. Forbes Winslow says, "Cigarette smoking is one of the chief causes of insanity."

In view of these and like statements, from other eminent authorities, would it not be a fine idea for your crime commission of eminent jurists to make a careful study of the bearing of cigarette smoking upon the criminal? And especially Mr. Hoover, since there are forty states of our Union which are trying to protect their future citizens from the cigarette evil by passing laws prohibiting the sale of cigarettes and cigarette papers to their youths?

If cigarette smoking helps to produce criminals, it may be necessary to prohibit this evil before our crime wave can be ultimately solved (?)

With great faith in the success of your administration, I am,

Most cordially,

Alva P. Jones.

Superintendant,
National Cigarette Law Enforcement League.

APJ/MS.

Alva P. Jones, National Cigarette Law Enforcement League; Woman's Home Missionary Society; Mr. & Mrs. William Wilson to Herbert Hoover

Oklahoma City, OK ★ *May 25, 1929*
Baltimore, MD ★ *June 15, 1932*
Philadelphia, PA ★ *June 15, 1932*

Prohibition was supposed to usher humanity into sunny meadows of sobriety, productivity and morality, thereby making the world—or at least the United States—a better place. It didn't work.

Within a short time after the 18th Amendment banned the manufacture, sale or transportation of intoxicating beverages, what Missouri Senator James A. Reed called "the leprosy of hypocrisy" made a mockery of Prohibition's noble goals. Speakeasies flourished—more than 32,000 of them in New York City alone, by one estimate. Organized crime experienced a huge growth spurt. Millions of respectable citizens became scofflaws, while rum-runners, moonshiners and bootleggers were honored for their services to the vast community of the thirsty.

Americans who had had enough of the so-called great experiment—including government officials who wanted the tax revenues that alcohol sales could generate, as well as the hordes of men and women who just wanted a legal drink—made Prohibition a major issue in the 1932 Presidential election. At the Republican National Convention in Chicago, *Time* magazine reported, debate was punctuated by shouts of "We want Repeal" from the gallery. After adopting a platform that half-heartedly called for modification of Prohibition, delegates dutifully, if glumly, chose the embattled incumbent Herbert Hoover as their candidate for President.

The two telegrams on the following pages, sent on the day of Hoover's renomination, illustrate the division within the GOP: Members of a church in Baltimore urge the President to "stand firm" on Prohibition, while a couple from Philadelphia simultaneously insists on Repeal as a way to "preserve the Republican Party."

In the end, neither plea mattered. Hoover lost all but six states to Democrat Franklin D. Roosevelt. Just a month after Roosevelt took office, Congress legalized the manufacture and sale of beer. And on December 5, 1933, Prohibition officially ended with the ratification of the Twenty-first Amendment.

The Reverend Alva P. Jones takes a somewhat different position on Prohibition in a letter written in 1929. As superintendant of the National Cigarette Law Enforcement League, he asserts that all the fuss about the evils of drink is merely distracting people from a much more serious issue: the evils of tobacco. "Concerning 'Acrolein,' one of the 20 different poisons in the smoke of a cigarette," he notes, "Mr. Edison says, 'I really think acrolein often makes boys insane.'" Jones closes his letter by assuring Hoover of his "great faith in the success of your administration"—but five months later the stock market crashed, and three years after that came the Roosevelt landslide. The sight of FDR with his jauntily angled cigarette holder must have sent chills down the Reverend Jones's spine.

OPPOSITE: *Twenty names on the letterhead add strength to his writer's plea to Herbert Hoover.*

PATRONS ARE REQUESTED TO FAVOR THE COMPANY BY CRITICISM AND SUGGESTION CONCERNING ITS SERVICE

1201S

CLASS OF SERVICE

This is a full-rate Telegram or Cablegram unless its deferred character is indicated by a suitable sign above or preceding the address.

WESTERN UNION

NEWCOMB CARLTON, PRESIDENT — J. C. WILLEVER, FIRST VICE-PRESIDENT

SIGNS

DL = Day Letter
NM = Night Message
NL = Night Letter
LCO = Deferred Cable
NLT = Cable Night Letter
WLT = Week-End Letter

The filing time as shown in the date line on full-rate telegrams and day letters, and the time of receipt at destination as shown on all messages, is STANDARD TIME.

Received at 708 14th St., N. W. Washington, D. C. 1932 JUN 15 PM 7 36

BRC51 15 5 EXTRA=BALTIMORE MD 15 729P

MINUTES IN TRANSIT

FULL-RATE	DAY LETTER

HON HERBERT HOOVER=

PRESIDENT UNITEDSTATES WASHN=

CONGRATULATIONS STAND FIRM FAVOR PROHIBITION AS NOW EMBODIED IN CONSTITUTION=

WOMANS HOME MISSIONARY SOCIETY CLIFTON AVE ME CHURCH

BALTIMORE.

PATRONS ARE REQUESTED TO FAVOR THE COMPANY BY CRITICISM AND SUGGESTION CONCERNING ITS SERVICE

1201 S

CLASS OF SERVICE

This is a full-rate Telegram or Cablegram unless its deferred character is indicated by a suitable sign above or preceding the address.

WESTERN UNION

8A

SIGNS

DL = Day Letter
NM = Night Message
NL = Night Letter
LCO = Deferred Cable
NLT = Cable Night Letter
WLT = Week-End Letter

NEWCOMB CARLTON, PRESIDENT   J. C. WILLEVER, FIRST VICE-PRESIDENT

The filing time as shown in the date line on full-rate telegrams and day letters, and the time of receipt at destination as shown on all messages, is STANDARD TIME.

Received at 708 14th St., N. W. Washington, D. C.

1932 JUN 15 AM 8 52

MINUTES IN TRANSIT

FULL-RATE	DAY LETTER

PA65 27 7 EXTRA=GO PHILADELPHIA PENN 15 839A

HONORABLE HERBERT CLARK HOOVER=

THE WHITE HOUSE WASHN=

GOD MOVES IN A MYSTERIOUS WAY HIS WONDERS TO PERFORM REPEAL 18TH AMENDMENT AND PRESERVE THE REPUBLICAN PARTY=

MR AND MRS WILLIAM ELMER WILSON 3424 NORTH BOUVIER ST.

Justice

RESPECTFULLY REFERRED FOR CONSIDERATION.

Lawrence Richey

Secy. to the President

Mitchell, S. Dak.,

April 26, 1932

Honorable Herbert Hoover,

President of the United States,

The White House,

Washington, D. C.

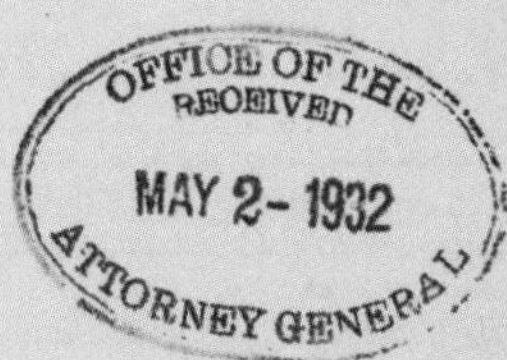

Dear Sir:

We, as citizens of the state of South Dakota, hereby wish to protest against any action that you, as chief executive of our nation, might take to release Al Capone from confinement because of his reported willingness to aid in the search for the kidnaped son of Mr. and Mrs. Charles A.Lindberg.

While our sympathy goes out to Mr. and Mrs. Lindberg in their loss, we feel that presidential action to free this notorious criminal even temporarily, to assist individuals, would be a serious mistake. We believe that it would encourage further acts of kidnaping violence from gangsters, and that it would be wholly unwise.

W. E. H.

Most respectfully yours,

RECEIVED
MAY 3 1932
CRIMINAL DIVISION

MAY 4 1932

Mitchell, SD ★ April 26, 1932

ON THE NIGHT OF MARCH 1, 1932, SOMEONE kidnapped the 20-month-old son of aviation icon and national hero Charles Lindbergh. On May 12, the baby's body was found in the woods near his home.

The crime gripped America as no other had. For four years the story played out in newspapers and on radio like an epic drama, offering a large cast of fascinating characters (including an army of amateur sleuths), badly misspelled ransom notes, an eerie interlude in a dark cemetery, bundles of marked currency, plenty of false leads and dead-end trails, and a circus-like trial that drew celebrity spectators to a cramped New Jersey courtroom. Even now, seven decades after a 35-year-old German-born carpenter named Bruno Hauptmann was executed for the crime, the what-ifs of the case continue to fuel heated discussion.

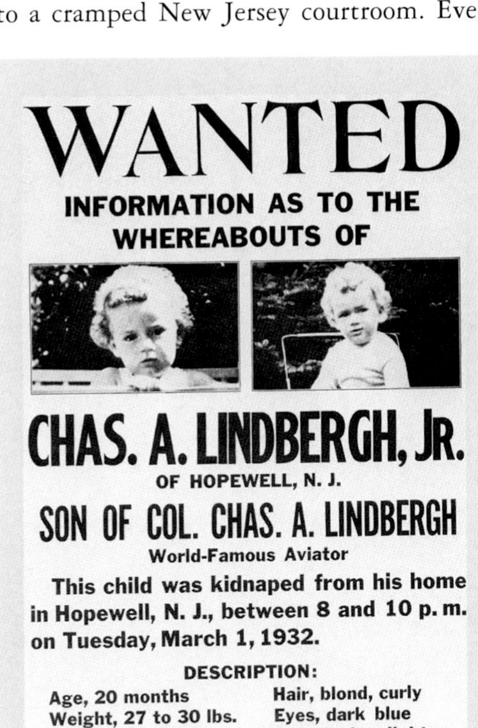

When Lucky Lindy's baby disappeared, America's best known gangster, Al Capone, was locked up in Chicago's Cook County Jail, awaiting a transfer to the federal penitentiary in Atlanta to begin serving an 11-year sentence for tax evasion. When he heard about the kidnapping, Capone promptly offered a $10,000 reward for information leading to the safe return of the child. Then, apparently assuming (as did many other people) that organized crime was involved, he claimed that he would personally nab the guilty mobsters if the feds would only release him from prison for two weeks.

The press ballyhooed Capone's offer, sparking a lively public debate on whether it should be accepted—and at this point, some "citizens of South Dakota" weighed in with this letter to President Herbert Hoover.

Using a typewriter that clearly has a mind of its own, they tell the President in no uncertain terms that they aren't happy about the possible release. Reminding Hoover that Capone is a "notorious criminal," they say that turning him loose would merely encourage more misdeeds. With admirable Midwestern taciturnity, they tell the President that springing this particular jailbird would be "wholly unwise."

As it turned out, the South Dakotans needn't have worried. Lindbergh contacted the IRS agent who had put Scarface Al behind bars and was assured that no gangster could be trusted and that Capone would flee the country as soon as the jailhouse door opened. Lindbergh later said that he never intended to ask for Capone's release.

OPPOSITE: *This letter bears the markings of an assortment of receiving offices within the federal government.*
ABOVE: *A shocked nation yearned to find the kidnapped Lindbergh baby alive.*

Argenta, Ark ~~June 2~~ 1899

Argenta

Ag

Hon. Wm McKinley
President of the U.S.

The leaders in the mob that killed 20 Colored men in April '99. in Little River co. Ark. were John Sanders, Jim Sanders, Eli Britt, John Hawkins. Colored men forced to assist were Elias Coons, Dave Rif.

After they killed the men the mob forced their wives and daughters to yeld to their beastly desiers. then beat them and some of them died from the effect of the cruel treatment. Please if possible do something for us.

Henry Johnson
Argenta
Ark.

P.S. Please answer soon and let us know what to do about it.

71

Henry Johnson to William McKinley
Ara Lee Settle to Warren G. Harding
Horace Robinson to Herbert Hoover

Argenta, AR ★ June 5, 1899
Washington, D.C. ★ June 8, 1922
Boston, MA ★ November 20, 1929

The dictionary definition of lynching —"putting a person to death for an alleged offense without a legal trial"—fails to convey the brutality of the act or the horror it aroused in the minds of those who were most likely to be its victims.

While the practice of lynching had existed in America since the eighteenth century, it became a much more frequent occurrence after the Civil War as white Americans sought to reassert their supremacy over blacks who were seeking—and often gaining—improved political, economic and social status. By the beginning of the twentieth century, the threat of lynching had become a terrifying fact of life for African Americans living in the South.

A study published in 1930 by the Commission on Interracial Cooperation reported that 3,724 people had been lynched since 1889, though the true total was by some accounts as high as 5,000. More than four-fifths of the victims were African Americans. Of the thousands of people who carried out or witnessed these killings, only 49 were indicted; of these, only four were actually sentenced.

The agony and outrage sparked by what anti-lynching crusader Ida B. Wells called "our country's national crime" are evident in these three letters written over a 30-year span.

Henry Johnson's brief 1899 letter to President William McKinley indicates that Johnson witnessed the killing of "20 colored men" in southwestern Arkansas. Besides offering chilling details of the crime, he courageously names the four men who led the murderous mob and implores the President, "Please if possible do something for us."

In her 1922 letter to President Warren G. Harding, teenager Ara Lee Settle pleads for support of the Dyer Bill, which aimed to punish authorities who failed to prevent lynching. Reminding Harding that black people helped build and sustain the nation ("During the world war, Negro boys also sacrificed their lives as well, and as bravely as the white man...") she says that as long as these hideous crimes continue, the phrase "sweet land of liberty" is nothing more than an empty promise.

Horace Robinson's letter to President Herbert Hoover, written in 1929, shows how little has changed in the seven years since Ara Lee Settle sat down at her typewriter. Having heard of another lynching in Florida, the 20-year-old Robinson funnels his emotional turmoil into a single question: "Are the members of my Race and I to be murdered and hacked by other Americans whose faces are white, but whose souls are of the blackest?"

Given the temper of the times, it is unlikely that Henry Johnson's letter prompted any meaningful response from the McKinley White House.

Despite Ara Lee Settle's appeal to Harding, the Dyer Bill never made it out of the Senate.

Horace Robinson's poignant question still hangs in the air.

OPPOSITE: *Henry Johnson's plaintive letter, daring to call lynchers by name, probably fell on deaf ears.*

158260

Armstrong Technical High School,
Washington, D. C.,
June 18, 1922.

Hon. Warren G. Harding,
President of the United States,
The White House,
Washington, D. C.

Dear Sir:

I am taking the liberty of intruding this letter upon you, because I feel that the issues involved are as important as any questions that have ever been pressed upon you. It is to urge your support of the Dyer Bill.

Mr. President, lynching has been committed in the south for many years, but when the last presidential election took place, practically every colored boy and girl in America was for Warren G. Harding as president. Why did we want you? The answer was: He is a Republican and will stop that terrible crime - lynching. You were elected, but now and then there could be heard of a few lynchings. Mr. President, why do they lynch the Negro? Has not he done his full share, or bit, in the making of this new land? When America was fighting for independence, was not Crispus Attucks, a negro, the first man killed? There are many others that could be named, but time and space will not permit me. When the trumpet was blown for civil strife, did not the Negro give his life as well as the Anglo-Saxon? During the world war, Negro boys also sacrificed their lives as well, and as bravely as the white man, that democracy might rule the earth. This reminds me of our glorious song "My Country 'tis of Thee, Sweet land of Liberty." Mr. President, you are aware of the fact that we have not our full liberty but still we sing the song by faith in the future. ABP

I admit that there are some lawless Negroes in America, as well as whites, capable of committing horrible crimes. All people are not as good as others, but, Mr. President, what good does lynching do? One man may be lynched for a crime of which another has committed. It does not tend to make a nation better, it only brings race prejudice and hatred. What good or use is the law, if the lynchers are going to put the law in their own hands. Mr. President, imagine yourself about to be lynched for something of which you know nothing about. Men sieze you from some place of refuge, carry you to the heart of the town, place a rope around you and burn you, while men, women and children are jeering amidst all your pain and agony. It is enough to make one ashamed not to use his full influence against this horrible crime.

A bill has been introduced in Congress by Representative Dyer (a Republican) to prevent lynching, or make it a criminal offense. Mr. President, it is incumbent upon you, the chief executive of all Americans to urge the passage of this bill. If lynching is permitted in the south, finally it will spread to the north, doing nothing but kindling the flames of racial and personal hatred, and sowing the seeds of internal strife. There are some courageous and conscientious senators who are in favor of the passage of the bill, but, Mr. President, we are looking to

see 158260-10

. . . Mr. President, lynching has been committed in the south for many years, but when the last presidential election took place, practically every colored boy and girl in America was for Warren G. Harding as president. Why did we want you? The answer was: He is a Republican and will stop that terrible crime--lynching. You were elected, but now and then there could be heard of a few lynchings. Mr. President, why do they lynch the Negro? Has not he done his full share or bit in the making of this new land? When America was fighting for independence, was not Crispus Attucks, a negro, the first man killed? There are many others that could be named, but time and space will not permit me. When the trumpet was blown for civil strife, did not the Negro give his life as well as the Anglo-Saxon? During the world war, Negro boys also sacrificed their lives as well, and as bravely as the white man, that democracy might rule the earth. This reminds me of our glorious song "My Country 'tis of Thee, Sweet land of Liberty." Mr. President, you are aware of the fact that we have not our full liberty but still we sing the song by faith in the future.

I admit that there are some lawless Negroes in America, as well as whites, capable of committing horrible crimes. All people are not as good as others, but, Mr. President, what good does lynching do? One man may be lynched for a crime of which another has committed. It does not tend to make a nation better, it only brings race prejudice and hatred. What good or use is the law if the lynchers are going to put the law in their own hands. Mr. President, imagine yourself about to be lynched for something of which you know nothing about. Men seize you from some place of refuge, carry you to the heart of the town, place a rope around you and burn you, while men, women and children are jeering amidst all your pain and agony. It is enough to make one ashamed not to use his full influence against this horrible crime.

A bill has been introduced in Congress by Representative Dyer (a Republican) to prevent lynching, or make it a criminal offense. Mr. President, it is incumbent upon you, the chief executive of all Americans to urge the passage of this bill. If lynching is permitted in the south finally it will spread to the north, doing nothing but kindling the flames of racial and personal hatred, and sowing the seeds of internal strife. There are some courageous and conscientious senators who are in favor of the passage of the bill, but, Mr. President, we are looking to you to see it through. If this country had more men such as Mr. Dyer it would be "Sweet land of Liberty".

One might say, push the bill away until a more opportune time presents itself when they would be more able to debate on it. But as a well known man has said, "Today is the only real day promised". Why not do that today and hurl lynching into a bottomless pit to remain forever? Mr. President, we are looking and pleading to you.

During the war the colored people were very patriotic, they bought Liberty Bonds, War Saving Stamps, Thrift Stamps, had meatless, sugarless, wheatless days, also they crocheted, knitted and embroidered for the boys over there while they were fighting for "dear old America", but mind you some of the same Colored boys have since returned to America and been lynched in a way that has been heretofore explained.

When lynching has been expurged, then we may all sing from our hearts with a true meaning:

"My Country 'tis of thee, Sweet Land of Liberty, Of thee I Sing.
Land where my fathers died, Land of the Pilgrims pride,
Frome every mountain side, Let Freedom ring.

Once more, Mr. Harding, we are looking to you, to you, to you.

Respectfully yours,

Ara Lee Settle, Section C, 15 years of age

OPPOSITE: *Wise beyond her 15 years, Ara Lee Settle makes both reasoned and impassioned arguments for a bill to end the horrors of lynching.*

Hon Wm McKinley, President of the U.S.

The leaders in the mob that killed 20 colored men in April '99 in Little River Co. Ark were John Sanders, Jim Sanders, Eli Britt, John Hawkins. Colored men forced to assist were Elias Coons, Dave Rex.

After they killed the men the mob forced their wives and daughters to yield to their beastly desires, then beat them and some of them died from the effect of the cruel treatment.

Please if possible do something for me.

Henry Johnson, Argenta, ARk.

P.S. Please answer soon and let me know what to do about it.

★★★

Dear Sir,

I, a Negro of twenty years, have just learned of another lynching of a member of my Race, which took place in Florida a few days ago. Although I dislike to bother you Sir, I am compelled to appeal to you to stop lynching in the United States of any man, regardless of race or color. I feel that you, as President of this nation, are better able to stop this outrage than any other person.

Are the members of my Race and I to be murdered and hacked by other Americans whose faces are white, but whose souls are of the blackest? Are we, who after having suffered numerous insults at the hands of the white race, who have, nevertheless fought and died for the Red, White and Blue to be continually restricted our natural rights.

Sir, I see only one way which will end lynching. That is for the President of the nation to take an active part against those states of the Union that allow such atrocious crimes.

Sir, do you think that because a woman of your Race is attacked by a man of my Race that this man should be put to death without even having a trial? Is not the woman's life as seriously endangered whether it be a white or a black man?

Of course, I believe that any man who commits such a crime should be given at least a life sentence at hard labor, but I do not think he should be killed by a lawless, blood-thirsty gang.

Sir, I appeal to you, I beg of you to protect my Race, who after all, are citizens of America as well as the white Race.

Sir, do you think that I would leave a white person in water where that person is struggling for his life, when I know that I can save him? No, Sir. I would not. For I would realize that although he is not a member of my Race, he is a human being, therefore he deserves to be saved.

Sir, I trust you will pardon me for taking up some of your valuable time, but I felt that I would be unable to do any constructive thinking until I had made an appeal to you on behalf of my race and me.

Respectfully yours,
Horace Robinson

OPPOSITE: *In 1929, America wasn't ready to hear Horace Robinson's eloquent plea for equality.*

218 - W. Canton St.
Boston, Mass.
November 20, 1929

Mr. Herbert Hoover, President
of the United States of America

Dear Sir:

I, a Negro of twenty years, have just learned of another lynching of a member of my Race, which took place in Florida a few days ago. Although I dislike to bother you Sir, I am compelled to appeal to you to stop lynching in the United States of any man, regardless of race or color. I feel that you, as President of this nation, are better able to stop this outrage, than any other person.

Are the members of my Race and I, to be murdered and hacked by other Americans whose faces are white, but whose souls are of the blackest! Are we, who after having suffered numerous insults at the hands of the white race, who have, nevertheless, fought and died for the Red, White and Blue

AMELIA EARHART

Do what we can and contact Mr Putnam

2 West 45th Street,
New York City.

November 10, 1936.

Dear Mr. President:

Some time ago I told you and Mrs. Roosevelt a little about my confidential plans for a world flight. As perhaps you know, through the cooperation of Purdue University I now have a magnificient twin-motor, all-metal plane, especially equipped for long distance flying.

For some months ~~we~~ Mr. Putnam and I have been preparing for a flight which I hope to attempt probably in March. The route, compared with previous flights, will be unique. It is east to west, and approximates the equator. Roughly it is from San Francisco to Honolulu; from Honolulu to Tokio -- or Honolulu to Brisbane; the regular Australia-England route as far west as Karachi; from Karachi to Aden; Aden via Kartoon across Central Africa to Dakar; Dakar to Natal, and thence to New York on the regular Pan American route.

Special survey work and map preparation is already under way on the less familiar portion of the route as, for instance, that in Africa.

The chief problem is the jump westward from Honolulu. The distance thence to Tokio is 3900 miles. I want to reduce as much as possible the hazard of the take-off at Honolulu with the excessive over-load. With that in view, I am discussing with the Navy a possible refueling in the air over Midway Island. If this can be arranged, I need to take much less gas from Honolulu, and with the Midway refueling will have ample

Amelia Earhart to Franklin D. Roosevelt

New York, NY ★ November 10, 1936

In a country that has known an endless parade of flash-in-the-pan celebrities, Amelia Earhart was a bona fide heroine. Some tried to hang the nickname "Lady Lindy" on her, but it didn't fit. She was unmistakably herself.

Tall and slim, with a steady gaze and a tomboy's grin and tousled hair that she obviously didn't pay much attention to, she looked like someone whom friends would describe as "a great gal." She worked as a nurse's aide, went to college, became a social worker—and then everything changed when she took a ride in an airplane in 1920. "By the time I had got two or three hundred feet off the ground," she later wrote, "I knew I had to fly."

By 1936, having won just about every existing aviation medal, she had fixed her sights on the biggest remaining challenge: She wanted to be the first woman to fly around the world. She planned to follow an east-to-west route, flying from California to Hawaii, then to Japan (or possibly Australia), Africa, and South America, before turning north to New York. The flight would be enormously risky from start to finish, of course, but one problem loomed particularly large: If she tried to carry enough fuel to get across the long stretch of ocean west of Honolulu, she risked overloading her plane.

In this letter to President Roosevelt, she summarizes her dilemma and presents one possible solution: If the President gives his approval, the Navy could refuel her plane in the air over Midway Island. She does some expert buttering up ("knowing your own enthusiasm for voyaging, and your affectionate interest in Navy Matters"), tells him that success in this project "might, I think, win for the Service further popular friendship," and assures him that the flight is a noncommercial venture being undertaken "because I feel that women...have to do things to show what women can do."

Roosevelt granted her request—but the midair refueling became unnecessary when Earhart learned about a new landing strip on tiny Howland Island that she could use. As it happened, her round-the-world flight never got that far: At the end of the first leg, her plane was damaged in a crash at Honolulu and had to be shipped back to California for repairs.

A few weeks later, Earhart was ready for another try. She and navigator Fred Noonan took off from Miami, flying west to east this time, on June 1. By the end of the month they had reached Lae, New Guinea, with no major mechanical problems. On July 2 they took off for their next landing spot—Howland Island—and were never seen again.

. . . will have ample gasoline to reach Tokio. As mine is a land plane, the seaplane facilities at Wake, Guam, etc., are useless. . . . Some new seaplanes are being completed at San Diego for the Navy. They will be ferried in January or February to Honolulu. It is my desire to practice actual refueling operations in the air over San Diego with one of these planes. That plane subsequently from Honolulu would be available for the Midway operation. . . . Like previous flights, I am undertaking this one solely because I want to, and because I feel that women now and then have to do things to show what women can do. . . .

P.S. – My plans are for the moment entirely confidential--no announcement has been made.

OPPOSITE: *Amelia Earhart's request for help earned a coveted notation from FDR: "Do what we can ..."*

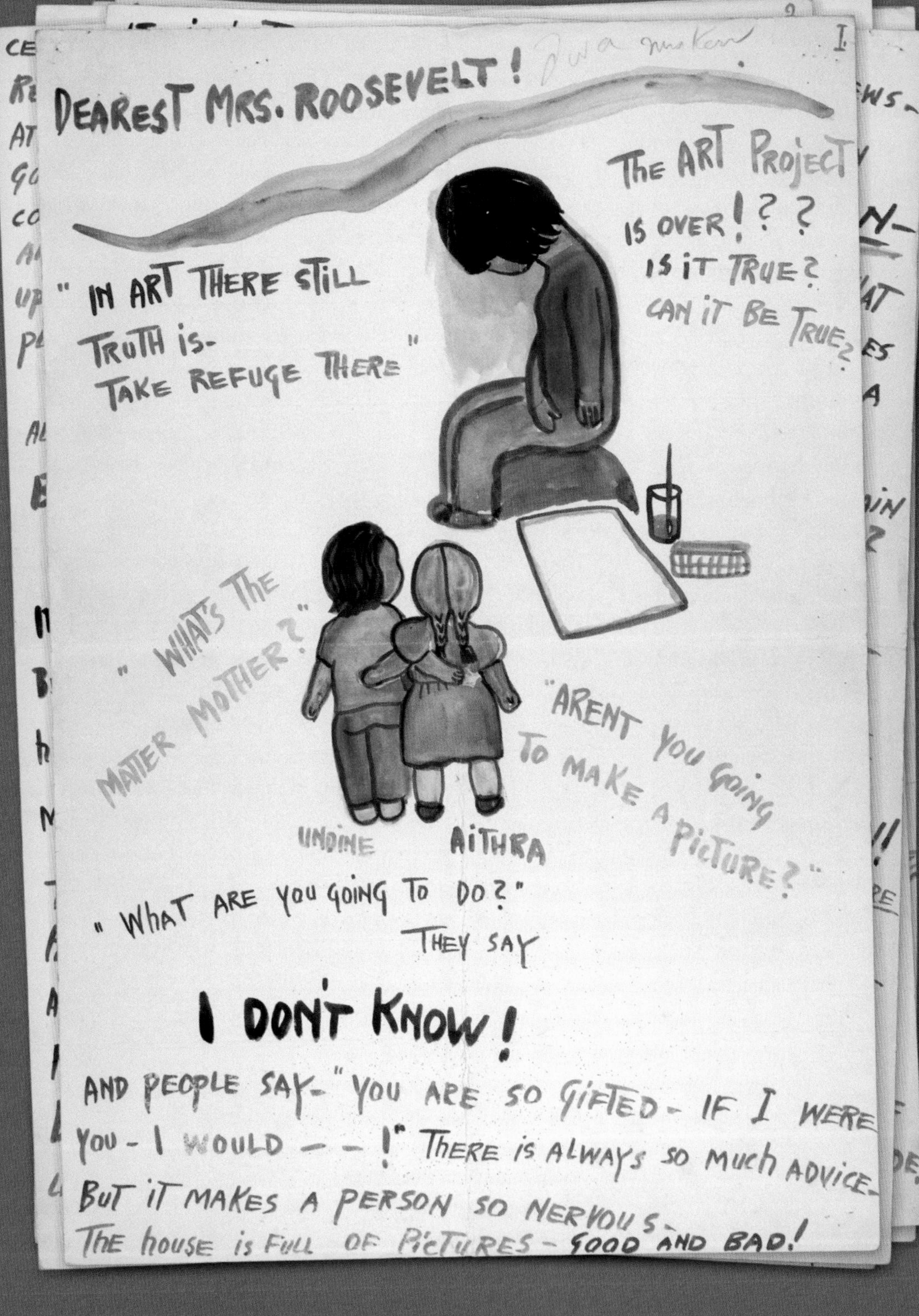
I.
DEAREST MRS. ROOSEVELT!
THE ART PROJECT IS OVER!??
IS IT TRUE?
CAN IT BE TRUE?
" IN ART THERE STILL TRUTH IS-
TAKE REFUGE THERE"
" WHAT'S THE MATTER MOTHER?"
"ARENT YOU GOING TO MAKE A PICTURE?"
UNDINE
AITHRA
" WHAT ARE YOU GOING TO DO?"
THEY SAY
I DON'T KNOW!
AND PEOPLE SAY- "YOU ARE SO GIFTED - IF I WERE
YOU - I WOULD - - !" THERE IS ALWAYS SO MUCH ADVICE-
BUT IT MAKES A PERSON SO NERVOUS-
THE HOUSE IS FULL OF PICTURES - GOOD AND BAD!

Gisella (Lacher) Loeffler to Eleanor Roosevelt

Los Griegos ★ *July 27, 1939*

Of the myriad alphabet-soup agencies created by Roosevelt's New Deal, few aroused stronger feelings than the Federal Art Project (FAP). Contemporary critics charged that the program was a wasteful boondoggle that produced amateurish works of flagrantly radical (and heavily pro-New Deal) propaganda. Supporters countered that in addition to putting artists to work—its primary purpose—the program also gave the nation some of its most significant pieces of public art. Today, it is generally agreed that the estimated 2,500 murals, 17,700 sculptures, 108,000 easel paintings, and 240,000 prints produced under the FAP's auspices constitute a priceless legacy and a joyous celebration of America's history, diversity, and creativity.

Established in 1935, the FAP eventually employed some 6,000 people, more than half of them directly involved in the production of art. One of them was Gisella Loeffler, an Austrian-born artist who moved to Taos, New Mexico, after seeing an exhibition of works by Taos painters. In addition to easel paintings and book illustrations, she also executed murals for several hospitals and schools, all of them in a charmingly naïve style that frequently incorporated images from Austrian, Mexican, and Native American folklore.

This letter, written to Eleanor Roosevelt in 1939, reflects Loeffler's shock on learning that the FAP was being shut down. "The Art Project is over!?? Is it true? Can it be true?" she asks, then answers her own question: "It is a dreadful blow; I don't know what to do?" She had reason to be concerned. Economic conditions had improved somewhat in recent months, but the Depression had by no means loosed its hold on New Mexico. Even if she moved out of the state, finding buyers for her work would not be easy—and she had two small children to support.

Loeffler's letter is ten pages long, embellished with brightly colored drawings depicting the artist and her daughters. In one of the illustrations, a thunderstorm is raging and the roof is leaking—but Loeffler's grief and dismay doubtless have something to do with her assertion that "it is raining out side and inside."

Dearest Mrs. Roosevelt!

The ART Project is over!?? Is it true? Can it be true?

"In art there still truth is. Take refuge there"

"What's the matter Mother?"

"Aren't you going to make a picture?"

"What are you going to do?" They say

I don't know!

And people say "You are so gifted--If I were you--I would--!" There is always so much advice. But it makes a person so nervous. The house is full of pictures--good and bad! It is just three days now since the bad news. People that have been on the project more than 18 months--must go off for 30 days! Then--I have been thinking-thinking-thinking-about what to do next. Go to a big city--and show the pictures somewhere--(but that takes money)

OPPOSITE: *In search of a sympathetic ear, Gisella Loeffler writes "to the First Lady of the Land" about the Federal Art Project's demise.*

Illustrate a book--Plenty of funny experiences right in this little adobe village-but that takes time-and again what will there be to live on in the meanwhile?? Why must it end this way?? I have just finished illustrating a book of Spanish games-in New Mexico-before that I did tempera panels for The Socorro School of Mines-before that the murals at The Carrie Tingley Hospital at Hot Springs-on the art project in New Mexico-it is a dreadfull blow! I don't know what to do? Several years ago-before the art projects-I decorated Dr. Villary Blair's operating room at the Barnes Hospital in St. Louis. It was the first operating room ever decorated-and was reproduced at the World's Fair in Chicago. Most of my work is for children-I just love to do things to make children happy! About 6 years ago I decorated the dining room at The Michael's School for Crippled Children in St. Louis. That was a government project--but a different kind-than the one I have been on for three-years-now!

Certainly-this all sounds very selfish--but really I have worked hard and conciencciously-at first we lived in Taos-then my daughter Undine got rheumatic fever-we had to leave Taos and come to Albuquerque-poor child was in bed a year and a half-and her heart was badly affected-she is up now and feels pretty strong and well-but of course plenty of harm was done--

Yes-I scold and scold myself! Truly I did all I could-for my little girl-and for the work but now-I feel so foolish and bewildered! If we could live like our Mexican neighbors on beans and tortillas-and coffee-perhaps we could have saved. A little bit-but that kind of diet makes us feel sick. Other wise we have learned to live very simply-and our life here has had so much charm-The country is beautiful. The air smells of pinon smoke. The people sing such pretty Spanish songs-and we just love to go to the Bailes and Fiestas-and dance la varsoviana-and la schotte-and las chapenecas! . . .

Los Griegos New Mexico July 27-1939

It is raining out side and inside.

We live in an adobe house-when the sun out of doors glares and burns-it is cool and dusky inside. But now there is a fierce thunderstorm and the roof is leaking.

So we are busy putting pails and pans under the worst leaks-Aithra has brought her bunny in-he is eating a grape leaf. Undine is burning a piece of cedar to make the house smell better-and to chase out all the evil spirits. Most of the adobe houses have blue painted around the door and window sills-that also is to keep out devils-it would be better to do something to keep out the rain-but the people here say "All mud roofs leak-it can't be helped!" The Mexicans have their wooden Santos to protect them-Santo Ni o-San Antonio San Isidro San Jose Guadalupe. For every trouble there is a Santo!

The Indians have their many Katchinas-and sacred corn-and snakes and turtles - and turquoise and the bear--and the deer-and their koshari-so many wonderworking powers!

A koshari-is a sort of ghost-he is very funny and makes people laugh-but also he has the power to take what he wishes! Pottery-and melons and soda pop! . . .

And the sun shining again-and the churchbells clankling-and children laughing-it is hard to realize anything dark and gloomy!

And Otonacio has promised to terra-vista our walls on the inside of the house-there are long muddy steaks - where the muddy water leaked down! We thank Otonacio for his good intentions! But on the inside we wonder just what will be--

OPPOSITE: *Pictures speak louder than words in Gisella Loeffler's colorfully illustrated letter to Eleanor Roosevelt.*

LOS GRIEGOS NEW MEXICO JULY 27-1939

IT IS RAINING OUT SIDE AND INSIDE

WE LIVE IN AN ADOBE HOUSE - WHEN THE SUN OUT OF DOORS GLARES AND BURNS - IT IS COOL AND DUSKY INSIDE. BUT NOW THERE IS A FIERCE THUNDER STORM AND THE ROOF IS LEAKING.

5.

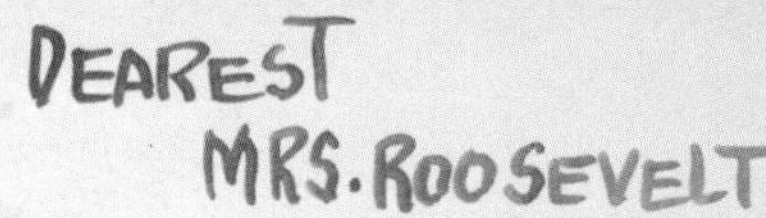

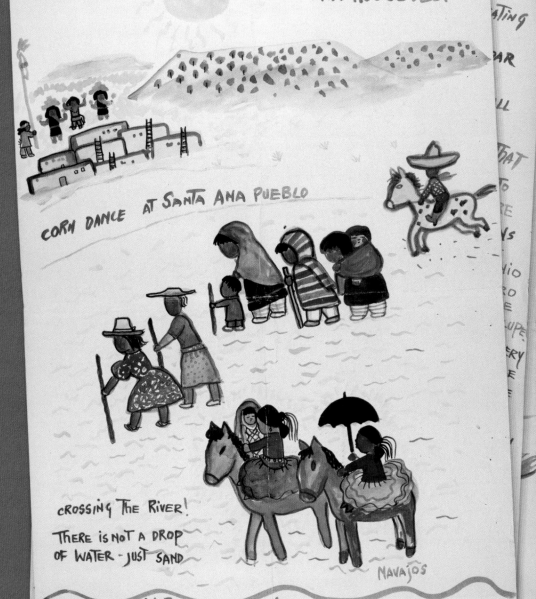

CORN DANCE AT SANTA ANA PUEBLO

CROSSING THE RIVER!

THERE IS NOT A DROP OF WATER - JUST SAND

NAVAJOS

So NOW — !!??? ???!

I COULD MAKE A PICTURE BOOK FOR LITTLE CHILDREN THAT ARE NOT ABLE TO COME OUT HERE IN THE ...

POTTERY - AND MELONS AND SODA POP!

Why am I writing to the First Lady of the land?

One of my little girls has been reading an old fashioned story about a poor troubled person who went to the Queen-and knelt before her-shy and sad-and sincere and hopeful-

Perhaps the Queen said "What can you do?"

No. Otonacio never worries-the rain is over and he is putting a little mud on the house-every once in a while Otonacio sits down to rest-and sing a pretty song-

"Hay Corazon que te vas para nunca volver nome digas adious"

"Adious mi chaparita no llores par tu pancho que se si va del rancho mui pronto volvera"

With all the pretty songs in the air-and yesterday we went to see a corn dance at Santa Ana Pueblo. We thought that it was a good thing for the Indians to pray-and sing and drum and dance for rain! It was so hot and dry and sandy and windy.

And today we have a deluge-there is a big lake all around us-water-water every where-the pinon wood is floating around in the back yard-we don't dare open the door-"There is much to see and hear"

Dearest Mrs. Roosevelt

Corn dance at Santa Ana Pueblo

Crossing the river! There is not a drop of water-just sand

So now-!!??????!

I could make a picture book for little children that are not able to come out here in the glistening desert-to hear and see the Indians drum and sing and dance.

When I was painting on the walls of The Michael's School for Crippled Children in St. Louis-the poor little sick children used to watch me paint - and I would tell them-about my grandfather's Gasthaus in Austria-"Kiady" gingerbread hearts-decorated Easter eggs-Grampus "Das Kriskindel" About the big-deep forests-and the red mushrooms with the white spots-and the good-good little strawberries-and the sweet little blue forget-me-nots-and sing them little old folk songs-

Then I would tell them about the Southwest-How the Indians bake bread in round adobe ovens out of doors-and how the Pueblo is on the inside-and about the wonderful silver bracelets and rings and necklaces the Navajos make-and about the rugs they weave-and how they spin the wool from their own sheep-and make dyes from-Chamiso and Indigo-and walnut hulls and bugs and leaves and things-

Then about the black pottery-and red pottery and pottery with beautiful designs-all made by busy little-brown loving Indian hands-and about-deer dances and corn dances-and ceremonial robes-and how they grow corn-red - and blue and purple and yellow-how the women grind it-into flour and make thin corn tortillas-

I'd like to make a book-or work with little tired and sick children-paint for them. And they for me-

Very sincerely,

Gisella L. Lacher

R.R. 12 Box 120-Los Griegos via Albuquerque New Mexico

OPPOSITE: *Signing this letter "Gisella L. Lacher," the Austrian-born artist was better known by the surname Loeffler.*

4 City ave
New Britain Conn
August 7, 1941.

Mrs Franklin D. Roosevelt

Dear First Lady,

I am a widow; my husband died nine months ago, and since then I have received my Social Security each month, fifteen dollars and ninety three cents.

I want to express my thankfulness to our President for being the means of this big help in being able to

Petra E. Harthun to Eleanor Roosevelt

New Britain, CT ★ August 7, 1941

Much has been written in recent years about the complicated and somewhat thorny nature of the domestic relationship between Franklin and Eleanor Roosevelt. Most Americans in the 1930s and '40s didn't know the details of their life as husband and wife, of course—but they sensed that the President and First Lady, however else one might characterize them, were partners. They knew that the wheelchair-bound President counted on his energetic wife to be his eyes and ears and legs, and that she, for her part, relished the role and respected the trust that he placed in her. They knew that she influenced his thinking on topics that interested her—and there were plenty of them. They knew that he listened to her.

It's not surprising, therefore, that people who wanted to get a message to the President often enlisted the First Lady as their messenger. This letter, from a woman in Connecticut, describes a family not unlike thousands of others in Depression-era America. The writer is a widow. She has taken her son and his little daughter into her home, for which she pays $25 a month in rent. Unable to find work in his field, her son has taken a job that pays just 43 cents an hour. Life isn't easy, but they're getting by.

Surprisingly, the letter isn't a plea for help. Instead, it's a warm expression of thanks.

Every month she receives a Social Security payment of $15.93. It isn't much (especially by today's standards) but it's a "big help in being able to carry on." She knows the President is responsible for her having it. She blesses him in her prayers every day, and she wants his wife to tell him so.

Mrs Franklin D. Roosevelt
Dear First Lady,

I am a widow, my husband died nine months ago, and since then I have received my Social Security each month, fifteen dollars and ninety three cents.

I want to express my thankfulness to our President for being the means of this big help in being able to carry on.

My son and his little girl lives with me, he is a telegraphist by trade, but being unable to find that kind of work, is at present working as a gatetender for the R.R. at 0.43 cents an hour, 8 hour day. We would have to part, go each our own way, if it were not for this money that help us pay the rent, $25.00 a month.

Please forward my deep appreciation.

I am yours respectfully,
Petra Engebretson Harthun

God bless the President and his dear ones. That's my little girls and my prayer every day.

OPPOSITE: *Eleanor Roosevelt must have appreciated this poignant letter of thanks for the benefit of Social Security.*

JHS

COLEGIO DE DOLORES
APARTADO 1
SANTIAGO DE CUBA

DIVISION OF
NOV 25 1940
THE AMERICAN REPUBLICS
DEPARTMENT OF STATE

President of the United States.
If you like, give me a ten dollars bill green american, in the letter, because never, I have not seen a ten dollars bill green american and I would like to have one of them.
My address is:
Sr. Fidel Castro
Colegio de Dolores.
Santiago de Cuba
Oriente. Cuba.
I don't know very English but I know very much Spanish and I suppose you don't know very Spanish but you know very English because you are American but I am not American.

(Thank you very much)
Good by. Your friend,

Castro
Fidel Castro

If you want iron to make your sheaps ships I will show to you the bigest (minas) of iron of the land. They are in Mayarí. Oriente Cuba.

much but I do not think
that I am writting to the

FIDEL CASTRO TO FRANKLIN D. ROOSEVELT

Santiago de Cuba ★ November 6, 1940

AS A GROWN MAN, HE WANTED BIG THINGS—building a tough guerrilla army, for instance, and getting rid of longtime dictator Fulgencio Batista, and transforming Cuba from a capitalist vacationers' playground to a socialist workers' paradise. But that was much later. In November 1940, Fidel Castro's wishes were more modest. He was 12 years old, and all he wanted was ten dollars.

It's a bit hard to imagine what drove young Fidel to ask the President of the United States for a long-distance cash donation. It wasn't the desperation of poverty, since Castro's parents were sufficiently well-off to ensure that their son got a good education in Jesuit schools and, later, the University of Havana. Besides, it appears that what he had in mind wasn't a handout but a quid pro quo exchange: "If you want iron to make your ships," he tells Roosevelt, "I will show to you the bigest (*minas*) of iron of the land. They are in Mayari [near Castro's birthplace] Oriente Cuba."

Perhaps the letter was a routine classroom assignment: *"Today, students, you will improve your English skills by writing a letter to someone in the United States."* If so, the young scholar's letter reveals that he needed the practice: "I don't know very English," he admits.

Or maybe the whole thing was simply adolescent bravado, a youngster's attempt to show his friends that he wasn't about to stand in awe of any *norteamericano*—even one who lived in the White House. If so, it was an attitude that Castro was to embrace again in later life, as president of Cuba and revolutionary icon.

It's equally hard to avoid speculating about what might have happened if Roosevelt had granted Castro's request. The long-running U.S. trade embargo, the Bay of Pigs invasion, the Cuban Missile Crisis, the Mariel boatlift, the Elian Gonzalez saga—is it possible that all of it could have been avoided if FDR had simply tucked a ten-spot into an envelope and mailed if off to the Colegio de Dolores in Santiago? No, of course not. But still...

My good friend Roosevelt:

I don't know very English, but I know as much as write to you.

I like to hear the radio, and I am very happy, because I heard in it that you will be President for a new (periodo).

I am twelve years old. I am a boy but I think very much but I do not think that I am writing to the President of the United States.

If you like, give me a ten dollar bill green american, in the letter, because never; I have not seen a ten dollar bill green american and I would like to have one of them.

My address is:

Sr. Fidel Castro / Colegio de Dolores / Santiago de Cuba / Oriente, Cuba

I don't know very English but I know very much Spanish and I suppose you don't know very Spanish but you know very English because you are American but I am not American. (Thank you very much) Good by. Your friend, Fidel Castro

If you want iron to make your ships I will show to you the bigest (minas) of iron of the land. They are in Mayari Oriente Cuba.

OPPOSITE: *Fidel Castro reached across as yet unwritten pages of history in this letter to FDR.*

Justice

RESPECTFULLY REFERRED
FOR ACKNOWLEDGMENT
AND CONSIDERATION

"Hottentot"

AN EXTERNAL REMEDY
SERIAL NO. 30154.

JUL 24 9-23

THE WHITE HOUSE
JUL 21 1912
RECEIVED

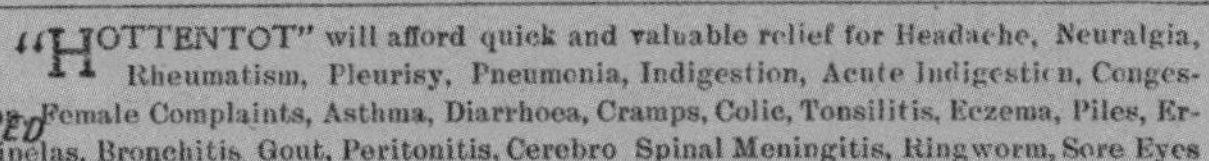

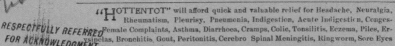

"HOTTENTOT" will afford quick and valuable relief for Headache, Neuralgia, Rheumatism, Pleurisy, Pneumonia, Indigestion, Acute Indigestion, Congestion, Female Complaints, Asthma, Diarrhoea, Cramps, Colic, Tonsilitis, Eczema, Piles, Erysipelas, Bronchitis, Gout, Peritonitis, Cerebro Spinal Meningitis, Ringworm, Sore Eyes Soft Corns, Bunions, etc.

"Hottentot" is manufactured only by C. DEARMAN, Tulsa, Oklahoma. P. O. Box 183.

OFFICE 212 N. FRANKFORT ST. TELEPHONE 1188.

Tulsa, Oklahoma, U. S. A. 7/18/12.

Hon, W.H.Taft, President of the United States of America.
Washington, D.C.

Honored Sir:-- I am asking you in the interest of the qualified Negro voters of the State of Oklahoma and more ~~espe-cially~~ especially the city of Tulsa, Okla to arrange with the Department of Justice in a way whereby immediate action will be taken to secure the right of every qualified Ngro voter in the State of Oklahoma and especially in the city of Tulsa, Okla. to vote in the coming elections without being intimidated and otherwise prevented from voting.

The tactics of the election officials in the city of Tulsa, Okla. now, are as follows: As pertaining to the Negroes each and every one must register only at the court house, regardless of how many times they have here-to-fore voted,.

It is stated by the election officials that any one not registering during the present registration will not under any circumstances be allowed to vote in the coming election,

Now before any Negro can register he must go into a little side room and read and write to the entire satisfaction of one or two white men, if it takes six hours continous reading and writing to satisfy them there is no one to object but the Negro trying to become qualified to vote, and his objections dont amount to any thing unless he pledges to support the democratic ticket, the majority if not all of which the election officials are. ~~The which~~ they allowed my writing to pass which is very poor and which you will find enclosed, they refused to allow other negroes writing to pass that to my mind is much better than my writing, Why? because I kick good and hard when ever it is necesary, and vote just as I please. But the majority of negroes will not kick either thru fear or indiference and those are the ones that I am praying and pleading for. The question that I often ask my self is, that if the continued oppression of and the discrimination against the negro should at some future day cause war, would those that are foremost in oppressing and discriminating against the negro, be foremost on the battle field, ~~I say~~ well I have an idea that they would be the very first to beat a hasty retreat at the first sound of the bugle.

Hoping that immediate action will be taken,
Very truly yours.

C. Dearman.

150719-62

DEPARTMENT OF JUSTICE
JUL 24 1912
MAIL & FILES DIVISION

Harr-Logan

C. DEARMAN TO WILLIAM H. TAFT
GEORGE A. MURRAY TO WOODROW WILSON

Tulsa, OK ★ July 18, 1912 ★ ★ ★ Washington, D.C. ★ February 14, 1920

IN THE FIRST DECADES OF THE TWENTIETH century, black Americans were subjected to a wide range of indignities and discriminatory practices that were sanctioned by law. Frustration over these legal barriers to equality is the subject of these two letters.

The first comes from businessman C. Dearman, manufacturer of a nostrum called "Hottentot" that offers relief from a startling array of ailments from bunions to meningitis. Writing to President Taft, Dearman recounts the tactics employed by election officials in Tulsa to ensure that black residents are "intimidated and otherwise prevented from voting." He tells Taft that he is willing to "kick good and hard" to protect his own rights, but many others who "will not kick either thru fear or indifference" need the President's help.

Dearman's comment that "continued oppression of and...discrimination against the negro" might "at some future day cause war" proved tragically prophetic. On May 31, 1921, a young black man was arrested by the Tulsa police for allegedly assaulting a white woman. When a mob gathered outside the jail, it was confronted by a group of black citizens who were determined to prevent a lynching. Violence erupted, and a wave of shooting and arson swept through the city's African-American neighborhoods. By the time the National Guard restored order, more than a thousand homes and businesses lay in ruins and at least 300 people were dead.

The second letter, written in 1920 by a Washington attorney, offers an unusual—but eminently rational—argument for eliminating segregation: It costs too much.

The Supreme Court's 1896 decision in the case of *Plessy* v. *Ferguson* had held that legally mandated "separate" facilities for blacks and whites were not unconstitutional as long as they were "equal." For the next half-century, this ruling was used to justify segregation in places such as schools, restaurants, and restrooms—as well as railroad cars, which had been the original subject of the Plessy case.

In his letter to President Wilson, George H. Murray attacks the "separate but equal" doctrine on the basis of its dollars-and-cents impact on America's railroads: It leads to costly and wasteful duplication of equipment and services. The $25,000,000 spent on maintaining separate cars for black and white passengers, he argues, would be better used to provide higher wages for railroad workers.

Murray doesn't try to persuade Wilson that separate facilities are inherently unequal. The Supreme Court addressed that issue decisively in its 1954 ruling in *Brown* v. *Board of Education*.

The question that I often ask my self is, that if the continued oppression of and the discrimination against the negro should at some future day cause war, would those that are foremost in oppressing and discriminating against the negro, be foremost on the battle field, well I have an idea that they would be the very first to beat a hasty retreat at the first sound of the bugle. Hoping that immediate action will be taken, Very truly yours, C. Dearman

---

OPPOSITE: *Two generations ahead of his time, C. Dearman petitioned Taft to protect the "qualified Negro voter."*

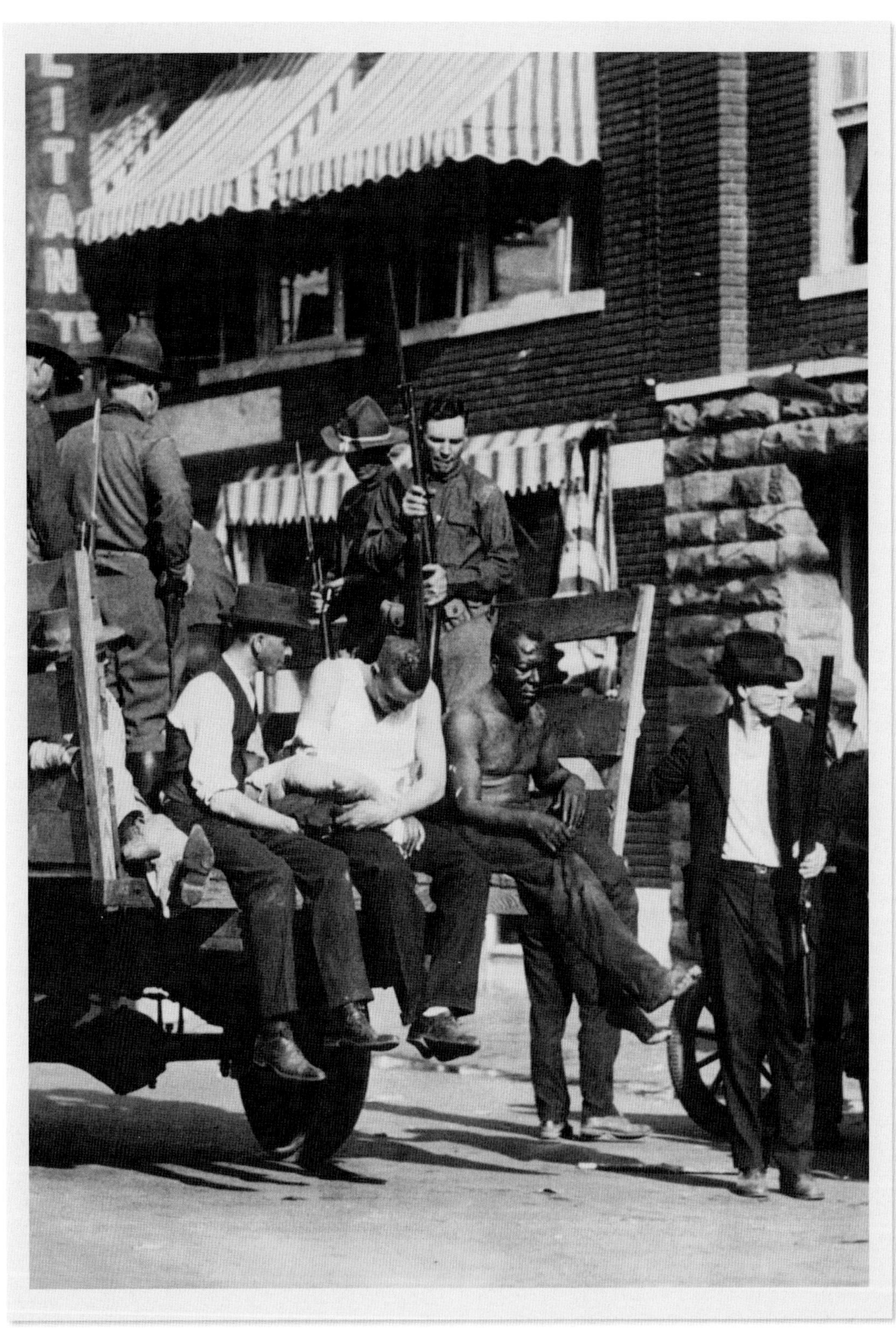

ABOVE: *Oklahoma's governor declared martial law during the 1921 Tulsa race riots; these prisoners nurse their wounds in the back of an Army truck.*

137609

H. LA[illegible]ER, CHAIRMAN
L. M. HERSHAW, VICE CHAIRMAN
DANIEL MURRAY, TREASURER
J. E. JOHNSON, SECRETARY
GEO. H. MURRAY, GEN'L COUNSEL

The Colored American Council

(INCORPORATED)

1215 SEVENTEENTH STREET, N. W.

WASHINGTON, D.C.

CH'M COM. ON FINANCE
MORRIS S. KOONCE
CH'M COM. ON STATE CO-OPERATION
WALTER J. SINGLETON
CH'M COM. ON PUBLICITY
VIRGIL A. FRANKLIN
CH'M COM. ON ORGANIZATION
EX-JUSTICE E. M. HEWLETT

17 1920 February 14,1920.

Hon. Woodrow Wilson,
President of the United States,
Executive Mansion,
Washington, D.C..

Dear Sir:

In connection with the threatened railroad strike, I am prompted to invite the attention of the President to the possibilities of the elimination of the costly separate car passenger service maintained by Federal taxation in the Southern interstate traffic district..

This service is supported by governmental guarantee at an annual cost of twenty five million dollars ($25,000,000) which estimate does not include four states using the service but credited to the western district.

It serves no useful,American purpose but forms according to current opinion a fertile field for propaganda aimed at national disintegration. Its elimination would free for wage increases to railway workers,$25,000,000.

On its face its elimination constitutes a proposal which is at once fair to the roads, the railworkers and the American people. It is an economy which requires no outlay of capital to effect and I trust that your Excellency will give its possibilities due consideration.

George H. Murray

General Counsel.

AMERICAN JEWISH CONGRESS

330 WEST 42nd STREET NEW YORK CITY

CABLE ADDRESS 'CONGRESS'
TELEPHONE LONGACRE 5-2600

Office of Dr. Wise
40 West 68 Street,
December 2, 1942.

The President
The White House
Washington, D. C.

Dear Boss:

I do not wish to add an atom to the awful burden which you are bearing, with magic and, as I believe, heaven-inspired strength at this time. But you do know that the most overwhelming disaster of Jewish history has befallen Jews in the form of the Hitler mass-massacres. Hitler's decision was to exterminate the Jewish people in all Hitler-ruled lands, and it is indisputable that as many as two-million civilian Jews have been slain.

I have had cables and underground advices for some months, telling of these things. I succeeded, together with the heads of other Jewish organizations, in keeping these out of the press and have been in constant communication with the State Department, particularly Under Secretary Welles. The State Department has now received what it believes to be confirmation of these unspeakable horrors and has approved of my giving the facts to the press. The organizations banded together in the Conference of which I am Chairman, feel that they wish to present to you a memorandum on this situation, so terrible that this day is being observed as a day of mourning and fasting throughout the Jewish world. We hope above all that you will speak a word which may bring solace and hope to millions of Jews who mourn, and be an expression of the conscience of the American people.

I had gathered from the State Department that you were prepared to receive a small delegation, which would include representatives of the American Jewish Committee, the American Jewish Congress, the B'nai B'rith. It would be gravely misunderstood if, despite your overwhelming preoccupation, you did not make it possible to receive our delegation and to utter what I am sure will be your heartening and consoling reply.

As your old friend, I beg you will somehow arrange to do this.

Ever yours,

PRESIDENT

SSW:S

Stephen S. Wise to Franklin D. Roosevelt

New York, NY ★ December 2, 1942

When the first sketchy reports began to reach the United States, they were so horrific that no one believed them. Soon, however, it was clear that the unimaginable was true: Adolf Hitler and the Nazis had embarked on a merciless campaign to exterminate the Jews of Europe. All of them.

When Rabbi Stephen Wise, the most widely respected American Jewish leader of his day, received reliable information on Hitler's plan in August 1942, he shared it with the U.S. State Department. In late November, Wise was told that the State Department had received information that would "confirm and justify your deepest fears." He promptly wrote to President Roosevelt.

In his letter, Wise does not offer many details of "the most overwhelming disaster of Jewish history." Instead, he praises the President for the "magic and, as I believe, heaven-inspired strength" with which he is leading the nation, and asks him to meet with a "small delegation" of Jewish leaders. His immediate hope is that Roosevelt will issue a statement condemning the Nazi mass murders, but it is clear that he ultimately expects much more from the man he considers an old friend.

The meeting took place on December 8. After a prayer of benediction by an orthodox rabbi, Wise gave the President a 12-page memorandum on the Nazi genocide and begged him "to do all in your power to bring this to the attention of the world and to do all in your power to make an effort to stop it." Thereafter, Roosevelt did most of the talking (one member of the delegation reported that "of the 29 minutes spent with the President, he addressed {us} for 23 minutes"), closing by assuring his visitors, "We shall do all in our power to be of service to your people in this tragic moment."

Despite Wise's hopes and the President's words, action was a long time coming: Not until January 1944 did Roosevelt finally establish the War Refugee Board. By the war's end, the Board had helped rescue about 200,000 Jews.

Shortly before his death in 1949, Rabbi Wise summed up his experience in urging decisive American action to thwart the Holocaust: "The tale might be less tragic if the help of men had been less scant and fitful."

. . . I do not wish to add an atom to the awful burden which you are bearing with magic and, as I believe, heaven-inspired strength at this time. But you do know that the most overwhelming disaster of Jewish history has befallen Jews in the form of the Hitler mass-massacres. Hitler's decision was to exterminate the Jewish people in all Hitler-ruled lands, and it is indisputable that as many as two million civilian Jews have been slain. . . . The State Department has now received what it believes to be confirmation of these unspeakable horrors and has approved of my giving the facts to the press. The organizations banded together in the Conference of which I am Chairman, feel that they wish to present to you a memorandum of this situation, so terrible that this day is being observed as a day of mourning and fasting throughout the Jewish world. We hope above all that you will speak a word which may bring solace and hope to millions of Jews who mourn, and be an expression of the conscience of the American people. . . .

OPPOSITE: *With the ease of an old friend, Rabbi Wise addresses President Roosevelt as "Dear Boss."*

The White House
Washington

WB83 26 NT FEB 24 6 18 AM 1942

PPF 200
RADIO ADDRESS
2 23
PRO "M"

BRIDGEPORT CONN FEB 23

PRESIDENT ROOSEVELT

WHITE HOUSE

JUST HEARD YOUR SPEECH IT CHEERED ME UP RECEIVED NOTICE TODAY THAT MY SON WAS KILLED IN SERVICE OF THE UNITEDSTATES AT PEARL HARBOR DECEMBER 7TH

J B MANUAL.

The White House
Washington

WB83 26 NT FEB 24 6 18 AM 1942

PPF 200
RADIO ADDRESS
2 23
PRO "M"

BRIDGEPORT CONN FEB 23

PRESIDENT ROOSEVELT

WHITE HOUSE

JUST HEARD YOUR SPEECH IT CHEERED ME UP RECEIVED NOTICE TODAY THAT MY SON WAS KILLED IN SERVICE OF THE UNITEDSTATES AT PEARL HARBOR DECEMBER 7TH

J B MANUAL.

J. B. Manual to Franklin D. Roosevelt

Bridgeport, OH ★ February 23, 1942

PERHAPS IT WAS BECAUSE HE LED THEM through unprecedented hard times and war, or because he showed them that if you put your mind to it, you could bear any load—even the unending burden of being crippled. Or maybe it was simply because he really seemed to care about them. Whatever the reason, a special bond developed between the American people and Franklin D. Roosevelt during FDR's twelve years as President. The unique nature of that bond was never captured more succinctly—or heartbreakingly—than in this brief telegram from a man in Bridgeport, Connecticut.

On February 23, 1942, J. B. Manual was notified that his son had been killed in the Japanese attack on Pearl Harbor eleven weeks earlier. That evening he sat beside the radio to listen to one of the thirty-odd "fireside chats" that Roosevelt delivered between 1933 and 1945.

In this Washington's Birthday broadcast, the President took on the dual role of cheerleader and comforter. He urged Americans to follow Washington's "model of moral stamina" in fighting the war that raged all over the world. He castigated those who "wanted the American eagle to imitate the tactics of the ostrich" and insisted that "we prefer to retain the eagle as it is—flying high and striking hard." Acknowledging that 2,340 men had been killed at Pearl Harbor, he reminded his listeners that "there is something larger and more important than the life of any individual or of any individual group—something for which a man will sacrifice...not only his pleasures, not only his goods, not only his associations with those he loves, but his life itself." He offered a firm assurance: "Soon, we and not our enemies will have the offensive; we, not they, will win the final battles; and we, not they, will make the final peace."

Roosevelt's words must have opened Manual's heart like a scalpel. What he heard, coupled with what he was feeling, moved him to send this telegram to the White House. It carries two messages, one of grief and one of faith. What is truly extraordinary is the order in which they are conveyed: Faith comes first.

Embedded in the last sentence is a telling phrase: Manual's son didn't just die, but gave his life "in service of the United States." In the depths of pain, some comfort.

OPPOSITE: *A grieving father speaks with the courage and faith that helped win World War II.*
ABOVE: *Rising to the occasion, Franklin Roosevelt regularly consoled, rallied, and inspired a nation at war.*

R + file

RESPECTFULLY REFERRED FOR ACKNOWLEDGEMENT AND CONSIDERATION

RECEIVED NOV 26 1943

Route 1
Childersburg, Ala.
Nov. 12, 1943

Pres. United States
White House
Washington, D.C.

Dear Sir:

I am nearing my seventeenth (17) Birthday and would like very much to be in the Armed Forces of the U.S. but Mother and Dad will not sign the necessary papers for me to enlist in the navy so I appeal to you to lower the draft age to seventeen (17) as soon as possible.

Yours very truly
French R. Massey

French R. Massey; Anna Rush; Carolyn Weatherhogg to Franklin D. Roosevelt

Childersburg, AL ★ November 12, 1943
Wenatchee, WA ★ November 18, 1943
Lincoln, NE ★ October 14, 1943

America's first national military conscription law was enacted in 1862, but it wasn't until World War I that the U.S. relied primarily on the draft to build and maintain its armed forces. The fall of France in 1940 spurred Congress to adopt the first peacetime draft, calling up men aged 21 to 35 for a one-year hitch. Just a year later, with the threat of war looming bigger every day, Congress voted—by a one-vote margin in the House of Representatives—to keep draftees in uniform beyond the end of their one-year term. After the Japanese attack on Pearl Harbor, all able-bodied men aged 18 to 38 were subject to conscription for the duration of the war.

As soon as the Selective Service System was established, Americans started voicing their dissatisfaction with the way it worked. These three letters to President Roosevelt encapsulate some of the major reasons for their frustrations and fears. All three were written in 1943, the peak year for conscription, when more than 3.3 million men were drafted.

Among those *not* called up that year was French Massey of Childersburg, Alabama, whose brief letter simmers with the impatience of youth. His complaint is a simple one: He's almost 17 and spoiling to fight, but his mother and father think he's too young. He wants the President to help him out by lowering the draft age—"as soon as possible."

Anna Rush of Wenatchee, Washington, has a different complaint: The wrong men are being drafted. Having been "deeply moved" by a newspaper article about a father of nine who was summoned to duty with the Navy, she pleads with the President to "release this poor father and let him go home to his children." Instead of calling up the likes of poor Armand Beliveau, she says, Selective Service should focus on drafting the many "young (childless) married men" whose country needs them "rite now."

Carolyn Weatherhogg of Lincoln, Nebraska, has fathers on her mind, too. Ten years old and worried about her daddy, she makes a suggestion that doubtless would have been cheered by everyone else whose last name begins with "W": draft fathers alphabetically.

Presumably, young French Massey had to wait another year before joining up. Mrs. Rush's plea was outweighed by the military's need to draft as many men as it could. And Carolyn Weatherhogg's dad was classified 4-F.

Almost 10 million men were drafted from 1940 through 1945. America's last draftee entered the Army in 1973.

Dear Sir,

I am nearing my seventeenth (17) Birthday and would like very much to be in the Armed Forces of the U.S. but Mother and Dad will not sign the necessary papers for me to enlist in the navy so I appeal to you to lower the draft age to seventeen (17) as soon as possible.

Yours very truly
French R. Massey

OPPOSITE: *Nearly 17 and itching to get in the fight, French Massey begs FDR to lower the draft age.*

Wenatchee - Wash.
Nov. - 18 - 1943 908 Ferry St

Dear President of the U.S.

I was deeply moved when I read this article in last evenings paper, I have two Sons in the U.S. Service and I know how hard it was to see them go, I can realize it was very hard for this father to leave his family, and I am pleading with you, dear President to release this poor father and let him go home to his children They need him, I'm sure; When we see so many young (Childless) Married men yes, so many of them here - these men should do their part in helping win this war, these men should go ahead of fathers with big families, yes, we plead for fathers. Our Country needs these young (Childless) married men and needs them - rite now, Please undertake Mr. President, Please.

FATHER OF 9 IS DRAFTED

MANCHESTER, N. H., (AP)—A mother and nine children, including six months old twins, bade au revoir today to the head of the family who is off to war with the navy.

Armand Beliveau, 34, chose a naval career after selective service called him.

"I'm willing to do my part to end the war," the father said as he left home, "but I feel there are a lot of younger men without families who could be taken before family homes like mine are disrupted."

In addition to the twins, a boy and a girl, Beliveau left seven other children whose ages ranged up to 11 years old.

for instance

Two Ask Divorce And Maiden Names

Cleo Sudderth filed suit for divorce from Eugene Sudderth in Chelan county superior court yesterday, charging non-support.

She charges cruelty and non-support and that he attacked her with a hand axe on Aug. 1, 1941.

They were married in 1941 and have no children or community property.

She asks return of her maiden name, Cleo Rausch.

Also filing for divorce was Mae Ruth Qualey from Clarence T. Qualey. They were married in Leavenworth in 1941 and have no children or community property.

She asks for her maiden name of Mae Ruth Smith.

Signed -

Mrs. Anna Rush.

Dear Mr. Roosevelt,

I am sending in a suggestion, that is draft fathers alphabetically.

I am ten years old, I life at 3800 K St., my phone number is 4-1226.

Carolyn Weatherhogg

10, Downing Street,
Whitehall.

May 1, 1944.

My dear Franklin,

You kindly sent me recently a portrait of yourself which I like very much and have hung in my bedroom. Here is a tit for your tat. I hope you will accept it, flattering though it be to me, and like it as much as I do yours.

Yours ever,

Winston S. C

The President of the United States of America.

WINSTON CHURCHILL TO FRANKLIN D. ROOSEVELT

10 Downing Street, Whitehall, London ★ May 1, 1944

IT WAS GRIT AND MANPOWER AND STRATEGY and industrial might that enabled the Allies to win World War II, of course, but many historians believe the deep friendship between Winston Churchill and Franklin D. Roosevelt played a major role in putting some heart behind all that muscle.

The exact nature of this "epic friendship," as one historian has described it, has come in for plenty of revisionist analysis—FDR was coy, Churchill was needy, that sort of thing—but what comes through in their correspondence is a strong relationship founded on mutual respect, the pursuit of a common goal, a shared love for the quirks and glories of the English language, and a genuine enjoyment of each other's company. Reading what they wrote and said to each other, it's easy to believe that when Churchill told Roosevelt, "Our friendship is the rock on which I build for the future of the world," he meant it.

Between September 1939 and April 1945 the two men exchanged almost 2,000 letters. Some of them deal with weighty matters of great historic significance—but this one sparkles with the high spirits of a schoolboy swapping photos with his chum. The second sentence alone makes this letter priceless.

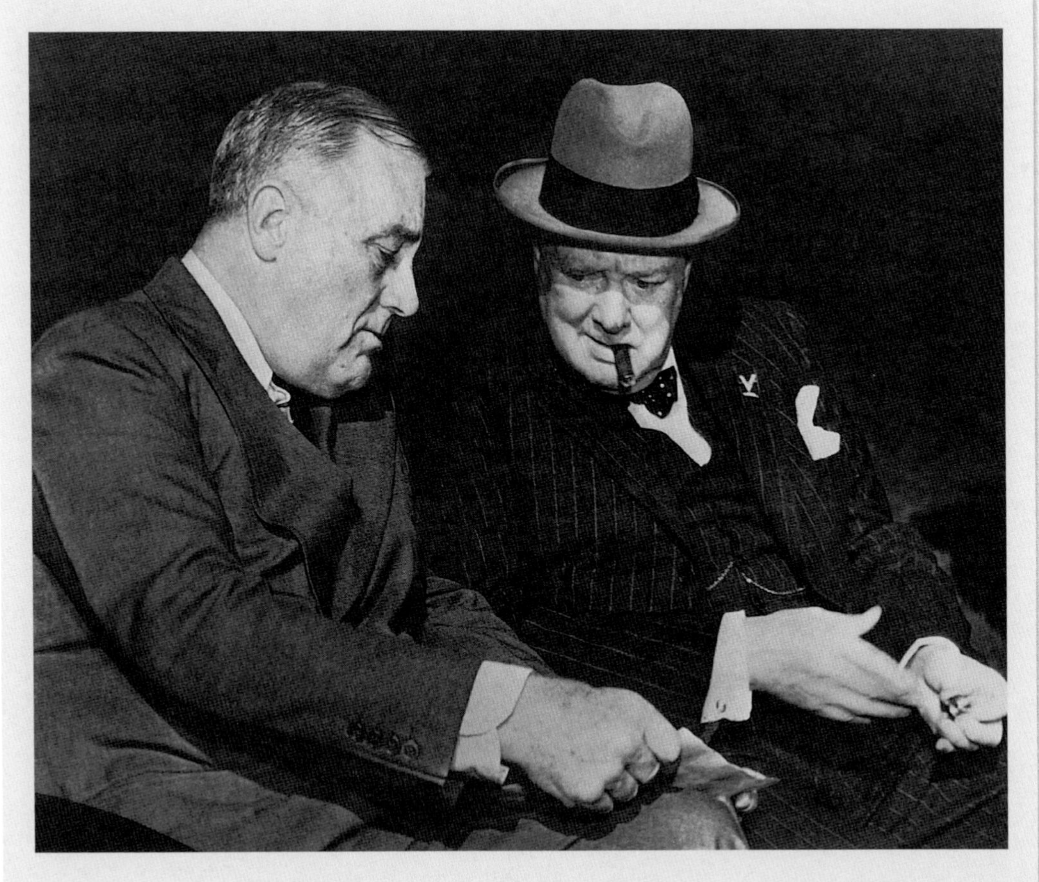

OPPOSITE: *No routing marks mar Churchill's letter to FDR, which doubtless traveled straight to the Oval Office.*
ABOVE: *Close friends, old warriors, and world leaders, FDR and Churchill were members of a club of two.*

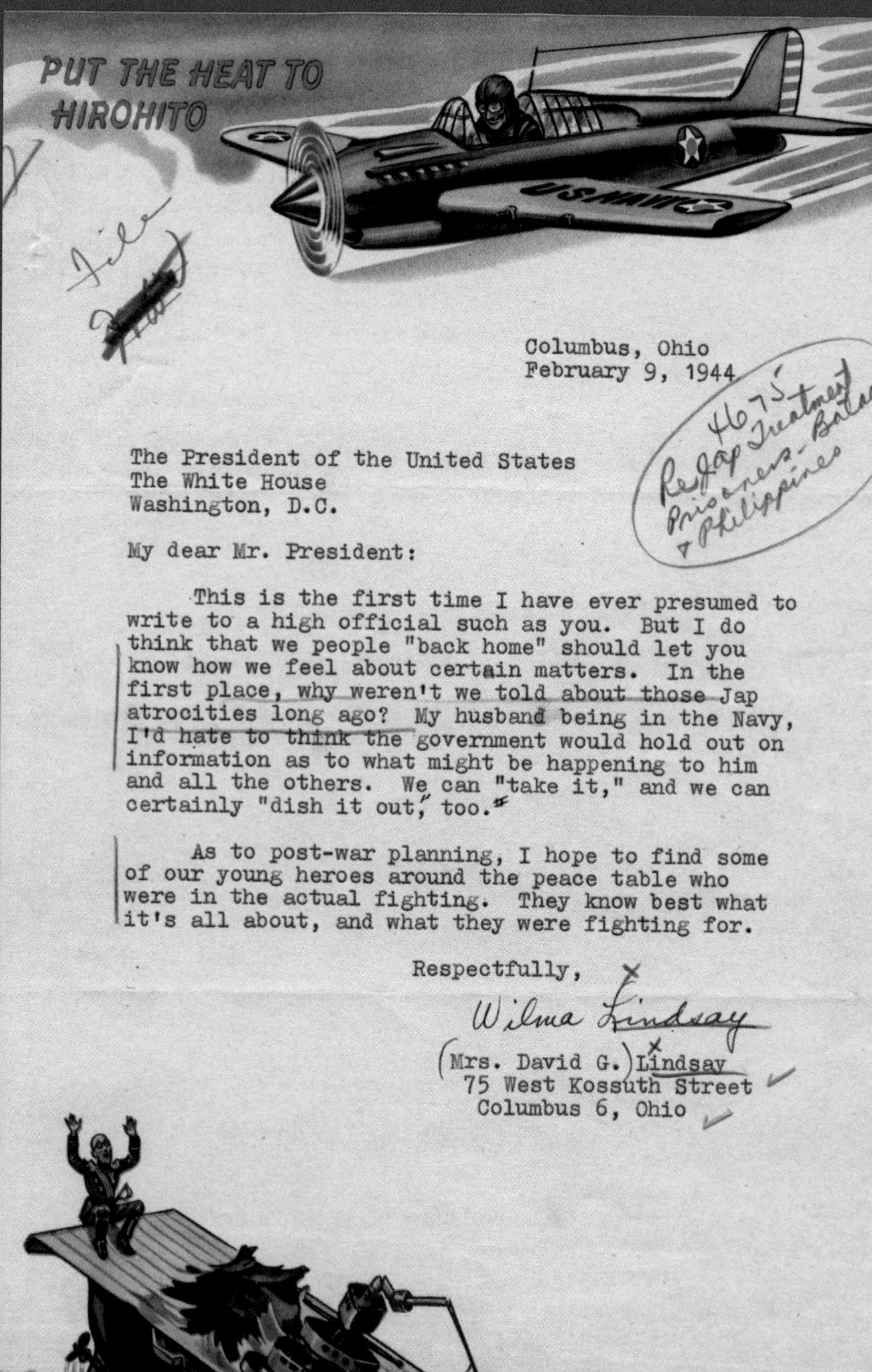
PUT THE HEAT TO
HIROHITO
U.S. NAVY

File

Columbus, Ohio
February 9, 1944

4675
Re Jap Treatment
Prisoners - Bataan
& Philippines

The President of the United States
The White House
Washington, D.C.

My dear Mr. President:

This is the first time I have ever presumed to write to a high official such as you. But I do think that we people "back home" should let you know how we feel about certain matters. In the first place, why weren't we told about those Jap atrocities long ago? My husband being in the Navy, I'd hate to think the government would hold out on information as to what might be happening to him and all the others. We can "take it," and we can certainly "dish it out," too.

As to post-war planning, I hope to find some of our young heroes around the peace table who were in the actual fighting. They know best what it's all about, and what they were fighting for.

Respectfully,

Wilma Lindsay

(Mrs. David G.) Lindsay
75 West Kossuth Street
Columbus 6, Ohio

Wilma Lindsay to Franklin D. Roosevelt

Columbus, OH ★ February 9, 1944

In an effort to stoke patriotic spirit and maintain support for the war effort, as well as to make Home Front citizens feel a sense of personal involvement in the struggle raging across the globe, advertisers and manufacturers during World War II splashed bellicose images across everything from magazine covers to costume jewelry. In this letter, the stationery's depiction of a grinning American pilot circling above a sinking Japanese aircraft carrier provides an appropriate frame for a wartime wife's anger and worry.

A few days earlier, a joint Army-Navy press release had given the public its first news of the infamous Bataan Death March in 1942, in which thousands of American and Filipino prisoners died at the hands of their Japanese captors. Shocked and outraged by the news, Wilma Lindsay of Ohio used a sheet of her "PUT THE HEAT TO HIROHITO" stationery to tell President Roosevelt how she felt.

First she wants to know why the news of Japanese atrocities in the Philippines wasn't released sooner. She assures the President, "We can 'take it,'" that facing the truth, however heartbreaking or horrifying, is easier than wrestling with imaginary demons—especially when your husband is in harm's way in some far-off place.

Then she expresses the hope that "men who were in the actual fighting" will be permitted to play a prominent role in shaping the postwar world. After 26 months of war, Mrs. Lindsay is allowing herself to believe that the fighting won't—can't—last forever and that America's "young heroes" will eventually come home.

OPPOSITE: *With fighting spirit, Mrs. Lindsay claims "We can 'take it,' and we can certainly 'dish it out, too.'"*
ABOVE: *Emperor Hirohito prepares his troops for war maneuvers that, a decade hence, will be all too real.*

Harold Ickes to Franklin D. Roosevelt

Washington, D.C. ★ *June 1, 1944*

In the spring of 1944, nobody knew that the war would drag on for another year, but many people sensed that the end might be in sight. Secretary of the Interior Harold Ickes decided it was time to right a wrong.

It began on February 19, 1942, when President Roosevelt signed Executive Order 9066, authorizing the Army to designate "military areas" from which "any or all persons may be excluded." While the order included no specific mention of Japanese Americans, they were its primary targets because their presence on the West Coast supposedly constituted a threat to national security. The commander of the Army's Western Defense Command went so far as to claim, "The very fact that no sabotage or espionage has taken place to date is disturbing and confirming indication that such action will take place."

Between March and November 1942, more than 110,000 people—most of them American citizens, none of them charged with a crime—were uprooted from their homes in Washington, Oregon, California, and southern Arizona. After a brief period in temporary detention centers, they were confined in ten War Relocation Camps that had been hastily set up in isolated locations from Idaho to Arkansas. Most of them had been there, living in harsh, crowded conditions, for almost two years when Ickes wrote this letter to President Roosevelt.

Ickes' message can be condensed to three words: Enough is enough. There is "no basis in law or in equity," he says, for perpetuating the order. He cites the fact that detainees' morale is deteriorating and children in the camps "are becoming a hopelessly maladjusted generation." He refuses to comment on "the justification or lack thereof for the original evacuation order" but tells the President that the government's action is likely to be ruled unconstitutional by the U.S. Supreme Court. An earlier draft includes a firm declaration that the continued detention "is inconsistent with the fundamental ideas of fairness and decency upon which civilization is based," but this statement is missing from the version sent to the President.

On December 18, as Ickes had predicted, the Supreme Court ruled in *Ex parte Endo* that the government could not legally detain loyal citizens against their will. The exclusion order was lifted, and evacuees were free to go home. The last camp closed in March 1946.

In the course of the war, only ten people were convicted of spying for Japan. None of them was a Japanese American.

. . . The difficulty which will confront these people in readjusting to ordinary life becomes greater as they spend more time in the centers. . . . I do say that the continued retention of these innocent people in the relocation centers would be a blot upon the history of this country. . . . (It is inconsistent with the fundamental ideas of fairness and decency upon which civilization is based. What has been done cannot be repaired, but I hope that you will see to it that history will not recite that these people were incarcerated and detained long after even the feeblest pretense could be made that there existed any military or security reason for this treatment; and that they were released only after the Supreme Court had branded their continued detention as lawless and unconstitutional.) *Bracketed text appears on the second page of Ickes' draft letter, and was left out of the final version.*

OPPOSITE: *This draft of a letter to FDR about the injustice of Japanese detention camps preserves Harold Ickes' revisions.*

DRAFT

My dear Mr. President:

I again call your attention to the urgent necessity of arriving at a determination with respect to revocation of the orders excluding Japanese Americans from the West Coast. It is my understanding that Secretary Stimson believes that there is no longer any military necessity for excluding these persons from the State of California and portions of the States of Washington, Oregon and Arizona. Accordingly, there is no basis in law or in equity for the perpetuation of the ban.

The reasons for revoking the exclusion orders may be briefly stated as follows:

1. The continued exclusion of American citizens of Japanese ancestry from the affected areas is clearly unconstitutional in the present circumstances. I expect that a case squarely raising this issue will reach the Supreme Court at its next term. I ~~believe~~ understand that the Department of Justice ~~will~~ agree? that there is little doubt as to the decision which the Supreme Court will reach in a case squarely presenting the issue.

2. I have been informally advised by officials of the War Department who are in charge of this problem that there is no substantial justification for continuation of the ban from the standpoint of military security.

3. The continuation of the exclusion orders in the West Coast areas is adversely affecting our efforts to relocate Japanese Americans elsewhere in the country. State and local officials are saying, with some justification, that if these people are too dangerous for the West Coast, they do not want them to resettle in their localities.

4. The psychology of the Japanese Americans in the relocation centers becomes progressively worse. The difficulty which will confront these people

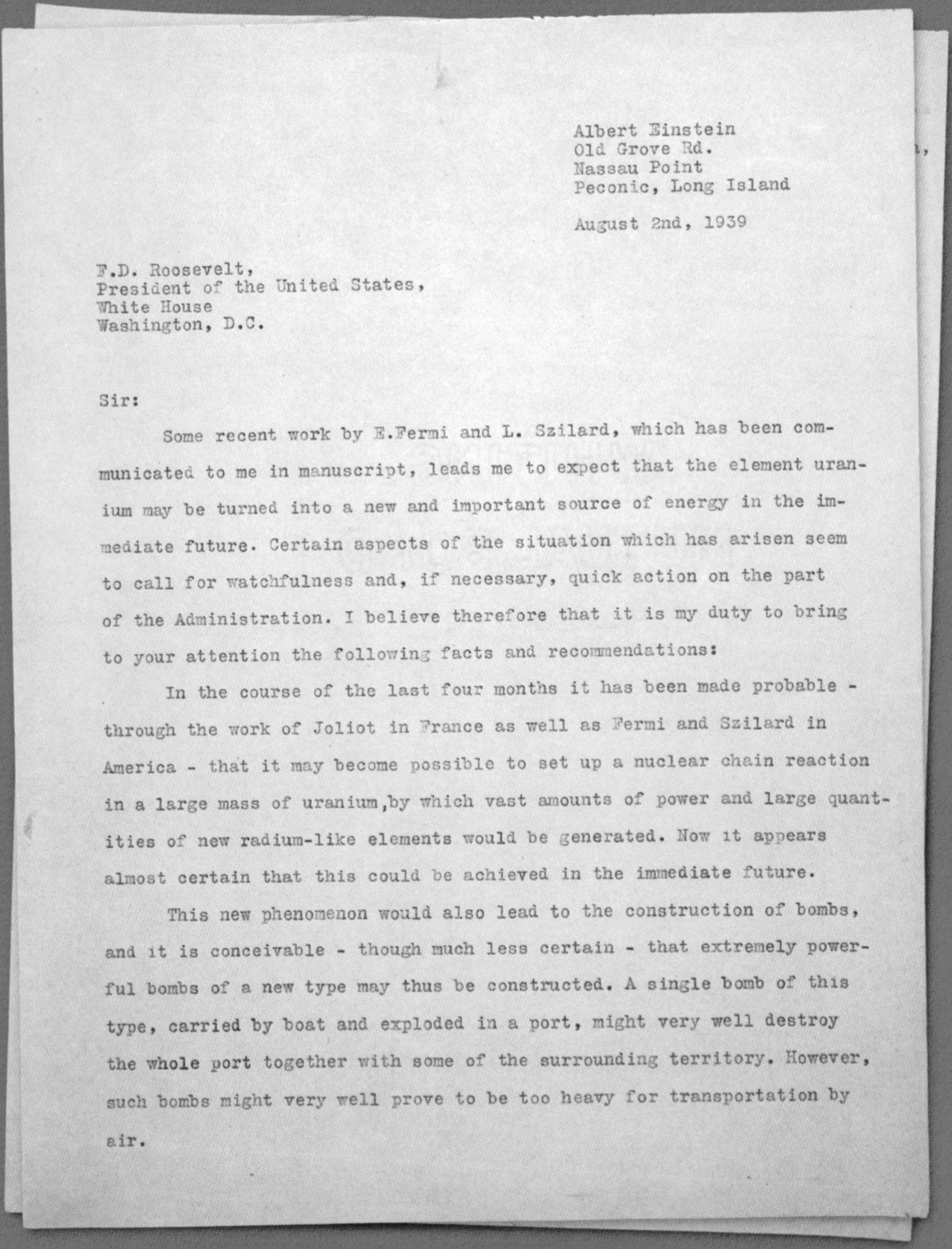

Albert Einstein
Old Grove Rd.
Nassau Point
Peconic, Long Island

August 2nd, 1939

F.D. Roosevelt,
President of the United States,
White House
Washington, D.C.

Sir:

Some recent work by E.Fermi and L. Szilard, which has been communicated to me in manuscript, leads me to expect that the element uranium may be turned into a new and important source of energy in the immediate future. Certain aspects of the situation which has arisen seem to call for watchfulness and, if necessary, quick action on the part of the Administration. I believe therefore that it is my duty to bring to your attention the following facts and recommendations:

In the course of the last four months it has been made probable - through the work of Joliot in France as well as Fermi and Szilard in America - that it may become possible to set up a nuclear chain reaction in a large mass of uranium,by which vast amounts of power and large quantities of new radium-like elements would be generated. Now it appears almost certain that this could be achieved in the immediate future.

This new phenomenon would also lead to the construction of bombs, and it is conceivable - though much less certain - that extremely powerful bombs of a new type may thus be constructed. A single bomb of this type, carried by boat and exploded in a port, might very well destroy the whole port together with some of the surrounding territory. However, such bombs might very well prove to be too heavy for transportation by air.

Albert Einstein to Franklin D. Roosevelt
Concerned Scientists to Harry S. Truman

Long Island, NY ★ August 2, 1939
Address Unknown ★ July 17, 1945

These two documents mark momentous stages in the birth of the nuclear age and the beginning of the swift slide into the Cold War.

Writing on August 2, 1939—just a month before Germany invaded Poland—Albert Einstein tells President Roosevelt that "the element uranium may be turned into a new and important source of energy in the immediate future" and that this could lead to the development of "extremely powerful bombs of a new type." He expresses no concern about the bomb's potential impact on world history—but, having fled Germany just before the Nazi takeover in 1933, he is understandably worried that Germany's research may be ahead of America's.

By the time twelve scientists send a petition to the White House six years later, America's top-secret effort to develop an atomic bomb—the innocuously titled Manhattan Project—has culminated in the detonation of a bomb known as "The Gadget" in the desert of New Mexico. The scientists' petition, written the day after the explosion at the so-called Trinity Site, begins with a plea for restraint: If America uses its frightful new weapon on Japan, it must "bear the responsibility of opening the door to an era of devastation on an unimaginable scale." Looking beyond the end of the current war, the scientists foresee a situation in which "rival powers" with nuclear capabilities will put America's cities "in continuous danger of sudden annihilation."

What makes these communications chilling is our knowledge of what happened next.

We now know, for instance, that Einstein overestimated Germany's progress toward the development of an atomic bomb, and that he was wrong in thinking that such a bomb might be too heavy for an airplane to carry. We also know, however, that he was dead right in his prediction of the weapon's awesome destructive power.

We know that the scientists failed to persuade Truman not to drop the bomb on Japan. We know, too, that they were correct in predicting that the U.S. could not retain for long its position as the world's only nuclear power. And finally, we know that they successfully evoked an image of the world to come—a world in which schoolchildren would be taught how to "duck and cover" and horrifying terms such as "fallout shelter" and "mutually assured destruction" and "nuclear winter" would enter the national vocabulary.

. . . The United States has only very poor ores of uranium in moderate quantities. There is some good ore in Canada and the former Czechoslovakia, while the most important source of uranium is Belgian Congo.

In view of this situation you may think it desirable to have some permanent contact maintained between the Administration and the group of physicists working on chain reactions in America. One possible way of achieving this might be for you to entrust with this task a person who has your confidence and who could perhaps serve in an inofficial capacity.
His task might comprise the following:

(continued on next page . . .)

OPPOSITE: *On the eve of World War II, Albert Einstein expresses concern about Germany's atomic ambitions.*

a) to approach Government Departments, keep them informed of the further development, and put forward recommendations for Government action, giving particular attention to the problem of securing a supply of uranium ore for the United States;

b) to speed up the experimental work, which is at present being carried on within the limits of the budgets of University laboratories, by providing funds, if such funds be required, through his contacts with private persons who are willing to make contributions for this cause, and perhaps also by obtaining the cooperation of industrial laboratories which have the necessary equipment.

I understand that Germany has actually stopped the sale of uranium from the Czechoslovakian mines which she has taken over. That she should have taken such early action might perhaps be understood on the ground that the son of the German Under-Secretary of State, von Weizs cker, is attached to the Kaiser-Wilhelm-Institut in Berlin where some of the American work on uranium is now being repeated.

Yours very truly,
Albert Einstein

★★★

. . . The development of atomic power will provide the nations with new means of destruction. The atomic bombs at our disposal represent only the first step in this direction, and there is almost no limit to the destructive power which will become available in the course of their future development. Thus a nation which sets the precedent of using these newly liberated forces of nature for purposes of destruction may have to bear the responsibility of opening the door to an era of devastation on an unimaginable scale.

If after this war a situation is allowed to develop in the world which permits rival powers to be in uncontrolled possession of these new means of destruction, the cities of the United States as well as the cities of other nations will be in continuous danger of sudden annihilation. All the resources of the United States, moral and material, may have to be mobilized to prevent the advent of such a world situation. Its prevention is at present the solemn responsibility of the United States singled out by virtue of her lead in the field of atomic power.

The added material strength which this lead gives to the United States brings with it the obligation of restraint and if we were to violate this obligation our moral position would be weakened in the eyes of the world and in our own eyes. It would then be more difficult for us to live up to our responsibility of bringing the unloosened forces of destruction under control.

In view of the foregoing, we, the undersigned, respectfully petition: first, that you exercise your power as Commander-in-Chief, to rule that the United States shall not resort to the use of atomic bombs in this war unless the terms which will be imposed upon Japan have been made public in detail and Japan knowing these terms has refused to surrender; second, that in such an event the question whether or not to use atomic bombs be decided by you in the light of the considerations presented in this petition as well as all the other moral responsibilities which are involved..

OPPOSITE: *A dozen scientists foretell the dangers of nuclear age in a letter stamped "Secret" upon receipt.*

July 17, 1945

A PETITION TO THE PRESIDENT OF THE UNITED STATES

Discoveries of which the people of the United States are not aware may affect the welfare of this nation in the near future. The liberation of atomic power which has been achieved places atomic bombs in the hands of the Army. It places in your hands, as Commander-in-Chief, the fateful decision whether or not to sanction the use of such bombs in the present phase of the war against Japan.

We, the undersigned scientists, have been working in the field of atomic power. Until recently we have had to fear that the United States might be attacked by atomic bombs during this war and that her only defense might lie in a counterattack by the same means. Today, with the defeat of Germany, this danger is averted and we feel impelled to say what follows:

The war has to be brought speedily to a successful conclusion and attacks by atomic bombs may very well be an effective method of warfare. We feel, however, that such attacks on Japan could not be justified, at least not unless the terms which will be imposed after the war on Japan were made public in detail and Japan were given an opportunity to surrender.

If such public announcement gave assurance to the Japanese that they could look forward to a life devoted to peaceful pursuits in their homeland and if Japan still refused to surrender our nation might then, in certain circumstances, find itself forced to resort to the use of atomic bombs. Such a step, however, ought not to be made at any time without seriously considering the moral responsibilities which are involved.

The development of atomic power will provide the nations with new means of destruction. The atomic bombs at our disposal represent only the first step in this direction, and there is almost no limit to the destructive power which will become available in the course of their future development. Thus a nation which sets the precedent of using these newly liberated forces of nature for purposes of destruction may have to bear the responsibility of opening the door to an era of devastation on an unimaginable scale.

If after this war a situation is allowed to develop in the world which permits rival powers to be in uncontrolled possession of these new means of destruction, the cities of the United States as well as the cities of other nations will be in continuous danger of sudden annihilation. All the resources of the United States, moral and material, may have to be mobilized to prevent the advent of such a world situation. Its prevention is at present the solemn responsibility of the United States--singled out by virtue of her lead in the field of atomic power.

The added material strength which this lead gives to the United States brings with it the obligation of restraint and if we were to violate this obligation our moral position would be weakened in the eyes of the world and in our own eyes. It would then be more difficult for us to live up to our responsibility of bringing the unloosened forces of destruction under control.

In view of the foregoing, we, the undersigned, respectfully petition: first, that you exercise your power as Commander-in-Chief, to rule that the United States shall not resort to the use of atomic bombs in this war unless the terms which will be imposed upon Japan have been made public in detail and Japan knowing these terms has refused to surrender; second, that in such an event the question whether or not to use atomic bombs be decided by you in the light of the considerations presented in this petition as well as all the other moral responsibilities which are involved.

R E Lapp
R S Mulliken
E P Wigner
George S. Monk
Leo Szilard

J. J. Nickson
W. H. Zachariasen
Francis R. Shonka
John A. Simpson, Jr
Walter Bartky
John R. Howe

Frank Foote

Guy von Dardel
% Onderdonk
815 North Tioga Avenue
Ithaca, New York

President Harry S. Truman
The White House
Washington, D.C.

Dear Mr. President:

I write to you concerning the whereabouts of my brother, Raoul Wallenberg, a Swedish citizen who went to Hungary in July, 1944 as the representative of President Roosevelt's War Refugee Board and who has been missing since the Soviet Foreign Office early in 1946 declared him to be under Russian protection.

I appeal to you because I believe that his fate, apart from being a source of continuous anguish to his family, also touches the conscience of this great democracy. I ask your aid because my brother's mercy mission -- which included the rescue of 20,000 Hungarian Jews -- was carried out under American auspices, and because two years of effort through regular diplomatic channels have failed.

The success of Raoul Wallenberg's humanitarian mission from July, 1944 until his disappearance on January 17, 1945 is a matter of public record. The War Refugee Board officially credits him with saving 20,000 lives; his former American associates in Stockholm as well as the people of Budapest estimate that perhaps 100,000 men, women and children owe their survival to him.

The manner in which he carried out his singular assignment has been described as unparalleled in both courage and resourcefulness. In the midst of furious battle and barbarous persecution, he literally snatched thousands of human beings from freight trains bound for Himmler's extermination camps. He furnished many thousands of otherwise doomed Hungarian Jews and anti-Nazis with documents of Swedish protective citizenship. He established an extraterritorial compound in the heart of Nazi-occupied Budapest and fought off German and Hungarian fascist marauders who tried to violate this sanctuary.

He set up hospitals, nurseries, schools and public soup kitchens to care for the hunted and the fear-ridden of Budapest. And when Fascist Premier Szalasi decreed in October 1945 that Swedish protective channels would no longer be honored -- an edict which spelled death to the surviving Jews of Budapest -- Raoul Wallenberg still found a way. With ingenuity and daring, he managed to forestall this cruel decree long enough to save many thousands from the final fires of Ausschwitz, Oswiecim and Dachau.

GUY VON DARDEL TO HARRY S. TRUMAN

Ithaca, NY ★ March 27, 1947

THIS 1947 LETTER TO PRESIDENT TRUMAN is a man's plea for help in finding his brother, one of the many thousands of family members who disappeared in the chaos that marked the end of the war in Europe. What sets this case apart is the fact that the missing man was one of the great heroes of the 20th century.

Guy von Dardel's letter recounts the facts: Raoul Wallenberg was a Swedish citizen who went to Budapest in July 1944 as a representative of the neutral government of Sweden and President Roosevelt's War Refugee Board. His mission was to aid and rescue Hungarian Jews, and he tackled the job with what von Dardel correctly describes as "unparalleled...courage and resourcefulness." He bought houses with embassy funds and installed Jewish refugees in them. He issued scores of "protective passports" to Jews, claiming they were Swedish subjects awaiting repatriation. He persuaded officials to cancel deportations by playing on their fears that they would later be accused of committing war crimes, and even convinced German and Hungarian authorities not to carry out their planned eradication of the Budapest ghetto and its 70,000 Jews. He is officially credited with saving 20,000 people from the Holocaust, but von Dardel notes that some sources "estimate that perhaps 100,000 owe their lives to him."

On January 17, 1945, Wallenberg went to meet with the commander of the Soviet forces who had recently moved into Budapest. He was never seen again. Von Dardel ends his letter by asking Truman's help "in obtaining the true facts."

Laboring under the threats and suspicions of the Cold War, the Soviets only gradually revealed their secrets. In 1957, they released a ten-year-old document in which a Russian prison official stated that Wallenberg had "died...in his cell." In 1989, they presented some of the diplomat's personal belongings to members of his family. Finally, in 1990, Russia formally acknowledged that Wallenberg and his driver had been "unjustifiably arrested by non-judicial bodies and deprived of their freedom for political reasons" and had been held "until their deaths in a Soviet prison."

By then, President Reagan had approved a special Act of Congress making Wallenberg an honorary U.S. citizen. One other foreigner—Winston Churchill—has been so honored.

. . . When the Germans were being driven from Budapest, Raoul remained at his post. On January 17, 1945 he went out to meet Marshal Malinovsky, the Soviet commander, in order to place his charges - thousands of men, women and children - under the protection of the Red Army.

Since leaving Budapest under Russian escort for Soviet headquarters, my brother has been missing. Rumors were circulated more than two years ago that he had been killed by Hungarian fascists. But while these rumors have never been supported by a shred of proof, a large body of evidence has come to the attention of the Swedish government which indicates that Raoul Wallenberg has been a Soviet prisoner since January, 1945.

The Soviet government has never retracted the admission by the Russian Foreign Office that Wallenberg was taken under Soviet protection more than two years ago. Nor has Moscow submitted any evidence to support the inspired rumors of his death at fascist hands. . . .

OPPOSITE: *After "two years of effort through ... diplomatic channels have failed," Raoul Wallenberg's stepbrother asks the President for help.*

Mädchenschule Pfaffenhofen
Landkreis Pfaffenhofen/Ilm

Laber Ella, 5. Kl
12 Jahre

Die 5. Klasse
dankt
für die gute Schulspeisung!

ELLA LEBER TO HARRY S. TRUMAN

Pfaffenhofen, Germany ★ 1948

IT'S TRUE: A PICTURE REALLY IS WORTH A thousand words.

Almost as soon as the fighting ended in 1945, the United States started working to help war-shattered Germany restart its economy and help the German people rebuild their lives. Today, discussion of America's contribution to postwar European recovery usually focuses on the amazing accomplishments of the Marshall Plan, which funneled an estimated $13 billion into various programs to help Europe get back on its feet. Less well known is the fact that the U.S. spent a nearly equal amount—almost $11 billion—on European recovery during the years between 1945 and 1948, before the Marshall Plan was launched.

Among these early and largely unheralded efforts was a program that got underway in the spring of 1947 to provide food to German schoolchildren. To mark the first anniversary of the program, more than a million Bavarian children took part in a drawing competition to show their gratitude for America's generosity. The fifty best drawings were sent to the White House. This joyous creation, the work of 12-year-old Ella Leber from the town of Pfaffenhofen, is one of them.

We don't know what Ella and her family endured during the war. We do know, because we can see it in her drawing, that she is glad to live once again in a world where people can smile and flowers can bloom.

OPPOSITE: *Ella Leber's bouquet of smiling faces offers thanks for good school lunches.*
ABOVE: *Beneficiaries of American largesse, schoolchildren in war-torn Greece line up for bread made from donated flour.*

JUST BETWEEN YOU AND ME —

Phyllis Bamberger
172 N. Ardmore R.D.
Col. 9. Ohio
Bexley

Dear President Truman,

When I read about your Cocker Spaniel named Feller I wanted to tell you about our Cocker Spaniel. He was 14 years old when he died and his name was Feller. Now we have another Cocker Spaniel named Feller 5 months old

Phyllis Bamberger to Harry S. Truman
Edwin Burtis; John Starnes to Lyndon B. Johnson
John Nabors to Dwight D. Eisenhower

Columbus, OH ★ *January 7, 1948*
El Paso, TX ★ *April 30, 1964* ★ ★ ★ *San Antonio, TX* ★ *June 20, 1966*
Address Unknown ★ *April 3, 1955*

For almost as long as there has been a White House, there have been pets in it.

The Executive Mansion was briefly home to an alligator that had been presented to John Quincy Adams by the Marquis de Lafayette. President Harding's Airedale had his own chair at Cabinet meetings, and Lyndon Johnson's dogs enjoyed an air-conditioned doghouse. Teddy Roosevelt's kids once rode their pony up the White House stairs. FDR and Richard Nixon made speeches about their dogs—a Scottie named Fala and a cocker spaniel named Checkers, respectively—and made front-page news. Among the many Coolidge pets was a raccoon named Rebecca who liked to drape herself around the President's neck. The Clintons' black-and-white cat Socks had his own fan club. Millie, the Bush family's springer spaniel, trumped them all by becoming a best-selling author.

These four letters depict the public's fascination with the critters (nonhuman, that is) that have occupied the White House in recent decades.

Despite having remarked, "If you want a friend in Washington, get a dog," Harry Truman preferred his White House pet-free. Phyllis Bamberger's letter was prompted by reports that the Trumans had received a puppy named Feller as a Christmas gift. Apparently feeling kinship with the Man in the White House, Phyllis informs the President that she has had not one but *two* Fellers, both of whom have given her much joy. Despite the fact that she used her most winsome stationery, Phyllis failed to forge a bond between the Trumans and their new dog. They gave Feller to their personal physician.

Lyndon Johnson loved his beagles Him and Her, but they caused him considerable grief in 1964. While chatting with a delegation on the White House lawn, Johnson lifted the dogs by their ears, setting off a chorus of howls—not only from the affronted beagles themselves but also from dog lovers everywhere. Edwin Burtis's letter is one of thousands that poured in. As president of the Texas Humane Federation, Burtis might have delivered a stern lecture—but instead, he merely offers some sage advice: "Please, Mr. President, don't ever again appear before a television with a dog."

Two years after the ear-pulling incident, Him was run over and killed on the White House grounds. In his letter to Johnson, John Starnes offers to replace the departed pooch with one of the puppies recently born to his dog Queenie. If the President accepts the offer, he will have "a Texan puppy." That's the good news. The bad news is that it'll cost him twenty-five bucks.

Another kid in Texas made an unsolicited contribution to the White House menagerie in 1955. After telling President Eisenhower, "I am one of your Dear admire," John Nabors remarks casually that he and his friends are "sending you this horn toad." The lizard's arrival prompted a memo from a member of the Secret Service staff: "It looks like I'll have to set up a Wildlife Division if many youngsters hear of this. We don't mind bloodworms, goldfish, turtles, frogs or mice, but we'll have to draw the line somewhere between baby alligators and tarantulas."

OPPOSITE: *"Just between you and me," Phyllis Bamberger extols the virtues of cocker spaniels to President Truman.*

Texas Humane Federation, Inc.
Organized 1937
A Federation of Texas Humane Societies
Affiliated with the American Humane Association
~~101 Vaughn Building~~
~~AMARILLO, TEXAS~~

April 30, 1964
3816 Hastings St
El Paso, Texas

To: Richard Nelson

President Lyndon B. Johnson,
The White House,
Washington, D.C.

Dear Mr. President:

We Texans are proud to have a native son reach the highest pinnacle of our national government. But, please, Mr. President, don't ever again appear before a television with a dog. We who are supporting you are having our troubles defending your conduct in your appearance on television with the beagles. Every Texan should know what the ears on a dog are for——they are not handles, they are to hear with.

Sincerely yours,

Edwin S. Burtis
President
Texas Humane Federation

OPPOSITE: *The President of the Texas Humane Federation informs the U.S. President what dogs' ears are for.*
ABOVE: *Lyndon Johnson had to live down this act of lifting his beagles up by their ears.*

REC'D JUN 20 '66

Dear President Johnson,

I'm sorry to hear your Beagle, Him was killed. My Dog Queenie had her first litter on April 28, 1966. I still have 3 males left, they are registered. I would like to sell you one for $25 dollars, Then you would have a Texan puppy.

Sincerelly yours,
John Starnes
231 Genevieve
San Antonio Tex.
TWa 27762 78214

OPPOSITE: *John Nabors later revealed that he and his three friends had dared one another to mail horned toads to various famous people. John was the only one with nerve enough to do it.*

Dear Ike

I am one of your Dear admire and I come from Texas you know Texas the biggest state I am enclosing a picture of me how do you like it. and I am makeing good Grades in school

Yours Turly

John.

P.S. and my freind

David

Billy

Jerry

and I am sending you this

Horn toad

to a good fellow

3 WE FACE THE SUNRISE — WE STRIVE FOR UNITY AMONG OUR PEOPLE

We Sken nen, We Kariwiio, We Kasatensara - Peace, Prosperity, Power and Equality to All

Akwesasne Mohawk Counselor Organization

(KA NIN KE A KA — PEOPLE OF FLINT)

Secretary
(Ra ia Tons)
Ray Fadden

St. Regis Mohawk Reservation
Hogansburg, New York

ackd 9/11/51 ohc

Sept.3,1951

President Harry Truman
Washington,D.C.
White House

emc

Dear President Truman,

The members of our Indian organization read of your act as regards Sgt.John R.Rice who died in action in Korea. We are ashamed that officials of Sioux City did the cruel thing that they did,refusing to bury an Indian in their cemetery. We were proud of you,Brother,when we read of you allowing our warrior to be buried in the Arlington Cemetery. We want you to know that we are grateful to you and appreciate it very much. May the Great Spirit bless your home for defending one of our people.

Cordially yours,

Ray Fadden

Ray Fadden,Sec.

Ray Fadden to Harry S. Truman

Hogansburg, NY ★ September 3, 1951

Old prejudices die hard. As this letter to President Truman indicates, prejudice against Native Americans was still very much alive in the middle of the twentieth century.

Sgt. John R. Rice, a decorated veteran of World War II, was killed on a Korean battlefield in 1950. His body was later shipped home for burial in Sioux City, Iowa, where his widow had bought a plot in Memorial Park Cemetery. At the funeral, a cemetery official grew suspicious when he noticed the large number of Native Americans present. Told that the dead man was part Indian, he promptly informed the Rice family that Memorial Park had a "Caucasians only" policy and Sergeant Rice would have to be buried elsewhere. The cemetery later insisted that its policy existed not "because of any prejudice against any race, but because people, like animals, prefer to be with their own kind."

Word of the incident spread quickly and soon reached the White House. When an angry President Truman offered to bury Sergeant Rice in Arlington National Cemetery, the members of a Mohawk tribal organization wrote to him from their reservation in New York.

The writers do not point out the irony in the fact that an Indian has been refused burial in a city named for an Indian tribe, nor do they vent the outrage they have every right to feel. Instead, on stationery whose pattern suggests birchbark, they merely express their gratitude in a few lines of great restraint and power. They refer to Rice as "our warrior" and call Truman "Brother"—titles that both men doubtless would have appreciated.

Two days after this letter was written, Sergeant Rice was laid to rest in the hallowed ground of Arlington with full military honors.

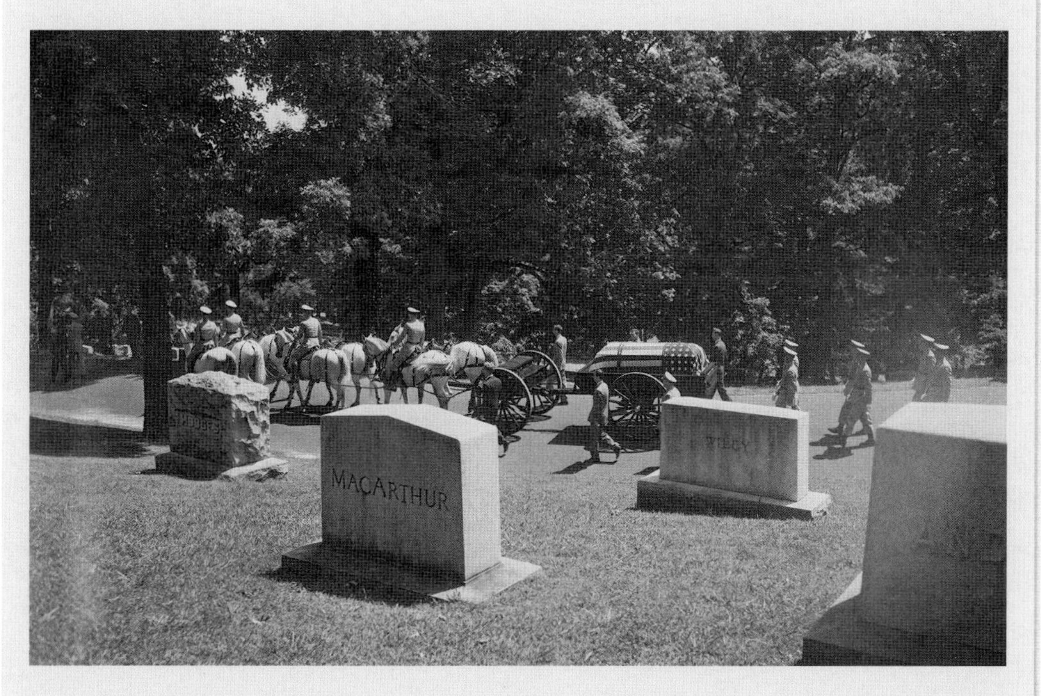

OPPOSITE: *Ray Fadden's brief letter about shameful bigotry is graced with dignity and admirable restraint.*
ABOVE: *In fields where heroes lie, Sgt. John Rice at last received a military burial.*

Cleveland School
Carteret, N.J.
January 31, 1949

Dear President Truman,

Our Second Grade class sold Hot Chocolate and Cookies for the March of Dimes. We made $20.60.

Ralph Ziegler to Harry S. Truman
Margaret M. Powers; Douw Fonda to Dwight D. Eisenhower

Carteret, NJ ★ *January 31, 1949*
Seattle, WA ★ *April 18, 1955*
Denver, CO ★ *August 8, 1955*

There was a time when the mere mention of the word "polio" was enough to make parents blanch and look around quickly to make sure their children were safe. The disease attacked nerve cells and sometimes the central nervous system, causing muscle wasting, paralysis, and in some children even death. No one knew how polio chose its victims or how it was transmitted, but everyone knew that there was no cure, that polio infections spiked dramatically in the hot summer months, and that children were especially susceptible.

Annual outbreaks of the disease increased in ferocity throughout the early 1950s. Millions of young kids spent hot summer days confined to the house because millions of parents feared that the neighborhood playground or swimming pool might harbor the virus that could leave their sons and daughters crippled or stuck in an iron lung for the rest of their lives.

Then, in the spring of 1955, came an electrifying announcement: Dr. Jonas Salk had developed a vaccine against the much-feared scourge, and tests had shown that it was amazingly effective. Immediately the federal government pushed to have huge quantities of the vaccine produced and distributed, and doctors' offices from coast to coast were soon filled with bawling children and their relieved parents. Reported cases of polio dropped from almost 29,000 in 1955 to fewer than 6,000 just two years later. The three letters here present a snapshot of polio's grip on the nation both in the years before and after the advent of the Salk vaccine.

In 1949, Mrs. Gallo's second-grade class sold hot chocolate and cookies to raise money for the March of Dimes, the organization famed for its national campaign against polio. In his letter to President Truman, young Ralph Ziegler expresses the hope that the $20.60 they earned "will help to make some crippled children well again." In fact, it was donations such as theirs that enabled the March of Dimes to support Dr. Salk's research.

Just six days after the announcement that the Salk vaccine had been proven "safe, effective and potent," Mrs. Edmund Powers writes to President Eisenhower that she is willing for her own small children to "forego their vaccinations" in order to give priority to "the most susceptible age group." While Mrs. Powers' unselfish offer was laudable, her fear that supplies of the vaccine might run out proved groundless: more than 450,000,000 doses were administered in four years.

Knowing that Eisenhower is planning a golfing vacation in Denver, Douw Fonda writes in the hope that the President "might give a very special wave" to a friend of his who lives near Ike's favorite golf course. The friend had been stricken with polio two years earlier—when he was a 20-year-old "good-looking, strapping young college football player"—and is now paralyzed. Fonda's letter is a sobering reminder that the vaccine came too late for many people. And, yes—President Eisenhower gave that wave.

OPPOSITE: *Second-grader Ralph Ziegler deserves an A for philanthropy in his letter to President Truman.*

2
5 encl. Re: Salk Vaccine injections

Mrs. Edmund A. Powers 2/4/20
3928 1/2 W. Othello St.
Seattle 6, Washington
April 18, 1955

Ackd 4-23-55 jsc

Dear Mr. President,

Enclosed you will find a picture of a one year old child receiving an injection of the limited supply of the Salk antipoliomyelitis vaccine.

As the mother of two children, (two years old and the other three and a half years old) I should like very much to have them immunized against this disease, but I am willing that they should forego their injections in order not to deprive other more susceptible children of their injections.

I consider the administration of the vaccine to other than the most susceptible age group to be a gross abuse, while the vaccine is in such limited supply.

I know that you are burdened with great and important

Fonda
esident

T. H. Fonda
Vice-Pres.-Treas.

S. J. Coleman
Secretary

Douw Fonda Company

Manufacturers' Representative

Telephone: TAbor 5-8289
1440 - 11th Street — Suite 206-208
Denver 4, Colorado

August 8, 1955

Ask:- Speak to Ptf. Arnold
Jim Rowley took care of
President wave
9/15/55

advised Mr. Fonda by phone 9/16/55

P E R S O N A L

President Dwight D. Eisenhower
c/o Mrs. John Sheldon Doud
750 Lafayette Street
Denver 18, Colorado

Dear President Eisenhower:

Although as President of The United States of America you are helping every American every day, I am wondering if, perhaps, while on your vacation in Denver this month you could help in particular one very courageous young man in his battle against polio. #

Two years ago Dick Markley, the son of Mr. and Mrs. S. A. Markley of 1075 East Oxford Avenue, Cherry Hills Village, was twenty years of age, a good looking, strapping young college football player. Then he was stricken with polio. He is now completely paralized. His young friends are wonderful to him and try to keep his spirits high, but his capacity for entertainment and diversion is extremely limited, being flat on his back unable to even use his hands or lift his head.

As he lives about 100 yards off the Cherry Hills Golf Course - between the 13th and 14th holes - his chief high point last summer was in watching for your foursome to come into view. I thought perhaps during your game this year you might give a very special wave in his direction as you pass his house. He spends a lot of his time on the patio watching others play golf. x PPF 52-E

Thanking you, President Eisenhower for this special favor and hoping that you will be able to give Dick a little something to brighten his life.

Very cordially yours,

Douw Fonda

Douw Fonda

DF/sjc

Incidently, neither Dick nor his family know I have written this letter.

Box 755
Noxon, Mont.

Dear President Eisenhower,

My girlfriends and I are writting all the way from Montana, We think its bad enough to send Elvis Presley in the Army, but if you cut his side burns off we will just die! You don't no how we fell about him, I really don't see why you have to send him in the Army at all, but we beg you please please don't give him a G. I. hair cut, oh please please don't! If you do we will just about die!

Presley
Presley
IS OURCRY
P-R-E-S-L-E-Y

E. P. LOVER

Elvis Presley
Lovers

Linda Kelly
Sherry Bare
Mickie Mattson

Linda Kelly; Sherry Bane; Mickie Mattson to Dwight D. Eisenhower

Noxon, MT ★ *1958*

The White House mailbox fills up with letters on all kinds of subjects, from government boondoggles to nuclear proliferation. This time it's sideburns.

Writing "all the way from Montana," three teenage girls let President Eisenhower know how very upset they are over Elvis Presley's imminent induction into the U.S. Army.

Actually, what bothers the girls most—so much, in fact, that they're barely able to keep from dropping dead right on the spot—is the fact that their idol's sideburns are going to wind up on the floor of an Army barbershop. It's really too too gruesome to contemplate.

In a closing salvo, they again deliver the threat employed by heartsick adolescents since time began—and then, just to make absolutely certain the President gets the message, they break into a peppy cheer. You can almost hear the pompoms rustling.

The much-dreaded G.I. haircut was caught on film, a fatherly barber seriously trimming away. The girls from Montana must have wept when they saw it. Elvis survived his hitch in the Army—and Linda, Sherry and Mickie undoubtedly managed to survive the two-year wait for his next record and movie.

His sideburns grew back.

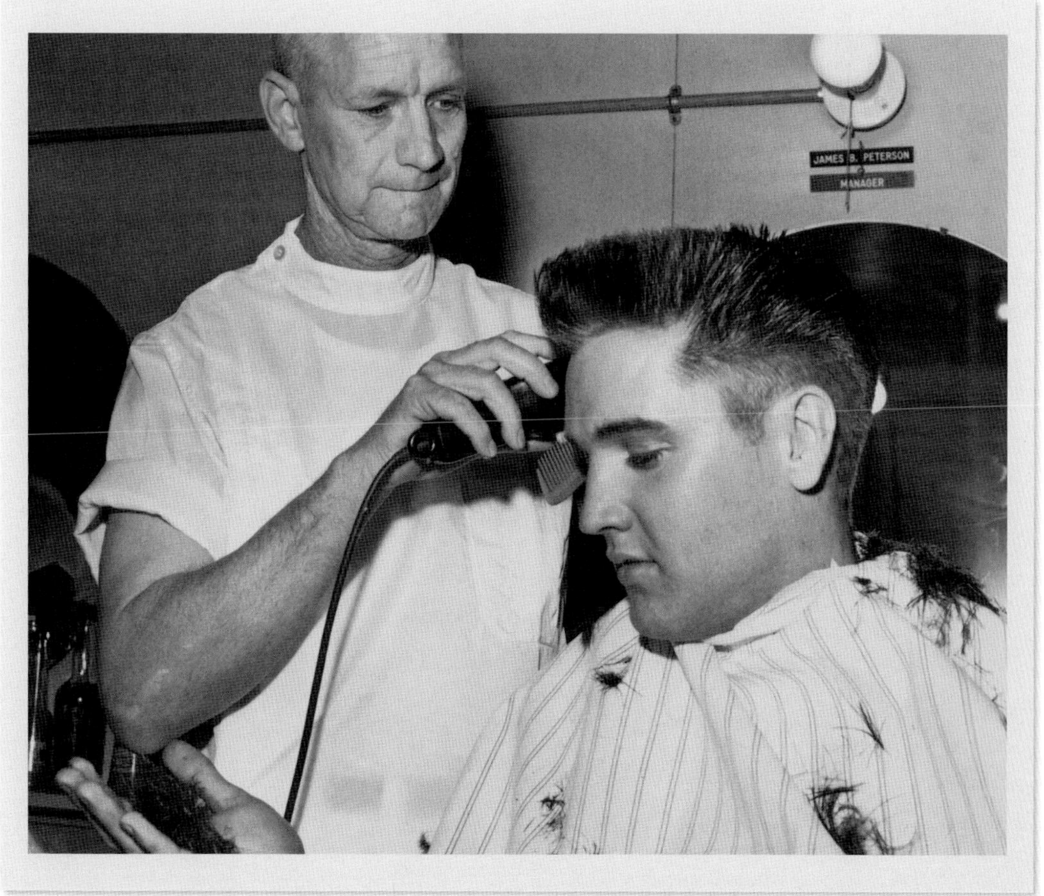

OPPOSITE: *Young "Elvis Presley Lovers" consider their idol's sideburns worthy of Presidential attention.*
ABOVE: *The tears of teenage girls fell with each lock as Elvis received his G.I. haircut.*

Jan. 24th
1960.

BUCKINGHAM PALACE

Dear Mr. President,

Seeing a picture of you in today's newspaper standing in front of a barbecue grilling quail, reminded me that I had never sent you the recipe of the drop scones which I promised you at Balmoral.

I now hasten to do so,

Queen Elizabeth II to Dwight D. Eisenhower

Buckingham Palace ★ January 24, 1960

When a woman shares a recipe with a friend, it's no big deal—unless the woman happens to be Queen of England and the friend happens to be President of the United States.

In this charming handwritten letter, Queen Elizabeth II tells President Eisenhower how to make up a batch of scones. Her recipe serves 16—royal residences do have large dining rooms, after all—so she tells him to use "less flour and milk" if he's baking for a smaller crowd. And if he should find there's no sugar in the Presidential pantry, she advises that "golden syrup or treacle" will do very nicely.

Think how gratifying it must be to tell your guests, "Aren't these scones yummy? Queen Elizabeth gave me the recipe."

Dear Mr. President,

Seeing a picture of you in today's newspaper standing in front of a barbecue grilling quail, reminded me that I had never sent you the recipe of the drop scones which I promised you at Balmoral.

I now hasten to do so, and I do hope you will find them successful.

Though the quantities are for 16 people, when there are fewer, I generally put in less flour and milk, but use the other ingredients as stated.

I have also tried using golden syrup or Treacle instead of only sugar and that can be very good, too.

I think the mixture needs a great deal of beating while making, and shouldn't stand about too long before cooking.

We have followed with intense interest and much admiration your tremendous journey to so many countries, but feel we shall never again be able to claim that we are being made to do too much on our future tours!

We remember with such pleasure your visit to Balmoral, and I hope the photographs will be a reminder of the very happy day you spent with us.

With all good wishes to you and Mrs. Eisenhower.

Yours sincerely,
Elizabeth R

DROP SCONES

Ingredients

4 teacups flour
4 tablespoons caster sugar
2 teacups milk
2 whole eggs
2 teaspoons bi-carbonate soda
3 teaspoons cream of tartar
2 tablespoons melted butter

Beat eggs, sugar and about half the milk together, add flour, and mix well together adding remainder of milk as required, also bi-carbonate and cream of tartar, fold in the melted butter.

Enough for 16 people.

OPPOSITE: *A handwritten note includes a recipe shared between friends—in this case, a Queen and a President.*

3

Telephone
MUrray Hill 2-0500

425 LEXINGTON AVENUE
New York 17, N. Y.

May 13, 1958

The President
The White House
Washington, D. C.

My dear Mr. President:

I was sitting in the audience at the Summit Meeting of Negro Leaders yesterday when you said we must have patience. On hearing you say this, I felt like standing up and saying, "Oh no! Not again."

I respectfully remind you sir, that we have been the most patient of all people. When you said we must have self-respect, I wondered how we could have self-respect and remain patient considering the treatment accorded us through the years.

17 million Negroes cannot do as you suggest and wait for the hearts of men to change. We want to enjoy now the rights that we feel we are entitled to as Americans. This we cannot do unless we pursue aggressively goals which all other Americans achieved over 150 years ago.

As the chief executive of our nation, I respectfully suggest that you unwittingly crush the spirit of freedom in Negroes by constantly urging forbearance and give hope to those pro-segregation leaders like Governor Faubus who would take from us even those freedoms we now enjoy. Your own experience with Governor Faubus is proof enough that forbearance and not eventual integration is the goal the pro-segregation leaders seek.

In my view, an unequivocal statement backed up by action such as you demonstrated you could take last fall in deal-

JACKIE ROBINSON TO DWIGHT D. EISENHOWER

New York, NY ★ May 13, 1958

ON MAY 12, 1958, THE NATIONAL NEWSPAPER Publishers Association, a federation of African-American community newspapers, sponsored a meeting of "Negro Leaders" in Washington. President Eisenhower was invited to speak.

After some remarks about "the problems of living in this world…under the threat of communism," Eisenhower moved to the topic of civil rights. "In such problems as this, there are no revolutionary cures," he said. "They are evolutionary." Citing the end of racial discrimination in the armed forces and the recent enactment of voting-rights legislation, he continued, "Such things as these mean progress. But I do believe that as long as they are human problems…we must have patience and forebearance. We must depend more on better and more profound education than simply on the letter of the law."

At least one member of the audience was offended by the President's words.

In 1958, Jackie Robinson was vice president of the Chock full o' Nuts coffee company—but he was far better known as the blazing Brooklyn Dodgers infielder who had broken Major League Baseball's color barrier a decade earlier. Since retiring from baseball, Robinson had become an outspoken champion of civil rights, and it was in this role that he wrote to the White House the day after the May 12 meeting.

Robinson's reaction to Eisenhower's call for patience—"I felt like standing up and saying, 'Oh no! Not again'"—sets the tone of the letter. "I respectfully remind you sir," he continues (you can almost see his jaw clenched in barely repressed anger), "that we have been the most patient of all people." Black citizens are no longer willing to "wait for the hearts of men to change," he says. "We want to enjoy now the rights that we feel we are entitled to as Americans." The key word in the sentence—"now"—isn't underlined, but its urgency is unmistakable.

Robinson's frustration was a harbinger of things to come. In the 1960s, smoldering discontent over the slow pace of progress in civil rights would erupt in flames on the streets of America's cities.

. . . I respectfully remind you sir, that we have been the most patient of all people. When you said we must have self-respect, I wondered how we could have self-respect and remain patient considering the treatment accorded us through the years.

17 million Negroes cannot do as you suggest and wait for the hearts of men to change. We want to enjoy now the rights that we feel we are entitled to as Americans. . . .

In my view, an unequivocal statement backed up by action such as you demonstrated you could take last fall dealing with Governor Faubus if it became necessary, would let it be known that America is determined to provide--in the near future--for Negroes--the freedoms we are entitled to under the constitution.

Respectfully yours,
Jackie Robinson

OPPOSITE: *The White House received Jackie Robinson's letter in May 1958, but it would take much longer for his message to be heard.*

The White House
Washington

1957 SEP 23 PM 6 57

TO : MR HAGERTY
FROM: GEN GOODPASTER
FOLLOWING TELEGRAM RECEIVED HERE:

WA024 PD
LITTLE ROCK ARK SEP 23 344PMC
THE PRESIDENT
THE WHITE HOUSE

THE CITY POLICE, TOGETHER WITH THE STATE POLICE, MADE A VALIANT EFFORT TO CONTROL THE MOB TODAY AT CENTRAL HIGH SCHOOL. IN THE FINAL ANALYSIS, IT WAS DEEMED ADVISABLE BY THE OFFICER ON THE GROUND AND IN CHARGE TO HAVE THE COLORED CHILDREN REMOVED TO THEIR HOMES FOR SAFETY PURPOSES.

THE MOB THAT GAGHERED WAS NO SPONTANEOUS ASSEMBLY. IT WAS AGITATED, AROUSED, AND ASSEMBLED BY A CONCERTED PLAN OF ACTION.

ONE OF THE PRINCIPAL AGITATORS IN THE CROWD WAS A MAN BY THE NAME OF JIMMY KARAM, WHO IS A POLITICAL AND SOCIAL INTIMATE OF GOVERNOR FAUBUS, AND WHOSE WIFE IS NOW WITH GOVERNOR'S PARTY AT THE SOUTHERN GOVERNOR'S CONFERENCE. KARAM HAS A LONG RECORD OF EXPERIENCE IN STRIKE-BREAKING, AND OTHER ACTIVITIES SUCH AS HE ENGAGED IN TODAY.

THE MANNER IN WHICH THE MOB WAS FORMED AND ITS ACTION, TOGETHER WITH THE PRESENCE OF JIMMY KARAM, LEADS TO THE INEVITABLE CONCLUSION THAT GOVERNOR FAUBUS AT LEAST WAS COGNIZANT OF WHAT WAS GOING TO TAKE PLACE.

DETAILED INFORMATION ON THE EVENTS OF THE DAY WILL BE TURNED OVER TO THE JUSTICE DEPARTMENT FOR SUCH ACTION AS THE FEDERAL GOVERNMENT DEEMS APPROPRIATE.

IF THE JUSTICE DEPARTMENT DESIRES TO ENFORCE THE ORDERS OF THE FEDERAL COURT IN REGARD TO INTEGRATION IN THIS CITY, THE CITY POLICE WILL BE AVAILABLE TO LEND SUCH SUPPORT AS YOU MAY REQUIRE.

I AM NOT MAKING THIS WIRE PUBLIC. THIS IS FOR YOUR INFORMATION AND FOR THE JUSTICE DEPARTMENT TO USE AS IT CONSIDERS NECESSARY

WOODROW W MANN, MAYOR LITTLE ROCK ARKANSAS.

END 645PGS.

OK DEWEY

Woodrow W. Mann to Dwight D. Eisenhower
Martin Luther King, Jr. to John F. Kennedy
Leah Russell to Dwight D. Eisenhower

Little Rock, AR ★ September 23, 1957 ★ ★ ★ Atlanta, GA ★ September 15, 1963
Miami, FL ★ September 25, 1957

THESE DOCUMENTS HIGHLIGHT TWO OF THE most important flash points in the struggle for civil rights that roiled and transformed America in the 1950s and '60s.

In 1957, three years after the Supreme Court's decision in *Brown* v. *Board of Education*, nine black students were set to start classes at Central High School in Little Rock, Arkansas. The day before the school year was to begin, however, Governor Orval Faubus called out the National Guard to surround the school and warned that if black students attempted to enter, "blood will run in the streets." After lawyers for the NAACP obtained an injunction forbidding the use of the National Guard to keep them out, the nine set out for Central High again on September 23. Despite the presence of an angry mob, they entered the building—only to be met with more violence from white students. When city police felt they could no longer control the mob, the students had to leave the school by a back door.

In a telegram sent to President Eisenhower that evening, Mayor Woodrow Mann summarizes the events of the day and assures the President that city police are ready to lend assistance if the government "desires to enforce the orders of the federal court."

Eisenhower responded by federalizing the Arkansas National Guard and dispatching the 101st Airborne Division to maintain order in Little Rock. In May, having endured eight months of harrassment, Ernest Green became the first black graduate of Central High.

By 1963, the focus of civil-rights activity had shifted from Arkansas to Alabama—and the level of violence had risen dramatically. In Birmingham, so many bombs were set off in the homes and businesses of those who threatened the traditional structure of white supremacy that the city became known as "Bombingham." Even people who had allowed themselves to become inured to the violence were horrified when, on September 15, a dynamite blast at the Sixteenth Street Baptist Church killed four young black girls who were sitting in a Sunday School class.

A telegram sent to President Kennedy by Dr. Martin Luther King, Jr. on the day of the bombing captures the revulsion felt by millions—and issues a warning. "I will sincerely plead with my people to remain non violent in the face of this terrible provocation," King says. But if the government fails to take forceful action, he foresees "the worst racial holocaust this nation has ever seen."

In 1977, Robert Chambliss was convicted of murder in the death of one of the girls. After the case was reopened in 1997, Thomas Blanton and Bobby Frank Cherry were also given multiple life sentences for their roles in the bombing.

The third document, sent to the White House by a teacher in Miami, suggests a simple way to help people get along with one another. In a brief essay written at the height of the violence in Little Rock, twelve-year-old Leah Russell, who is blind, says that if children were sent to school blindfolded, she is confident that "after they got to know each other there wouldn't be any more fights. …"

In his reply, Eisenhower asked the teacher to tell Leah that "she has already grasped one of the great moral principles by which we all should live."

OPPOSITE: *Back-to-school days in 1957 Little Rock were troubled times; the city's mayor explains police efforts to control a segregationist mob.*

GENERAL

HU 2/ST1

The White House
Washington

1963 SEP 15 PM 8 32

WA064 PD

ATLANTA GA 15 443P EST

THE PRESIDENT

THE WHITE HOUSE

DEAR MR PRESIDENT I SHUDDER TO THINK WHAT OUR NATION HAS BECOME WHEN SUNDAY SCHOOL CHILDREN AND THEIR TEACHERS ARE KILLED IN CHURCH BY RACIST BOMBS. THE SAVAGE BOMBING OF THE 16TH STREET BAPTIST CHURCH THIS MORNING IS ANOTHER CLEAR INDICATION OF THE MORAL DEGENERATION OF THE STATE OF ALABAMA AND GOVERNOR GEORGE WALLACE. MR PRESIDENT YOU MUST CALL FOR LEGISLATION EMPOWERING THE ATTORNEY GENERAL TO ENTER CASES WHERE ANY CIVIL RIGHTS VIOLATION OCCURS THE LIVES OF WOMEN AND CHILDREN ARE FAR MORE PRECIOUS THAN THE OFFENSE CREATED BY THE ELIMINATION OF OUTMODED CUSTOMS AND TRADITIONS. IN A FEW HOURS I WILL BE GOING TO BIRMINGHAM. I WILL SINCERELY PLEAD WITH MY PEOPLE TO REMAIN NON VIOLENT IN THE FACE OF THIS TERRIBLE PROVOCATION HOWEVER I AM CONVINCED THAT UNLESS SOME STEPS ARE TAKEN BY THE FEDERAL GOVERNMENT TO RESTORE A SENSE OF CONFIDENCE IN THE PROTECTION OF LIFE, LIMB AND PROPERTY MY PLEAS SHALL FALL ON DEAF EARS AND WE SHALL SEE THE WORST RACIAL HOLOCAUST THIS NATION HAS EVER SEEN AFTER TODAYS TRAGEDY, INVESTIGATION WILL NOT SUFFICE. THE NATION AND BIRMINGHAM NEEDS YOUR COMMITMENT TO USE EVERYTHING WITHIN YOUR CONSTITUTIONAL POWER TO ENFORCE THE DESEGREGATION ORDERS OF THE COURTS

DR MARTIN LUTHER KING JR PRES SOUTHERN CHRISTIAN LEADERSHIP CONFERENCE.

How To Stop Trouble
By Leah Russell, age 12

If I were president, I would have all the children blindfolded and send them to school. I would also send some of the colored children and have them blindfolded. I think that all of them would have a lot of fun and there wouldn't be any fights. Probably after they got to know each other there wouldn't be any more fights or anything like that.

GENERAL
PP2-2/ST32 (2)

NATIONAL ASSOCIATION FOR THE ADVANCEMENT OF COLORED PEOPLE

TWENTY WEST FORTIETH STREET • NEW YORK 18, N. Y. • BRyant 9-1400

November 5, 1964

The Honorable Lyndon B. Johnson
President of the United States
The White House
Washington, D. C.

Dear Mr. President:

The people have not spoken; they have shouted.

Congratulations!

Sincerely,

Roy Wilkins

Roy Wilkins
Executive Director

RW:mso

Roy Wilkins to Lyndon B. Johnson

New York, NY ★ November 5, 1964

In the 1964 presidential election, voters gave Lyndon Johnson the most one-sided victory in history. Johnson won 61 percent of the popular vote, a record that even his idol Franklin Roosevelt had never matched. The Republican candidate, Barry Goldwater, carried only six states.

Admittedly, Johnson was helped by the public's perception of Goldwater as a trigger-happy extremist—a perception that Goldwater fueled by peppering his campaign speeches with outrageous (and eminently quotable) statements that gave him a reputation for "shooting from the lip." But while some people undoubtedly voted *against* Goldwater, many more voted *for* the array of social programs and initiatives that Johnson bundled together as the foundation for his "Great Society." Chief among these in the minds of many Americans, black and white, was the commitment—codified in the Civil Rights Act of 1964—to throw the full weight of the federal government behind the struggle for racial equality.

For those who had labored long and hard to end decades of discrimination, Johnson's victory was both a vindication and a long-awaited promise of better days to come. This nine-word note from Roy Wilkins, head of the National Association for the Advancement of Colored People, captures the spirit of near-euphoria that prevailed two days after voters went to the polls.

The good feelings soon started to fade, of course—but for a while, Americans allowed themselves the luxury of optimism.

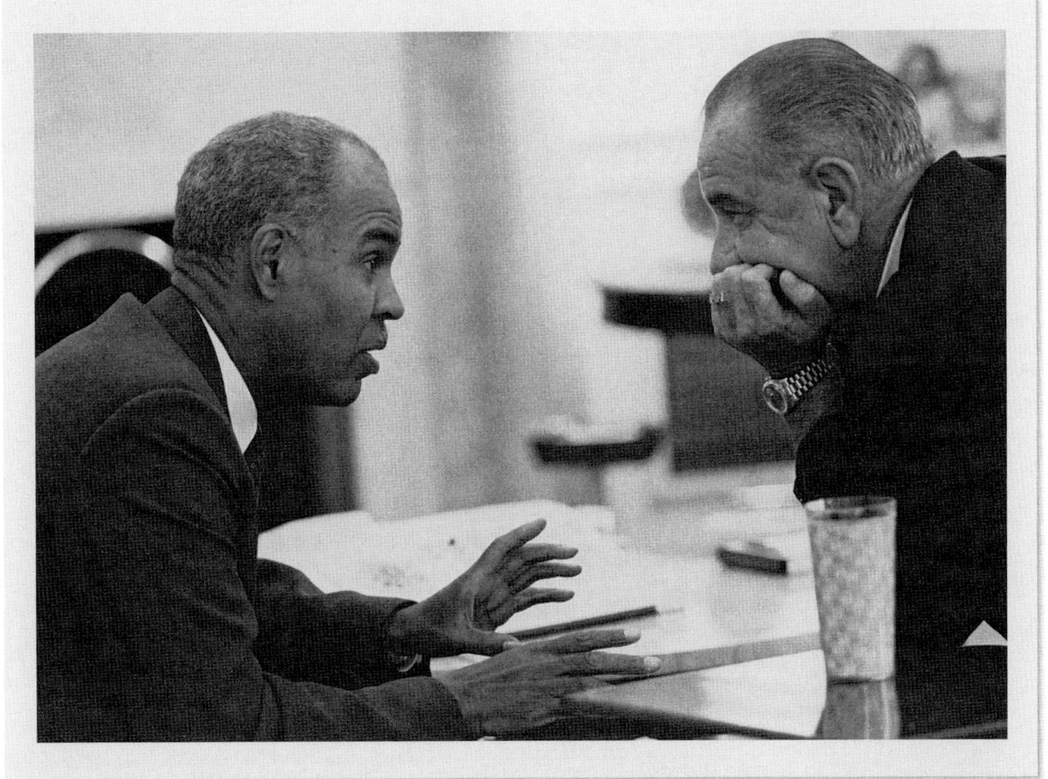

OPPOSITE: *Roy Wilkins of the NAACP offers short but sweet congratulations to LBJ after his landslide victory.*
ABOVE: *Eager to build his "Great Society," President Johnson gives Roy Wilkins his full attention.*

VIỆT-NAM DÂN CHỦ CỘNG HÒA

CHÍNH PHỦ LÂM THỜI

BO NGOAI GIAO

*

YKB-3739-1

HANOI FEBRUARY 28 1946

MAR 11 RECD

TELEGRAM

PRESIDENT HOCHIMINH VIETNAM DEMOCRATIC REPUBLIC HANOI

TO THE PRESIDENT OF THE UNITED STATES OF AMERICA WASHINGTON D.C.

ON BEHALF OF VIETNAM GOVERNMENT AND PEOPLE I BEG TO INFORM YOU THAT IN COURSE OF CONVERSATIONS BETWEEN VIETNAM GOVERNMENT AND FRENCH REPRESENTATIVES THE LATTER REQUIRE THE SECESSION OF COCHINCHINA AND THE RETURN OF FRENCH TROOPS IN HANOI STOP MEANWHILE FRENCH POPULATION AND TROOPS ARE MAKING ACTIVE PREPARATIONS FOR A COUP DE MAIN IN HANOI AND FOR MILLTARY AGGRESSION STOP I THEREFORE MOST EARNESTLY APPEAL TO YOU PERSONALLY AND TO THE AMERICAN PEOPLE TO INTERFERE URGENTLY IN SUPPORT OF OUR INDEPENDENCE AND HELP MAKING THE NEGOTIATIONS MORE IN KEEPING WITH THE PRINCIPLES OF THE ATLANTIC AND SAN FRANCISCO CHARTERS

RESPECTFULLY

HOCHIMINH

Hochiminh

Ho Chi Minh to Harry S. Truman
Ngo Dinh Diem to John F. Kennedy

Hanoi, North Vietnam ★ *February 28, 1946*
Saigon, South Vietnam ★ *February 23, 1963*

In 1946, most Americans knew little or nothing about Vietnam. They didn't realize (or care, probably) that during the preceding five years, while American troops had been fighting to push the Japanese out of the islands of the Pacific, Vietnam had been the scene of a fierce guerrilla war between Japanese forces and a ragtag organization known as the Vietminh. They were likewise unaware that a charismatic nationalist and ardent communist calling himself Ho Chi Minh ("he who enlightens") had announced the birth of the Democratic Republic of Vietnam, with himself as president, a few days after an atomic bomb fell on Hiroshima.

The French, on the other hand, did know about Ho Chi Minh. They saw him as an obstacle in their drive to reassert control over Vietnam, which had been part of France's colonial empire since the 1880s, and they moved to push him aside. By the end of 1945, French forces had reoccupied all of southern Vietnam and were ready to move against Ho's stronghold in the north.

In this 1946 telegram to President Harry Truman, Ho appeals for American help in maintaining the independence of his fledgling republic. Displaying a clear knowledge of world affairs and a shrewd appreciation for the value of seizing the moral high ground, he urges Truman to fulfill the promise of the 1941 Atlantic Charter, in which President Roosevelt and Prime Minister Churchill had endorsed "the right of all peoples to choose the form of government under which they shall live."

This was not Ho's first attempt to plead his country's case before a U.S. President: At Versailles in 1919, he had tried unsuccessfully to present a proposal for Vietnam's independence to Woodrow Wilson. When his second attempt, 27 years later, failed to persuade Truman to "interfere urgently" in Vietnam, Ho launched an all-out guerrilla campaign against the French. A stunning French defeat at Dien Bien Phu in 1954 set the stage for a peace conference that divided Vietnam into a communist North and a "free" South. A promised national election to reunify the country was never held.

In 1955, Ngo Dinh Diem (whom the French described as "not only incapable but mad") was elected president of South Vietnam and direct U.S. aid began to flow into the country. As conflict between the Diem regime and the communist Viet Cong escalated, American aid increased; by the end of 1962, more than 10,000 U.S. military personnel were stationed in Vietnam.

Sent on the occasion of the lunar new year known as Tet, Diem's 1963 letter to President Kennedy offers effusive expressions of gratitude for America's "strong and effective aid" coupled with assurances that the people of Vietnam are "more than ever determined to redouble their efforts and sacrifices in the year ahead. ..." It closes with a tribute to "the noble sons of America who have given their lives in our land. ..."

Later in 1963, President Diem was assassinated in a United States-sanctioned coup. Five years after this letter was written, another Tet holiday saw a nationwide communist offensive that killed scores of "noble sons of America" and sent public support for the war plummeting.

OPPOSITE: *Ho Chi Minh's 1946 telegram requesting U.S. aid raises the inevitable specter of "what if."*

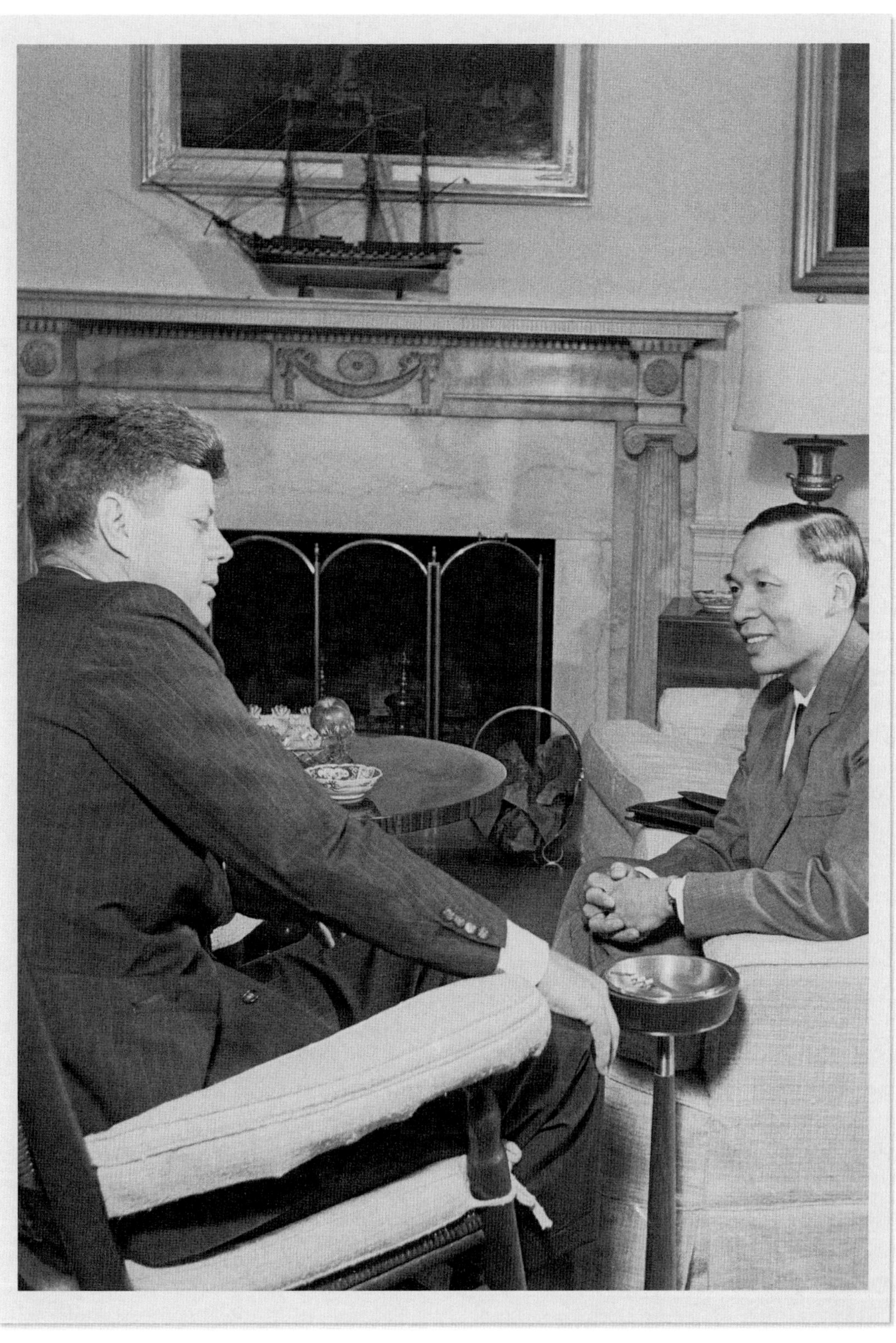

ABOVE: *Nguyyan Dinh Thuan, Chief Cabinet Minister to President Ngo Dinh Diem of South Vietnam, hand-delivered Diem's letter to President Kennedy.*
OPPOSITE: *Ngo Dinh Diem's letter drips with fulsome praise; soon his country would drip with American blood.*

4a

February 23, 1963

Dear Mr. President;

The whole Vietnamese people were deeply touched by the message which Your Excellency, as spokesman for the great American democracy, so kindly sent them on the occasion of their New Year Day.

They have welcomed this message as a magnificent and perfect expression of the comprehension and friendship of the American people who have supported them with strong and effective aid in these difficult days of their struggle against communist subversion and aggression.

This is indeed a major source of inspiration for my countrymen who are more than ever determined to redouble their efforts and sacrifices in the year ahead to come near to the final victory that will bring them security and peace, and promote social justice and collective ascent within the framework of the economic development of the country.

In the reverent memory of the noble sons of America who have given their lives in our land for the common cause, I want to thank you cordially, Dear Mr. President, for your wishes which express so well our common aspirations and hopes and to offer the gratitude and admiration of the Vietnamese people to the great nation and people "who have always been willing to pay the dearest costs for liberty."

Ngo-dinh-Diem
President of the Republic of Viet-Nam

9/11 2/22

February 18, 1963

Dear President Kennedy,

My brother, Specialist James Delmas McAndrew, was one of the seven crew members killed on January 11 in a Viet Nam helicopter crash.

The Army reports at first said that communist gunfire was suspected. Later, it said that the helicopter tradgedy was due to malfunction of aircraft controls. I've wondered if the "malfunction of aircraft controls" wasn't due to "communist gunfire." However, that's neither important now, nor do I even care to know.

My two older brothers entered the Navy and the Marine Corps in 1941 immediately after the war started - they served all during the war and in some very important battles - then Jim went into the Marines as soon as he was old enough and was overseas for a long time. During those war years and even all during the Korean conflict we worried about all of them - but that was all very different. They were wars that our country were fighting, and everyone here knew that our sons and brothers were giving their lives for their country.

I can't help but feel that giving one's life for one's country is one thing, but being sent to a country where half our country never even heard of and being shot at without even a chance to shoot back is another thing altogether!

Bobbie Lou Pendergrass to John F. Kennedy John Steinbeck; the Smothers Brothers to Lyndon B. Johnson

Santa Ana, CA ★ February 18, 1963
Long Island, NY ★ May 28, 1966
Los Angeles, CA ★ October 31, 1968

THE EMOTIONAL, SOCIAL AND POLITICAL turmoil caused by the ever worsening Vietnam War is traced in these three letters from the mid-1960s.

The first, sent to President Kennedy in 1963, voices the grief that was to visit so many American homes in the following years. Bobbie Lou Pendergrass writes that when her three brothers went off to fight in World War II and Korea, their worried family found some solace in the knowledge that those wars involved and united the whole nation in a common cause. Now, however, one brother has been killed in Vietnam, and the shattered family feels that he died for a murky cause in a country that "half our country never even heard of." Assuring the President that she is "a good Democrat—and I'm not criticizing," she expresses an opinion that eventually was shared by millions of others: "It seems to me that if we are going to have our boys over there, that we should send enough to have a chance—or else stay home." She goes on to ask: "If a war is worth fighting, isn't it worth fighting to win?"

In his response, Kennedy devoted several paragraphs to a defense of the American presence in Vietnam. Noting that 45 Americans had died in that far-off land thus far, he stated flatly that "full scale war in Viet Nam is at the moment unthinkable."

By the time the second letter was written in 1966, the death toll had skyrocketed and "full scale war" was a bloody reality. In that context, the letter is a thoughtful and moving expression of confidence, patriotism, and love. Famed author John Steinbeck thanks President Lyndon Johnson for meeting with him and his son at the White House. Speaking of his son, who is leaving soon for duty in Vietnam, Steinbeck offers a father's ultimate accolade: "I am pleased with this boy and proud." And to the President, whose policies are under vicious attack by antiwar demonstrators, he offers the ultimate comfort: "I assure you that only mediocrity escapes criticism."

Written two years later, the third letter offers a hint of just how widespread and virulent antiwar sentiment has become. In a remarkable apology, comedians Tom and Dick Smothers tell President Johnson they regret having made him the butt of so many jokes on their wildly popular televison show. "We disregarded the respect due to the office and the tremendous burden of running the country," they write. "Please know that we do admire what you have done for the country and particularly your dignity in accepting the abuses of so many people." They assure him that they are "now working for the election of Hubert Humphrey"—but their work couldn't stave off disaster for the Democrats in 1968.

Four days after Richard Nixon won the Presidency, Johnson wrote to thank the Smothers Brothers for their apology. "It is part of the price of leadership of this great and free nation to be the target of clever satirists," he told them. "If ever an Emmy is awarded for graciousness, I will cast my vote for you."

OPPOSITE: *In 1963, Bobbie Lou Pendergrass asks questions about Vietnam that would one day echo throughout the land.*

My brother, Specialist James Delmar McAndrew, was one of the seven crew members killed on January 11 in a Viet Nam helicopter crash.

The Army reports at first said that communist gunfire was suspected. Later, it said that the helicopter tradgedy was due to malfunction of aircraft controls. I've wondered if the "malfunction of aircraft controls" wasn't due to "communist gunfire." However, that's neither important now, nor do I even care to know.

My two older brothers entered the Navy and the Marine Corps in 1941 immediately after the war started--they served all during the war and in some very important battles--then Jim went into the Marines as soon as he was old enough and was overseas for a long time. During those war years and even all during the Korean conflict we worried about all of them--but that was all very different. They were wars that our country were fighting, and everyone here knew that our sons and brothers were giving their lives for their country.

I can't help but feel that giving one's life for one's country is one thing, but being sent to a country where half our country never even heard of and being shot at without even a chance to shoot back is another thing altogether!

Please, I'm only a housewife who doesn't even claim to know all about the international situation--but we have felt so bitter over this--can the small number of our boys over in Viet Nam possibly be doing enough good to justify the awful number of casualties? It seems to me that if we are going to have our boys over there, that we should send enough to have a chance--or else stay home. Those fellows are just sitting ducks in those darn helicopters. If a war is worth fighting--isn't it worth fighting to win?

Please answer this and help me and my family to reconcile ourselves to our loss and to feel that even though Jim died in Viet Nam--and it isn't our war--it wasn't in vain.

I am a good Democrat--and I'm not criticizing. I think you are doing a wonderful job--and God Bless You--

Very sincerely,

Bobbie Lou Pendergrass

. . . If Viet Nam should fall, it will indicate to the people of Southeast Asia that complete Communist domination of their part of the world is almost inevitable. Your brother was in Viet Nam because the threat to the Viet Namese people is, in the long run, a threat to the Free World community, and ultimately a threat to us also. For when freedom is destroyed in one country, it is threatened throughout the world.

I have written to you at length because I know that it is important to you to understand why we are in Viet Nam. James McAndrew must have foreseen that his service could take him into a war like this; a war in which he took part not as a combatant but as an advisor. I am sure that he understood the necessity of such a situation, and I know that as a soldier, he knew full scale war in Viet Nam is at the moment unthinkable.

I believe if you can see this as he must have seen it, you will believe as he must have believed, that he did not die in vain. Forty-five American soldiers, including your brother, have given their lives in Viet Nam. In their sacrifice, they have earned the eternal gratitude of this Nation and other free men throughout the world.

Again, I would like to express to you and the members of your family my deepest personal sympathy.

Sincerely, John F. Kennedy

OPPOSITE: *Kennedy expresses gratitude to the 45 Americans who have died in a conflict that would ultimately claim more than 50,000.*

EXECUTIVE

ND9-2-2/M*

C/F MAR 6 1963

Bobbie Lou

Dear Mrs. Pendergrass: *McAndrew, James D.

I would like to express to you my deep and sincere sympathy in the loss of your brother. I can, of course, well understand your bereavement and the feelings which prompted you to write.

The questions which you posed in your letter can, I believe, best be answered by realizing why your brother -- and other American men -- went to Viet Nam in the first place. When this is understood, I am sure that the other related questions will be answered.

Americans are in Viet Nam because we have determined that this country must not fall under Communist domination. Ever since Viet Nam was divided, the Viet Namese have fought valiantly to maintain their independence in the face of the continuing threat from the North. Shortly after the division eight years ago it became apparent that they could not be successful in their defense without extensive assistance from other nations of the Free World community.

In the late summer of 1955, with the approval of President Eisenhower, an Advisory Group was established in Viet Nam to provide them with adequate weapons and equipment and training in basic military skills which are essential to survival in the battlefield. Even with this help, the situation grew steadily worse under the pressure of the Viet Cong. By 1961 it became apparent that the troubles in Laos and the troubles in Viet Nam could easily expand. It is also apparent that the Communist attempt to take over Viet Nam, is only part of a larger plan for bringing the entire area of Southeast Asia under their domination. Though it is only a small part of the area geographically, Viet Nam is now the most crucial.

JOHN STEINBECK • *Box 1017, Sag Harbor, Long Island, New York*

28 MAY, 1966

DEAR MR. PRESIDENT:

I AM GRATEFUL TO YOU FOR RECEIVING MY SON AND ME. IT MEANT A GREAT DEAL TO BOTH OF US AND I AM SURE THAT SEEING YOU REASSURED HIM THAT RESPONSIBILITY IS BEHIND HIM AND BACKING HIM. HE HAD NEVER BEEN TO WASHINGTON BEFORE. FROM THE PLANE I TOOK HIM FIRST TO THE LINCOLN MEMORIAL. HE STOOD FOR A LONG TIME LOOKING UP AT THAT HUGE AND QUIET FIGURE AND THEN HE SAID, "OH! LORD! WE HAD BETTER BE GREAT."

YOU WILL UNDERSTAND, THAT I AM PLEASED WITH THIS BOY AND PROUD. HE KNOWS WHAT HE WANTS AND MUST DO. HE IS THROOUGHLY TRAINED TO DO IT. HE IS PROUD OF HIS UNIFORM AND PROUD OF HIS COUNTRY. HE GOES VERY SOON NOW, AND AS YOU MUST KNOW, MY HEART GOES WITH HIM. AND I WILL ASK YOU, SIR, TO REMEMBER YOUR PROMISE TO PRAY FOR HIM.

I KNOW THAT YOU MUST BE DISTURBED BY THE DEMONSTRATIONS AGAINST POLICYIN VIETNAM. BUT PLEASE REMEMBER THAT THERE HAVE ALWAYS BEEN PEOPLE WHO INSISTED ON THEIR RIGHT TO CHOOSE THE WAR IN WHICH THEY WOULD FIGHT TO DEFEND THEIR COUNTRY. THERE WERE MANY WHO WOULD HAVE NO PART OF MR. ADAMS' AND GEORGE WASHINGTON'S WAR. WE CALL THEM TORIES. THERE WERE MANY ALSO WHO CALLED GENERAL JACKSON A BUTCHER. SOME OF THESE SHOWED THEIR DISAPPROVAL BY SELLING BEEF TO THE BRITISH. THEN THERE WERE THE VERY MANY WHO DENOUNCED AND EVEN IMPEDED MR. LINCOLN'S WAR. WE CALL THEM COPPERHEADS. THEN THERE WERE THOSE WHO NOT ONLY DENOUNCED BUT DESTROYED PRESIDENT WILSON'S POLICY. BECAUSE OF VERY SPECIAL CIRCUMSTANCES, WE WILL NOT CALL THEM ANYTHING--- FOR A WHILE. I REMIND YOU OF THESE THINGS, MR. PRESIDENT, BECAUSE SOMETIMES, THE SHRILL SQUEAKING OF PEOPLE WHO SIMPLY DO NOT WISH TO BE DISTURBED, MUST BE SADDENING TO YOU. I ASSURE YOU THAT ONLY MEDIOCRITY ESCAPES CRITICISM.

AGAIN MY THANKS TO YOU, SIR. YOU GAVE MY BOY A PEDIMENT OF PRIDE, AND THAT A GOOD SOLDIER MUST HAVE.

AS ALWAYS, FAITHFULLY,

John Steinbeck

Rec'd CH 11/5

October 31, 1968

The President
The White House
Washington, D.C.

Mr. President:

During the past couple of years we have taken satirical jabs at you and more than occasionally overstepped our bounds. We disregarded the respect due the office and the tremendous burden of running the country because of our own emotional feelings regarding the war. We frequently disregarded the many, many good works and the progress the country has made under your administration.

We saw the television broadcast you made last night in behalf of the Democratic Party and Hubert Humphrey and were quite moved by your sincerity and by the content of the message. If the opportunity arose in this coming election to vote for you, we would.

Often an emotional issue such as the war makes people tend to over-react. Please accept our apology on behalf of the Smothers Brothers Comedy Hour for our over-reaction in some instances. Please know that we do admire what you have done for the country and particularly your dignity in accepting the abuses of so many people.

We are now working for the election of Hubert Humphrey and much of the enthusiasm we have for him is due to that broadcast of yours.

THE SMOTHERS BROTHERS COMEDY HOUR — 7800 BEVERLY BLVD., LOS ANGELES, CALIFORNIA 90036
COMEDIC PRODUCTIONS INCORPORATED

I am grateful to you for receiving my son and me. It meant a great deal to both of us and I am sure that seeing you reassured him that responsibility is behind him and backing him. He had never been to Washington before. From the plane I took him first to the Lincoln Memorial. He stood for a long time looking up at the huge and quiet figure and then he said, "Oh! Lord! We had better be great."

You will understand that I am pleased with this boy and proud. He knows what he wants and must do. He is thoroughly trained to do it. He is proud of his uniform and proud of his country. He goes very soon now, and as you must know, my heart goes with him. And I will ask you, sir, to remember your promise to pray for him.

I know that you must be disturbed by the demonstrations against policy in Vietnam. But please remember that there have always been people who insisted on their right to choose the war in which they would fight to defend their country. There were many who would have no part of Mr. Adams' and George Washington's war. We call them Tories. There were many also who called General Jackson a butcher. Some of these showed their disapproval by selling beef to the British. Then there were the very many who denounced and even impeded Mr. Lincoln's war. We call them copperheads. Then there were those who not only denounced but destroyed President Wilson's policy. Because of very special circumstances, we will not call them anything--for a while. I remind you of these things, Mr. President, because sometimes, the shrill squeaking of people who simply do not wish to be disturbed, must be saddening to you. I assure you that only mediocrity escapes criticism.

Again my thanks to you, sir. You gave my boy a pediment of pride, and that a good soldier must have.

As Always, faithfully,
John Steinbeck

★ ★ ★

During the past couple of years we have taken satirical jabs at you and more than occasionally overstepped our bounds. We disregarded the respect due the office and the tremendous burden of running the country because of our own emotional feelings regarding the war. We frequently disregarded the many, many good works and the progress the country has made under your administration.

We saw the television broadcast you made last night in behalf of the Democratic Party and Hubert Humphrey and were quite moved by your sincerity and by the content of the message. If the opportunity arose in this coming election to vote for you, we would.

Often an emotional issue such as the war makes people tend to over-react. Please accept our apology on hehalf of the Smothers Brothers Comedy Hour for our over-reaction in some instances. Please know that we do admire what you have done for the country and particularly your dignity in accepting the abuses of so many people.

We are now working for the election of Hubert Humphrey and much of the enthusiasm we have for him is due to that broadcast of yours.

We just saw your message on Viet Nam and with all America, are pleased at your determined move to halt the bombing in an effort to achieve peace.

Respectfully, Tom Smothers / Dick Smothers

OPPOSITE: *In saluting the Smothers Brothers' gracious apology, President Johnson shows genuine grace himself.*

THE WHITE HOUSE

WASHINGTON

November 9, 1968

Dear Messrs. Smothers:

I am very grateful for your kind and thoughtful letter.

To be genuinely funny at a time when the world is in crisis is a task that would tax the talents of a genius; to be consistently fair when standards of fair play are constantly questioned demands the wisdom of a saint.

It is part of the price of leadership of this great and free nation to be the target of clever satirists. You have given the gift of laughter to our people. May we never grow so somber or self-important that we fail to appreciate the humor in our lives.

If ever an Emmy is awarded for graciousness, I will cast my vote for you.

Sincerely,

Messrs. Tom and
Dick Smothers
7800 Beverly Boulevard
Los Angeles, California 90036

Council of Physical Fitness

3/18

1023 Berwick
Pontiac, Mich.
March 14, 1963

Open Letter to President Kennedy:
White House
Washington, D.C.

Dear Mr. Kennedy:

Your physical fitness program is in full swing and a very fine idea, except for one hitch. How can the women and teen-age girls be physically fit with deformed feet? It is impossible to find round toe, flat heel shoes to fit sub-teens in women's sizes, and difficult to find wedge or high heels with round toes. I'm sure you don't expect the army or marines to hike fifty miles in pointed toes, but even gym shoes and house slippers for women are pointed.

I have written letters to newspapers and shoe manufacturers without success. But the solution is simple for you. Please convince Mrs. Kennedy to buy and wear in public round toe shoes, and every style conscious woman will demand the manufacturers make them.

Please, Mr. President, do this favor for

Gladys D. McPherson; Richard Millington to John F. Kennedy

Pontiac, MI ★ March 14, 1963
Sacramento, CA ★ February 11, 1963

In recent years, revelations about the true state of John F. Kennedy's health have made it clear that our nation's youngest President suffered from a variety of ailments that required heavy medication and kept him in considerable pain. During Kennedy's years in the White House, these facts were masked by staff members and advisors, who presented to the public a carefully crafted image of the President as a vigorous, athletic man who enjoyed sailing, jogging on the beach, and playing touch football. As far as most people knew, Kennedy's only physical complaint stemmed from the most all-American of infirmities: a bad back.

Ironically, despite—or perhaps because of—his own health problems, Kennedy positioned himself as a champion of physical fitness for Americans, especially young people. In a 1961 speech at the National Football Foundation and Hall of Fame banquet, he said that America had become "a nation of spectators" whose only exercise came from "walking across the room to turn on our television sets." He wasn't exaggerating: Between 1948 and 1961, one out of every six men examined for military service was rejected as physically unfit.

To meet this challenge, Kennedy said, "we must...literally change the physical habits of millions of Americans." As a start, he urged members of his staff to shed five pounds. And he reinvigorated the President's Council on Physical Fitness (created during the Eisenhower Administration) as a vehicle for encouraging schoolchildren to get off the couch and onto the playing fields.

Most people applauded Kennedy's initiative, but some foresaw problems.

Like pointy-toed shoes, for example. Gladys McPherson writes that the President wouldn't "expect the army or marines to hike fifty miles in pointed toes" but she and her sister-citizens ("to whom God gave rounded feet instead of pointed ones") have to suffer every day. She suggests that Jackie Kennedy wear round-toed shoes to set an example for everyone.

Speaking of examples, Richard Millington points out that the sorry spectacle of "paunchy teachers" and Scoutmasters with "midriff bulge" makes it hard for kids to believe in the importance of exercise. His solution is a law requiring teachers "to keep themselves in the pink too."

Of course, neither suggestion ever stood a chance.

OPPOSITE: *Practical women have long asked McPherson's question: How can they walk in pointy-toed shoes?*
ABOVE: *Four student athletes hiked 220 miles from Vermont's Windham College to New York City in support of JFK's physical fitness program.*

Dear Mr. Kennedy,

Your physical fitness program is in full swing and a very fine idea, except for one hitch. How can the women and teen-age girls be physically fit with deformed feet? It is impossible to find round toe, flat heel shoes to fit sub-teens in women's sizes, and difficult to find wedge or high heels with round toes. I'm sure you don't expect the army or marines to hike fifty miles in pointed toes, but even gym shoes and house slippers for women are pointed.

I have written letters to newspapers and shoe manufacturers without success. But the solution is simple for you. Please convince Mrs. Kennedy to buy and wear in public round toe shoes, and every style conscious woman will demand the manufacturers make them.

Please, Mr. President, do this favor for the women of America to whom God gave rounded feet instead of pointed ones. We have suffered for a long time.

Respectfully yours,
Gladys D. McPherson

★★★

Dear President Kennedy,

I would like to know why, in this age of stress on physical fitness, there are still paunchy teachers around. These teachers are supposed to be good examples to us poor, disgusted kids. We kids do the exercise the teachers tell us, while the teachers stand around talking to other teachers. How are we supposed to believe exercises are worth it if the teachers don't seem to be interested?

I move that a new law be passed that requires teachers to keep themselves in the pink too. Thank you for your attention and please reply soon.

Sincerely yours,
Richard Millington

P.S. Even some of the Scoutmasters have midriff bulge.

OPPOSITE: *Richard Millington wants his teachers to practice as well as preach physical fitness.*

16

HEW

2571 Portola Way
Sacramento, Calif.
February 11, 1963

Dear President Kennedy,

I would like to know why, in this age of stress on physical fitness, there are still paunchy teachers around. These teachers are supposed to be good examples to us poor, disgusted kids. We kids do the exercises the teachers tell us, while the teachers stand around talking to other teachers. How are we supposed to believe exercises are worth it if the teachers don't seem to be interested?

I move that a new law be passed that requires teachers to keep themselves in the pink, too. Thank you for your attention and please reply soon.

Sincerely yours,
Richard Millington

P.S. Even some of the Scoutmasters have midriff bulge.

WHITEHALL 4-9000

Founded 1801

New York Post

75 WEST STREET . NEW YORK 6, N. Y.

THE WHITE HOUSE
OCT 3 2 24 PM '61
RECEIVED

Leonard Lyons

October 2, 1961.

Dear Mr. President:

In the event that you might be anxious about how you rate in history, I think you should know about this market: a manuscript and autograph framing shop on 53rd Street and Madison Avenue has a window display of framed presidential autographs. In each is either a tinted photo or a medallion of a President.

George Washington's sells for $175. U.S. Grant's sells for $55, Franklin D. Roosevelt's for $75, Teddy Roosevelt's for $67.50, John F. Kennedy's for $75.

Please don't bother to acknowledge this, for two reasons:

(1) You're too busy; and
(2) If you sign your name too often, that would depress the autograph market on E.53rd Street.

Sylvia joins me, of course, in sending you fondest regards.

Sincerely,

Leonard

President John F. Kennedy
The White House
Washington, D.C.

LEONARD LYONS TO JOHN F. KENNEDY

New York, NY ★ October 2, 1961
New York, NY ★ October 16, 1961

FROM 1934 TO 1974, LEONARD LYONS' column "The Lyons Den" in the *New York Post* was a popular source of news and gossip about the celebrities and hangers-on who dined and danced (and occasionally spilled their secrets) at Lindy's, the Stork Club, El Morocco, and other famed New York hot spots. With his sharp eye for news-worthy nuggets, Lyons spotted some Presidential autographs in a shop window on East 53rd Street one day—and decided to let President Kennedy know about it.

In the first shot of a volley that was to span more than a month, he cautions Kennedy that overuse of the Presidential pen could depress the market for his autograph, which currently commands the same price as Franklin Roosevelt's. When Kennedy responds with a note that is purposely unsigned, a tickled Lyons asks permission to publish it. Press secretary Pierre Salinger is given the privilege of delivering the punch line.

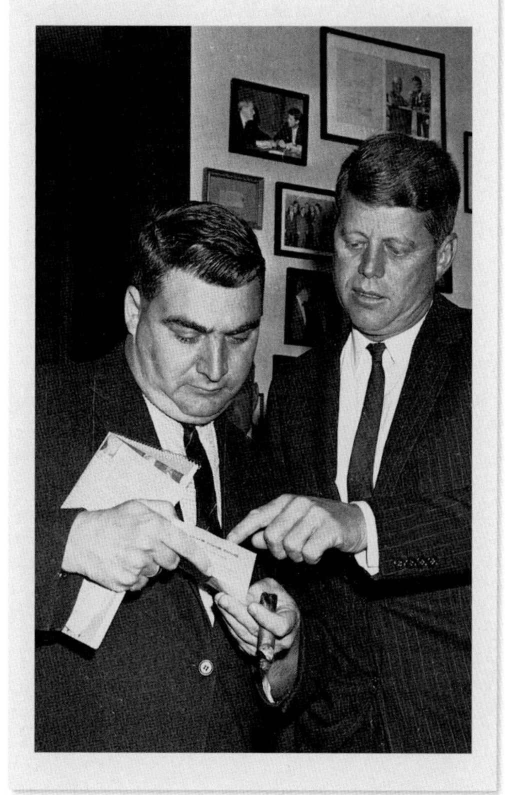

Dear Leonard:

With regard to your letter of October 16th, you have permission to print the President's response.

By having me write this letter, the President again avoided signing the letter.

Best regards,
Pierre Salinger
Press Secretary to
the President

OPPOSITE: *Columnist Leonard Lyons gives JFK the heads up regarding his apparent worth "on paper."*
ABOVE: *Press secretary Pierre Salinger (left) confers with his boss, President John F. Kennedy.*

EXECUTIVE

PR6

October 11, 1961

Dear Leonard:

I appreciate your letter about the market on Kennedy signatures. It is hard to believe that the going price is so high now. In order not to depress the market any further I will not sign this letter.

Best regards,

Not signed

Mr. Leonard Lyons
NEW YORK POST
75 West Street
New York 6, New York

JFK/PS/sm

WHITEHALL 4-9000

Founded 1801

New York Post

75 WEST STREET • NEW YORK 6, N. Y.

THE WHITE HOUSE
OCT 17 2 23 PM '61
RECEIVED

Leonard Lyons

October 16, 1961.

Dear Mr. President:

Sylvia and I laughed and laughed at your unsigned response regarding depressing the market for presidential autographs.

Naturally, such a communication is privileged; but, since it's so amusing, I am writing for permission to print it and share the amusing aspects with my readers.

I assume that your reply, one way or another, will be signed. Now that you know about the market, I hope you don't think I am seeking unjust enrichment. As a swap, therefore, I'm enclosing two Republican autographs -- Tom Dewey's and Richard Nixon's. Not that one of your autographs isn't worth two of theirs: it's just that yours will be signed "Jack" and theirs are signed in full.

With best regards,

Sincerely,

Leonard

Sincerely,

Dick Nixon

Richard Nixon

Sincerely yours

Thomas E. Dewey

HARRY S. TRUMAN
INDEPENDENCE, MISSOURI

June 28, 1962

Dear Mr. President:-

It looks as if the Republicrats have n't changed a bit since 1936. President Roosevelt had his troubles with them—so did I.

Mr. President, in my opinion you are on the right track. Don't let 'em tell you what to do. You tell them, as you have! Your suggestions for the public welfare, in my opinion, are correct. This is a personal and confidential statement for what it may be worth. You know my program with these counterfeits was "Give 'em Hell" and if

Presidential Advice

Harry S. Truman to John F. Kennedy ★ *Independence, MO* ★ *June 28, 1962*
Herbert Hoover to Harry S. Truman ★ *New York, NY* ★ *December 19, 1962*
Barry Goldwater to Gerald Ford ★ *Washington, D.C.* ★ *May 7, 1976*
Richard Nixon to Ronald Reagan ★ *New York, NY* ★ *August 13, 1987*

The American Presidency is the world's most exclusive men's club. It's hardly surprising, therefore, that the members of this fraternity would offer advice to one another.

It is unclear what triggered Harry Truman's handwritten note to President Kennedy in June 1962, but there were plenty of issues—from a stock-market slump to a threatened strike by flight engineers—swirling around the White House at the time. Whatever it was that prompted him to write, he tells Kennedy he is "on the right track" and urges him to adopt the well-known Truman strategy: "Give 'em Hell and if they don't like it, give them more of the same." He closes by telling the President "I admire your spunk"—high praise indeed from a man who had plenty of spunk himself.

It is a bit surprising that Barry Goldwater, who went down to crushing defeat in 1964, should presume to offer advice on running a successful Presidential campaign, but that's exactly what he does in his 1976 letter to President Ford. He tells Ford that his speeches "are a little bit too long" and need to be "more punchy"—advice that campaign audiences doubtless would have appreciated. As for dealing with Ronald Reagan, who had assumed Goldwater's ultra-conservative mantle and was challenging Ford for the Republican nomination, Goldwater tells the President bluntly, "You are not going to get the Reagan vote...so get after middle America."

The subject of Richard Nixon's 1987 letter to President Reagan is the Iran-Contra affair, in which members of the administration illegally sold weapons to Iran and used proceeds to assist Nicaraguan anticommunists known as Contras. Referring to Reagan's August 12 television address marking the conclusion of congressional committee hearings on Iran-Contra, Nixon congratulates the President for having "sounded and looked strong" and adds that the committee "labored for nine months and produced a stillborn midget." His advice: "Don't ever comment on the Iran-Contra matter again."

The 1962 letter from Herbert Hoover to Harry Truman doesn't offer advice. It is a heartfelt expression of gratitude from one former President to another. Recalling his years as a political pariah, Hoover thanks Truman for having given him a chance to re-enter "the only profession I know, public service." The message: Even a Chief Executive needs help, and the unlikeliest friend may end up the closest one.

It looks as if the Republerats haven't changed a bit since 1936. President Roosevelt had his troubles with them--so did I. Mr. President, in my opinion you are on the right track. Don't let 'em tell you what to do. You tell them, as you have! Your suggestions for the public welfare, in my opinion, are correct. This is a personal and confidential statement for what it may be worth. You know my program with these counterfeits was "Give 'em Hell" and if they don't like it, give them more of the same. I admire your spunk as we say in Wisconsin.
Sncerely,
Harry S. Truman

OPPOSITE: *From one President to another, Truman urges Kennedy to override the "Republerats" who troubled both him and FDR in the past.*

BARRY GOLDWATER
ARIZONA

THE PRESIDENT HAS SEEN....

5-7

COMMITTEES:
AERONAUTICAL AND SPACE SCIENCES
ARMED SERVICES
PREPAREDNESS INVESTIGATING SUBCOMMITTEE
TACTICAL AIR POWER SUBCOMMITTEE
INTELLIGENCE SUBCOMMITTEE
MILITARY CONSTRUCTION SUBCOMMITTEE
RESEARCH AND DEVELOPMENT SUBCOMMITTEE

United States Senate
WASHINGTON, D.C. 20510

May 7, 1976

The President
The White House
Washington, D.C. 20500

Dear Mr. President:

I hope this reaches you before you depart for Nebraska for I would like to reiterate a couple of things I said to you on the phone the other day.

You are the President. Do not stupe to arguing with another candidate. Your speeches are a little bit too long. Get a good speech that is short and use it and use it and use it. Reagan's trick, as you know, is to have a whole handful of cards and he shuffles out whatever comes out to be ten minutes of speaking, and I don't think this deck has changed much over the years. Your speech writer has to be more punchy. It has to sound like you and no matter how much you have to rehearse it, do it.

You are not going to get the Reagan vote. These are the same people who got me the nomination and they will never swerve, but ninety per cent of them will vote for you for President, so get after middle America. They have never had it so good. They are making more money and they are not at war and, for God's sake, get off of Panama, but don't let Reagan off that hook.

God speed and with best wishes,

Barry

Barry Goldwater

HERBERT HOOVER

The Waldorf-Astoria Towers
New York 22, New York
December 19, 1962

Dear Mr. President:

I have received your book. It is a real contribution to the American people, and I greatly treasure its inscription. Indeed, it goes into the file of most treasured documents.

This is an occasion when I should like to add something more, because yours has been a friendship which has reached deeper into my life than you know.

I gave up a successful profession in 1914 to enter public service. I served through the First World War and after for a total of about 18 years.

When the attack on Pearl Harbor came, I at once supported the President and offered to serve in any useful capacity. Because of my varied experience during the First World War, I thought my services might again be useful, however there was no response. My activities in the Second World War were limited to frequent requests from Congressional committees.

When you came to the White House within a month you opened the door to me to the only profession I knew, public service, and you undid some disgraceful action that had been taken in the prior years.

For all of this and your friendship, I am deeply grateful.

Yours faithfully,

Herbert Hoover

The Honorable Harry S. Truman
Independence, Missouri

RICHARD NIXON

August 13, 1987

26 FEDERAL PLAZA
NEW YORK CITY

533859
5200
SP1169
FG002-36
PR007-02
PR005-02

CJ

No Reply
fchonded

Dear Ron,

The speech last night was one of your best. What was even more important than what you said was that you sounded and looked strong. You gave the lie to the crap about your being over-the-hill, discouraged, etc.

If I could be permitted one word of advice: Don't ever comment on the Iran-Contra matter again. Have instructions issued to all White House staffers and Administration spokesmen that they must never answer any question on or off the record about that issue in the future. They should reply to all inquiries by stating firmly and categorically that the President has addressed the subject and that they have nothing to add.

The committee labored for nine months and produced a stillborn midget. Let it rest in peace!

Sincerely,

Dick

The Honorable
Ronald Reagan

★ ★ ★

. . . When the attack on Pearl Harbor came, I at once supported the President and offered to serve in any useful capacity. Because of my varied experience during the First World War, I thought my services might again be useful, however there was no response. . . . When you came to the White House within a month you opened the door to me to the only profession I knew, public service, and you undid some disgraceful action that had been taken in the prior years.

For all of this and your friendship, I am deeply grateful.

Yours faithfully,

Herbert Hoover

★ ★ ★

. . . You are the President. Do not stupe to arguing with another candidate. Your speeches are a little bit too long. Get a good speech that is short and use it and use it and use it. . . . You are not going to get the Reagan vote. These are the same people who got me the nomination and they will never swerve, but ninety per cent of them will vote for you for President, so get after middle America. They have never had it so good. . . .

Barry Goldwater

★ ★ ★

. . . They should reply to all inquiries by stating firmly and categorically that the President has addressed the subject and that they have nothing to add.

The committee labored for nine months and produced a stillborn midget. Let it rest in peace!

Richard Nixon

OPPOSITE: *Ronald Reagan phoned his reply to Nixon's letter offering praise and advice about the Iran-Contra affair.*

Beloved —

You are as brave a man as Harry Truman — or FDR — or Lincoln. You can go on to find some peace, some achievement amidst all the pain. You have been strong, patient, determined beyond any words of mine to express.

Lady Bird Johnson to Lyndon B. Johnson

August, 1964

We shouldn't be reading this letter. It is too personal, too intimate to be subjected to our curious gaze—even now, more than four decades after it was written.

In August 1964, Lyndon Johnson had been President for only nine months. During that time, he had helped shepherd America through its grief over the assassination of President Kennedy, developed and proclaimed his vision of what he called "the Great Society," declared "unconditional war on poverty," and persuaded Congress to pass the most sweeping civil-rights legislation in the nation's history. The nonstop rush of history-in-the-making that characterized the period was encapsulated in the events of a single day, August 4. That morning, Johnson was told that for the second time in two days, North Vietnamese torpedo boats had attacked American ships in the Gulf of Tonkin; in the afternoon, while meeting with his advisors to formulate a response to the Tonkin Gulf incident, he received word that the bodies of three civil-rights workers missing since June had been found in Mississippi.

Johnson loved a challenge, relished the rough-and-tumble of political life. But he also had, in the words of one historian, "a huge, unappeasable hunger to be loved" and a deep need for reassurance and encouragement. As the 1964 election drew closer, that need grew particularly strong. Lady Bird Johnson, who was the President's closest advisor as well as his wife, sought to meet it with this letter.

She tells him that he is a worthy successor to those who had occupied the White House before him, including the two—Lincoln and FDR—whom Johnson especially idolized. She praises his good qualities and assures him that "most of the country" is behind him. If he quits now, she says, "Your friends would be frozen in embarassed silence and your enemies jeering." She applauds his bravery, but her steadfast reassurance underscores her own courage: "I am not afraid of Time or lies or losing money or defeat."

Apparently, these words were exactly what Johnson needed to hear. He delivered a rousing acceptance speech at the Democratic Convention, waged a barn burner of a campaign, and won the election in a landslide.

Beloved -

You are as brave a man as Harry Truman--or FDR--or Lincoln. You can go on to find some peace, some achievement amidst all the pain. You have been strong, patient, determined beyond any words of mine to express.

I honor you for it. So does most of the country.

To step out now would be wrong for your country, and I can see nothing but a lonely waste land for your future. Your friends would be frozen in embarassed silence and your enemies jeering.

I am not afraid of Time or lies or losing money or defeat.

In the final analysis I can't carry any of the burdens you talked of--so I know its only your choice. But I know you are as brave as any of the thirty-five.

I love you always

Bird

OPPOSITE: *From the greeting—"Beloved"—to the close, Lady Bird's letter to her husband glows with devotion and support.*

AmericanAirlines

In Flight...

Altitude; (1)

Location;

Dear Mr. President:

First I would like to introduce myself. I am Elvis Presley and admire you and Have ~~Great~~ Respect for your office. I talked to Vice President Agnew in Palm Springs 3 weeks ago and expressed my concern for our country. The Drug Culture, The Hippie Elements, The SDS, Black Panthers, etc do <u>not</u> consider me as their enemy or as they call it The Establishment. <u>I call it America ~~and~~</u>

Elvis Presley to Richard Nixon

Washington, D.C. ★ *December 21, 1970*

On December 21, 1970, a man walked up to the northwest gate of the White House and handed this letter to the guard on duty.

Handwritten on American Airlines stationery and addressed to President Richard Nixon, the letter begins with a simple declaration: "First I would like to introduce myself. I am Elvis Presley. ..." It goes on to state the writer's desire to "help the country out" by being named a "Federal Agent at Large." As proof that he is qualified for the assignment, Presley says that he has "done an in depth study of Drug abuse and Communist Brainwashing techniques" and notes that "the Drug Culture, the Hippie Elements, the SDS, Black Panthers, etc. do *not* consider me as their enemy or as they call it The Establishment."

When Nixon's appointments secretary learned that The King wanted to see The Chief, he wrote a memo to chief of staff H. R. Haldeman suggesting that the meeting might be a good thing. "If the President wants to meet with some bright young people outside of the Government," he said, "Presley might be a perfect one to start with." Haldeman wrote "You must be kidding" in the margin—but he approved the meeting.

In the Oval Office, Presley showed Nixon some badges he had received from various law enforcement agencies, criticized the Beatles, and reiterated his eagerness to fight drug use and restore faith in America. For his part, Nixon admired Presley's cuff links, praised his public-spiritedness and, in the words of an aide who was present, "indicated that he was aware of how difficult it is to perform in Las Vegas"—though precisely *how* he gained this awareness is unclear. As one might expect, photos of the occasion show Elvis Presley looking very showbiz and Richard Nixon looking, as he often did, slightly uncomfortable.

After the meeting ended, there was an exchange of gifts. Presley gave the President a World War II-era Colt 45; in return, he received a badge from the Bureau of Narcotics and Dangerous Drugs. In a brief follow-up letter sent a few days later, Nixon thanked the King of Rock and Roll for the gun and wished him "a happy and peaceful 1971." No mention was made of Presley's offer to sign up for a hitch in the anti-drug army.

OPPOSITE: *The bizarre side of Elvis lives on in his letter offering to serve as a federal undercover agent.*
ABOVE: *In a surreal version of "The King and I," President Nixon poses with Elvis Presley.*

Dear Mr. President,

First I would like to introduce myself, I am Elvis Presley and admire you and have great respect for your office. I talked to Vice President Agnew in Palm Springs 3 weeks ago and expressed my concern for our country. The Drug Culture, the Hippie Elements, the SDS, Black Panthers, etc. do NOT consider me as their enemy or as they call it The Establishment. I call it America and I love it. Sir I can and will be of any service that I can to help the country out. I have no concerns or motives other than helping the country out. So I wish not to be given a title or an appointed position. I can and will do more good if I were made a Federal Agent at Large, and I will help out by doing it my way through my communications with people of all ages. First and foremost, I am an entertainer but all I need is the Federal credentials. I am on the plane with Sen. George Murphy and we have been discussing the problems that our country is faced with. So I am staying at the Washington hotel room 505-506-507--Have 2 men who work with me by the name of Jerry Schilling and Sonny West. I am registered under the name of Jon Burrows. I will be here for as long as it takes to get the credentials of a Federal agent. I have done an in depth study of drug abuse and communist brainwashing techniques and I am right in the middle of the whole thing, where I can and will do the most good. I am glad to help just so long as it is kept very private. You can have your staff or whomever call me anytime today, tonight or tomorrow. I was nominated this coming year one of America's Ten Most Outstanding Young Men. That will be in January 18 in my home town of Memphis Tenn. I am sending you the short autobiography about myself so you can better understand this approach. I would love to meet you just to say hello if you're not to Busy.

Respectfully
Elvis Presley

P.S. I believe that you Sir were one of the Top Ten Outstanding Men of America also. I have a personal gift for you also which I would like to present to you and you can accept it or I will keep it for you until you can take it.

OPPOSITE: *The "personal gift" Elvis speaks of was a weapon: a World War II-era Colt 45.*

AmericanAirlines

In Flight...

Altitude;

Location; 5

~~approach~~

approach. I would love to meet you just to say hello if you're not to Busy.

Respectfully

Elvis Presley

P.S. I believe that you Sir were one of the Top Ten Outstanding Men of America also.

I have a personal gift for you also which I would like to present to you and you can accept it or I will keep it for you until you can take it.

The White House
Washington

WHA007 KA005 1971 JUL 16 PM 2 43
K LLD037 POM PD KANSAS CITY MO 16 1242P CDT
PRESIDENT RICHARD NIXON
THE WHITE HOUSE WASHDC
HAVE FUN IN RED CHINA. HOPE THEY KEEP YOU
MARYANN GRELINGER.

The White House
Washington

WHA008 (04)PA013 SYA023 KA428 1971 JUL 16 PM 2 43
K LLA005 POM PD KANSAS CITY MO 15
PRESIDENT NIXON
WASHDC
YOU ARE A SELL-OUT A JACKASS AND A DOLT
MRS JOHN SHIELDS.

3

2

Mary Ann Grelinger; Mrs. John Shields to Richard Nixon

Kansas City, MO ★ *July 16, 1971*

People who disliked Richard Nixon—and there were lots of them—kept finding new reasons to fire their disapproving salvos at him. His 1972 trip to China gave them plenty of ammunition.

In a startling departure from twenty years of official policy that had mostly treated "Red China" as either dangerously bellicose or virtually nonexistent, Nixon told Congress in February 1970 that his Administration had indicated to China "our willingness to have a more normal and constructive relationship." Over the next few months, the U.S. exchanged a flurry of secret messages with leaders in Beijing, eased and then ended longstanding travel and trade restrictions, and dispatched a ping-pong team as the first group of Americans to visit China since 1949. Then, in a television address on July 15, 1971, Nixon announced that he and his wife would go to China early the following year.

Extensive media coverage of the eight-day visit in February 1972 offered Americans glimpses of a vast world behind a door that had long been closed—and not everyone liked seeing that door swing open. Some had bitter memories of China's involvement in the Korean War, while others reached further back to fan their long-smoldering outrage over America's failure to halt Mao Tse-tung's 1949 takeover. Many felt that "normalization" of relations with Communist China amounted to a betrayal of longtime ally Nationalist China—especially after the United Nations voted to admit the People's Republic and expel Taiwan.

Nixon called his visit "the week that changed the world." He was right, but some thought it was not a change for the better. The July 15 announcement of the upcoming trip prompted these telegrams, in which two women from Kansas City exercise their cherished right to let the President know, in no uncertain terms, what they think.

One adopts a wry tone, first wishing Nixon a "fun" trip, then sticking in the knife: "Hope they keep you."

The other doesn't mince words, doesn't even mention the visit to China before launching a stream of epithets: *sell-out*, *jackass*, *dolt*. Not particularly eloquent, not at all original, certainly not very respectful of the President or conducive to productive discourse—but admirably straightforward nonetheless.

OPPOSITE: *In their hearts they think he's wrong—two telegrams from Kansas City castigate Nixon.*
ABOVE: *Looking cheerful, Richard and Pat Nixon pose on China's Great Wall during their famous 1972 visit.*

P-883

Dear Mr. President,
I like your courage to pardon former President Nixon. Although I dont like to hear your speeches. You know I'am only 10 years old. I wish you would write me back.

Yea Alabama

Thank You,
Jackie Ann Lucas
Head of President Ford Commity

Yea Birmingham Americans

(P.S. I'am a Republacan)

(Sorry I don't know how to spell Republacan)

(P.S. please send me your autograph)

(I'am from)
(Wright School!!!)

Jackie Ann Lucas; Robert Lind; Anthony Ferreira to Gerald Ford

Birmingham, AL ★ *November, 1974*
Address Unknown ★ *September, 1974*
Fair Lawn, NJ ★ *September 11, 1974*

On August 8, 1974, just one month after being sworn in as President following Richard Nixon's unprecedented resignation, Gerald Ford stunned Americans by granting "a full, free, and absolute pardon" to Nixon "for all offenses against the United States which he...has committed or may have committed or taken part in...."

In his 1983 autobiography, *A Time to Heal*, Ford revealed that he steadfastly continued to believe that Nixon had played no role in the Watergate break-in and subsequent cover-up—until August 1, when he learned that newly transcribed White House tapes "contained the so-called smoking gun" that confirmed Nixon's involvement. Ford quickly sought advice on the possibility (and advisability) of his issuing a pardon. When he was told that court proceedings against the former President could drag on for as long as six years, he realized that "it would be virtually impossible for me to direct public attention on anything else" and concluded that he had to "get the monkey off my back one way or the other."

Announcing and justifying his action in a somber television address, Ford stated his belief that "Richard Nixon and his loved ones have suffered enough." He had been advised, Ford said, that "many months and perhaps more years will have to pass before Richard Nixon could obtain a fair trial by jury in any jurisdiction of the United States"—a period during which "ugly passions would again be aroused." What Ford called the "long national nightmare" of Watergate "could go on and on and on," he told his audience, "or someone must write the end to it. I have concluded that only I can do that, and if I can, I must."

The pardon was not the kind of issue on which kids might be expected to weigh in, but many of them—like thousands of adults—hastened to share their opinions with the White House.

Jackie Ann Lucas, a proud "Republacan" and head of the "President Ford Commity," admits that she doesn't think much of the new President as a speaker but applauds his courage anyway. Robert Lind supports Ford's pardon, characterizing Nixon as "an ok President" and noting compassionately that "evrewun makes mustackes." And Anthony Ferreira stakes a firm claim to the middle of the road, demonstrating a knack for diplomacy that doubtless has served him well in later life.

OPPOSITE: *Writing on the flip side of ruled paper, young Jackie Ann Lucas "hearts" Gerald Ford.*
ABOVE: *Ford's golden retriever, Liberty, seems to smile her approval in the Oval Office.*

Dear Mr. Ford, I think you did the right thig because he was an ok President. Some times he makes mistakes but evrewun makes mustackes.
from Robert Lind,

H.B. Milnes School
Fair Lawn N.J. 07410
Sept. 11, 1974

Dear President Ford,

I think you are half Right and half wrong.

yours Truly,
Anthony Ferreira

Mt. Olive Baptist Church

Rt. 23, Maryville Pike • Knoxville, Tennessee 37920 • 577-5559

Fred W. Randles
Minister of Music & Youth

August 13, 1975

Mrs. Gerald Ford
The White House
Washington, D.C.

Dear Mrs. Ford,

Your statements concerning abortion, the use of marijuana, and premarital sex came as no surprise to me as there is permissiveness in all levels of society. But, I do question the wisdom with which they were made, particularly from a person of your influence who should be an example before others. If you were seeking to find favor with the untold thousands of warped individuals and "liberated" women, I'm sure you have succeeded. I'm sure a sizable number of this group will be voting in 1976, but someday when God holds His final election, the majority of these won't be registered voters.

I respect your right to speak out on these subjects as provided by our Constitution. But, I must also remind you that many of us still believe in and hold in high esteem such statements as "In God We Trust." Are we trusting in God when we place our approval on the very things God abhors?

As a mother Mrs. Ford, would you honestly be so permissive towards premarital sex if Susan contracted a veneral disease from an affair or if use of marijuana led to a heroin habit for her? Even our society thinks ill of these situations, let alone what God thinks.

Let me remind you that Rome didn't fall to conquering nations, but rather to immoral decay from within. I love my country and the people in it but I fear for her future.

Prayerfully yours,

Tyson Garrison

Tyson Garrison,
Associate Pastor

Tyson Garrison; Dorothy Tabata to Betty Ford

Knoxville, TN ★ August 13, 1975
Baton Rouge, LA ★ August 18, 1975

America had never had a First Lady like Betty Ford. She was a former dancer, a divorcée, a feminist, a supportive wife and fond parent who was also an independent woman. Where most of her predecessors had been inconspicuous—sometimes to the point of invisibility—she relished the fact that her position gave her the power to make a difference.

People were especially impressed (or intensely annoyed) by her willingness to speak out on important issues. She lobbied for passage of the Equal Rights Amendment and urged her husband to consider women for positions in the Cabinet and on the Supreme Court. When she became addicted to pain medications, she admitted it—and eventually founded the Betty Ford Center to help others recover from drug and alcohol dependence. And when she was diagnosed with breast cancer and underwent a mastectomy, her candor led thousands of women to make appointments with their doctors.

On a Sunday evening in August 1975, she appeared on the popular CBS television program *60 Minutes* and set off a prime-time firestorm. She applauded the Supreme Court's decision in *Roe* v. *Wade*, told her interviewer she wouldn't be surprised to learn that her daughter had engaged in premarital sex, and implied that she didn't see much difference between young people's pot smoking and her own generation's beer drinking. Watching the interview, President Ford estimated that his wife's remarks had cost him ten million votes.

The White House was deluged with almost 35,000 telegrams and letters, both critical and supportive. These two are fairly typical: A Baptist minister in Tennessee scolds her for failing in her responsibility to "be an example before others," while a woman in Louisiana hopes that her "charming, refreshing" interview "may make it fashionable to speak the truth…."

A few months later, *Time* magazine named her Woman of the Year. In the 1976 Presidential election, Gerald Ford was turned out of office—but "Betty for President" buttons bloomed.

Dear Lady Ford, Regards on your TV interview--charming, refreshing! What courage you have for not doing the usual and pretending that certain issues simply do not exist. None of your answers were in "poor taste." By bringing taboo subjects out in the open, you may promote understanding and willingness to face problems that were previously unmentionable. As the first Lady, what you do can greatly infleunce women. <u>You have</u> cut down on deaths from breast cancer and now you may make it fashionable to speak the truth, in a tactful way, and to open the mind to understanding of one another!

Sincerely yours,
Mrs. Dorothy Tabata

OPPOSITE: *Pastor Tyson Garrison links Betty Ford's comments on* 60 Minutes *with "warped individuals and 'liberated' women."*

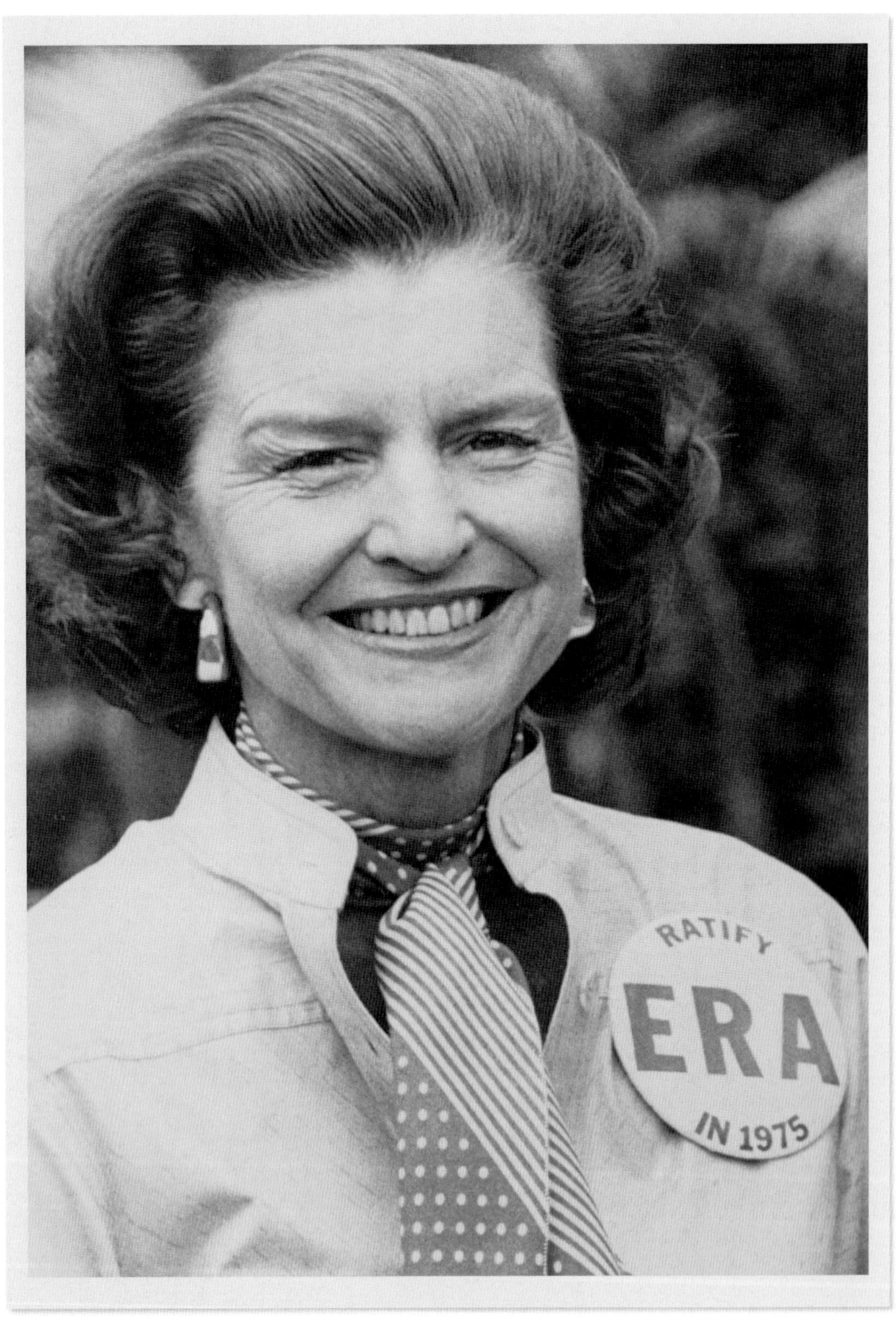

ABOVE: *Betty Ford spoke openly and wore a big button in favor of equal rights for women.*
OPPOSITE: *Showing her own steel-magnolia spirit, a Louisiana woman praises Betty Ford's honesty.*

12533 Parkciel Ave
Baton Rouge, La. 70816
August 18, 1975

Dear Lady Ford,

Regards on your TV interview — charming, refreshing! What courage you have for not doing the usual and pretending that certain issues simply do not exist. None of your answers were in "poor taste". By bringing taboo subjects out in the open, you may promote understanding and willingness to face problems that were previously unmentionable. As the First Lady, what you do can greatly infleunce women. You have cut down on deaths from breast cancer and now you may make it fashionable to speak the truth, in a tactful way, and to open the mind to understanding of one another!

Sincerely yours,

Mrs. Dorothy Tabate

LDM

Calcutta 17/11/79

Dear Mr. J. Carter,

God love you for the very beautiful message of love you have sent.

Right from the beginning of the work - your people through Catholic Relief Services - have shared the joy of feeding the Hungry Christ Clothing the Naked Christ and giving a home to the homeless Christ. In all these years, nearly 30 years. Your people have always been there. Thank God.

You will be glad to know our Sisters are with the "shut ins" at 335 East 145 St Bronx and in Detroit & St Louis

MOTHER TERESA TO JIMMY CARTER

Calcutta, India ★ November 17, 1979

IN ADDITION TO SERVING AS HEAD OF THE government and Commander in Chief of the armed forces, the President is also expected to provide leadership in moral and ethical issues. In this letter, a revered religious figure calls on the President to join her crusade against abortion.

In 1929, the woman who had been born Gonxha Agnes Bojaxhiu in Macedonia arrived in India, took her initial vows as a nun, and adopted the name Teresa. After several years as a teacher, she left the convent school and devoted herself to working among the poorest of the poor in the slums of Calcutta. In 1950 she received permission to found her own order, the Missionaries of Charity, which eventually spread its work around the world, caring for disaster victims, refugees, the homeless, alcoholics, and AIDS sufferers.

In her letter to President Carter, Mother Teresa bemoans the fact that Americans "suffer much" from "the murder of the unborn child" and asks the President to "abolish the law of abortion." Her plea must have touched Carter, who wastroubled by the issue of abortion. He maintained that his religious views made abortion abhorrent—but his responsibility as President was to support the Supreme Court ruling in *Roe* v. *Wade*, which affirmed a woman's right to legal abortion, as the law of the land.

In 1979, Mother Teresa was awarded the Nobel Peace Prize. Twenty-three years later, the same honor was bestowed on ex-President Carter. In his acceptance speech, Carter cited Mother Teresa as one who had proven that "even without government power—often in opposition to it—individuals can enhance human rights and wage peace effectively."

Dear Mr. J. Carter,

God love you for the very beautiful message of love you have sent.

Right from the beginning of the work--your people through Catholic Relief Services--have shared the joy of feeding the Hungry Christ, clothing the Naked Christ and giving a home to the homeless Christ. In all these years, nearly 30 years. Your people have always been there. Thank God.

You will be glad to know our sisters are with the "shut ins" at 335 East 145 St Bronx and in Detroit & St. Louis.

Your people suffer much from very deep poverty. The poverty of loneliness & fear of the shut ins--and the murder of the unborn child through fear of having to feed one more child--educate one more child--the child must die. I was so very surprised. The other day, when in my prayer I realized that it was the unborn St. John that 'lept with joy in his mother's womb when Mary the Mother of Jesus brought Him in Her womb to His home. I ask you for a gift. Abolish the law of Abortion in your country and you will have Peace. How will you meet God--What will you answer Him for all the murders of inocent unborn children done in your country--God has entrusted to you--Open your heart to the cry of the children.

I am praying for you that you may hear their cry and do something--that God may give you the light to see, the love to accept it and the courage to do it.

My prayer is with you.

God bless you

M Teresa

OPPOSITE: *Addressing the President as "Mr. J. Carter," Mother Teresa commends the charitable spirit of Americans.*

SAVE THE HOUSING INDUSTRY
Pass Brooke-Cranston and tax-EXEMPT
revenue bonds NOW.

Dear Jimmy
The general economy may be in a recession but housing
is in a depression. Immediate action must be taken to assist
our industry—it equals 5 Chrysler Corporations. Thousands
of jobs & companies are being lost along with the tax dollars
plus added costs in unemployment compensation. Available &
affordable funds must be made available now—a good start
would be Brooke-Cranston. Where do you expect our children
to live? This piece of 2x4 is not wasted if you get the message
and then put in your wood burning stove. L.W. McKENZIE Jr. V.P.

ROY KLOBER TO JIMMY CARTER
L. W. MCKENZIE, JR. TO JIMMY CARTER

Benton, AR ★ *1980* ★ ★ ★ *Lafayette, IN* ★ *1980*

AS COMMUNICATIONS GURU MARSHALL McLuhan proclaimed in 1964 in the pages of his landmark book *Understanding Media*, the medium is the message.

Here, the message is simple: The U.S. housing industry is in trouble. It is rendered memorable, however, by the medium: a length of two-by-four.

Roy Klober, who was from Benton, Arkansas, and L. W. McKenzie, Jr., a builder from Lafayette, Indiana, urge President Jimmy Carter to support the federal Emergency Mortgage Purchase Assistance program, popularly known as the Brooke-Cranston program, which sought to stimulate housing construction by purchasing and reselling residential mortgages at reduced rates.

Reflecting the carefully crafted down-home image of the Carter Administration, McKenzie begins with a breezy "Dear Jimmy." Acknowledging Carter's interest in energy conservation, he closes by noting that the two-by-four can be used as fuel in the President's wood-burning stove. As this was one of several hundred similar wooden messages sent to the President as part of a campaign organized by the National Association of Home Builders, workers in the White House mailroom probably would have been delighted to follow McKenzie's suggestion.

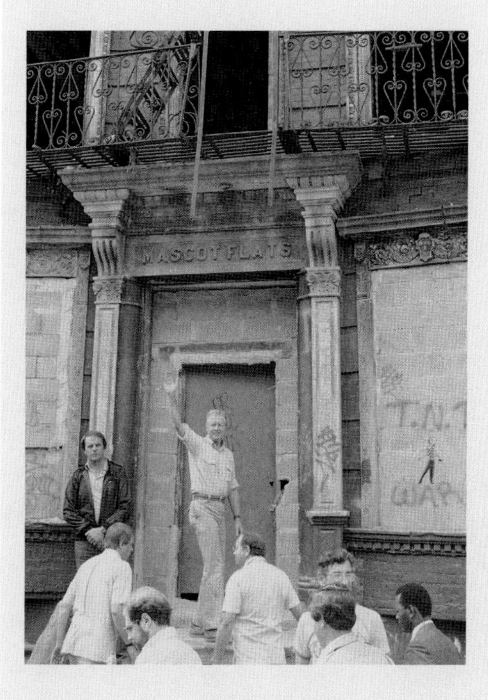

Dear Jimmy,

The general economy may be in a recession but housing is in a depression. Immediate action must be taken to assist our industry--it equals 5 Chrysler Corporations. Thousands of jobs & companies are being lost along with the tax dollars plus added costs in unemployment compensation. Available & affordable funds must be made available now--a good start would be Brooke-Cranston. Where do you expect our children to live? This piece of 2x4 is not wasted if you get the message and then put in your wood burning stove.

L.W. McKenzie Jr. V.P.

OPPOSITE: *More than 100 housing-industry workers wrote to Jimmy Carter on wooden "stationery" during an economic crisis.* ABOVE: *Champion of Habitat for Humanity, Carter has long renovated slums, like this one in New York City, and built homes for the poor.*

THE SECRETARY OF STATE

WASHINGTON

Monday, April 21

Dear Mr. President:

I have the greatest respect and admiration for you and it is with a heavy heart that I submit my resignation. It has been a privilege and a high honor to serve you and our nation. I look with pride and satisfaction at the many actions and new directions which have marked our foreign policy under your leadership. The Panama Canal Treaty, the Camp David Accords, the Egyptian-Israeli Peace Treaty, normalization of relations with the Peoples Republic of China, the strengthening of our military forces and our alliances, the negotiation of the Salt II Agreement, the Zimbabwe settlement, and the new thrust and direction given to our relations with the nations of the Third World are several of these major steps.

I know how deeply you have pondered your decision on Iran. I wish I could support you in it. But for the

Cyrus Vance to Jimmy Carter

Washington, D.C. ★ *April 21, 1980*

Breaking up is hard to do.

It's especially hard for a Secretary of State who finds that he cannot support a major policy decision by the President who appointed him.

The breakup between Cyrus Vance and Jimmy Carter originated in the most serious foreign crisis the United States had faced since the end of the Vietnam War. On November 4, 1979, a crowd of Iranian students siezed the American Embassy in Tehran and took 66 Americans hostage. After economic and diplomatic pressures failed to gain the hostages' freedom, Carter authorized a secret rescue mission. Vance vehemently opposed the action, and when Carter overruled his objections, the Secretary of State felt that he had no choice but to resign.

In this handwritten letter, Vance doesn't rehash the reasons for his split with his boss. He doesn't need to; it's an issue that he and the President have discussed countless times in the preceding days. Instead, he lists "with pride and satisfaction" the impressive achievements in foreign policy—including the Panama Canal Treaty, the Camp David accords, and the long-hoped-for peace treaty between Israel and Egypt—for which they have been responsible. With assurances of his continued "respect and admiration," he tells Carter that he is unable to provide "the public backing you need on an issue and decision of such extraordinary importance" and therefore must leave his post.

On April 24, three days after Vance's resignation, the rescue mission was launched. Operation Eagle Claw was a disaster from the start. When the rescue aircraft rendezvoused at a remote Iranian airstrip, three helicopters were put out of action and the mission was aborted; during the withdrawal, a collision killed eight U.S. servicemen. In Iran and elsewhere, anti-American media had a field day.

The Vance-Carter relationship wasn't the only political casualty of the Iran hostage crisis. Most analysts agree that Carter's inability to solve the crisis was a major factor in his 1980 defeat. After 444 days of captivity, the hostages were finally freed on the day of Ronald Reagan's inauguration in 1981. More than three decades later, America's relationship with Iran is still unhealed.

. . . I know how deeply you have pondered your decision on Iran. I wish I could support you in it. But for the reasons we have discussed I cannot.

You would not be well served in the coming weeks and months by a Secretary of State who could not offer you the public backing you need on an issue and decision of such extraordinary importance--no matter how firm I remain in my support on other issues, as I do, or how loyal I am to you as our leader. Such a situation would be untenable and our relationship, which I value so highly, would constantly suffer.

I shall always be grateful to you for having had the opportunity to serve. I shall always have for you the deepest respect and affection, and you know you can count on my support for your continued leadership of our nation.

Respectfully yours,

Cy

OPPOSITE: *Having reached an unbreachable divide with his President, Secretary of State Cyrus Vance respectfully resigns.*

Andy Smith

400 London Pride Road

Irmo, South Carolina 29063

April 18, 1984

Dear Mr. President,

My name is Andy Smith. I am a seventh grade student at Irmo Middle School, in Irmo, South Carolina.

Today my mother declared my bedroom a disaster area. I would like to request federal funds to hire a crew to clean up my room. I am prepared to provide the initial funds if you will privide matching funds for this project.

I know you will be fair when you consider my request. I will be awaiting your reply.

Sincerely yours,

Andy Smith

Andy Smith

ANDY SMITH TO RONALD REAGAN

Irmo, SC ★ April 18, 1984

ANDY SMITH OF SOUTH CAROLINA HAS A problem. And like millions of Americans before and since, he turns to the White House for help.

Andy's request is simple: His room is such a god-awful mess that his mother has declared it a disaster area, and he wants President Reagan to give him a federal grant to help pay for the cleanup.

If the seventh-grader's 1984 letter is the very epitome of *cute*, the President's response—shown here in draft form—is a model of easy wit and supreme graciousness.

Reagan first points out a couple of problems with Andy's application for funding assistance. First, the request must come from "the authority declaring the disaster"—namely, the exasperated Mrs. Smith. And second, a bumper crop of calamities has left disaster-relief funds "dangerously low." Still, there is a solution. Citing his administration's support for private-sector volunteerism, Reagan suggests that Andy roll up his sleeves and do the job himself.

Friends and foes alike often called Reagan "the Great Communicator." This letter shows why he deserved the title.

OPPOSITE: *Andy Smith speaks for children everywhere when he seeks emergency assistance to clean his room.*
ABOVE: *Under the watchful eye of the Secret Service, Ronald Reagan inspects a genuine disaster area.*

To Andy Smith

Dear Andy

I'm sorry to be so late in answering your letter but as you know I've been in China and found your letter here upon my return.

Your application for disaster relief has been duly noted but I must point out one technical problem; the authority declaring the disaster is supposed to make the request. In this case your mother.

However, setting that aside I'll have to point out the larger problem of available funds. This has been a year of disasters, 539 hurricanes as of May 4th and several more since, numerous floods, forest fires, drought in Texas and a number of earthquakes. What I'm getting at is that funds are dangerously low.

May I make a suggestion? This administration, believing that govt. has done many things that could better be done by volunteers at the local level, has sponsored a Private Sector Initiative Program, calling upon people to practice volunteerism in the solving of a number of local problems.

Your situation appears to be a natural. I'm sure your Mother was fully justified in proclaiming your room a disaster. Therefore you are in an excellent position to launch another volunteer program to go along with the more than 3000 already underway in our nation--congratulations.

Give my best regards to your Mother,

Ronald Reagan

OPPOSITE: *Displaying his famous charm, Reagan suggests to Andy Smith that he "volunteer" to keep his room clean.*

To Andy Smith 400 London Pride Rd.
Irmo So. Carolina 29063

Dear Andy

I'm sorry to be so late in answering your letter but as you know I've been in China and found your letter here upon my return.

Your application for disaster relief has been duly noted but I must point out one technical problem; the authority declaring the disaster is supposed to make the request. In this case your mother.

However setting that aside I'll have to point out the larger problem of available funds. This has been a year of disasters, 539 hurricanes as of May 4th and several more since, numerous floods, forest fires, drought in Texas and a number of earthquakes. What I'm getting at is that funds are dangerously low.

May I make a suggestion? This administration, believing that govt. has done many things that could better be done by volunteers at the local level, has sponsored a Private Sector Initiative Program, calling upon people to practice volunteerism in the solving of a number of local problems.

Your situation appears to be a natural. I'm sure your Mother was fully justified in proclaiming your room a disaster. Therefore you are in an excellent position to launch another volunteer program to go along with the more than 3000 already underway in our nation — congratulations.

Give my best regards to your Mother

Sincerely RR

KH
Smg-163

Patricia J. Elvin
2401 Bayshore Blvd. #512
Tampa, Fl 33629

November 27, 1990

George Bush
President of the United States
The White House
Washington, D.C. 20500

Dear President Bush,

I am writing to you out of a sense of conscience, aware that you may never even know of my letter, to urge you, none the less, to share with the American people your understanding and rationale for drawing on us to make war with Iraq. A pointed and difficult question, perhaps, and one which you may think you have been answering. However, Mr. President, the answer still is not clear and there is growing concern that we are perilously close to being at war and losing some of those whom we love for an uncertain purpose.

We are the people who elected you because we had more confidence in you than in the others who sought your office. We now want your confidence in us, not simply to follow your lead blindly, but to proceed in a direction because it is justifiably right.

I've often heard that although our justice system is flawed, or even wrought with error, that the jury, largely ignorant of the law in general and of the intricacies of the system, is usually accurate in deciding the truth of a case. This must

Patricia J. Elvin; Eric Colton to George H. W. Bush

Tampa, FL ★ November 27, 1990
Saudi Arabia ★ February 12, 1991

On August 2, 1990, Iraqi troops invaded Kuwait. Fearing that Saddam Hussein's militancy posed a threat to America's Middle Eastern allies and the region's oil supplies, George H. W. Bush organized a multinational coalition and began a massive buildup of troops and equipment in Saudi Arabia. After weeks of devastating air attacks on targets in Kuwait and Iraq, the ground offensive—Operation Desert Storm—was launched on February 24. Three days of fierce combat drove the invaders out of Kuwait, and fighting ended with Iraq's acceptance of cease-fire terms on March 3.

Every time a President makes the difficult decision to send American troops to fight on foreign soil, Americans flood the White House with heartfelt expressions of anger and support, grim resignation and anguish. The Gulf War was no exception.

Patricia Elvin's letter to President Bush expresses neither the gung-ho enthusiasm of a hawk nor the pained disapproval of a dove. Instead, it movingly conveys the bewilderment of a citizen who just wants to know *why*. She assures the President that "the American people, in general, are a reasonable lot"—but they "need to hear your full case against Iraq" in order to calm their fears about "being at war and losing some of those whom we love for an uncertain purpose."

Many Americans were to echo Elvin's concerns a few years later, in the context of another war against Iraq.

In the second letter, the uncertainties of

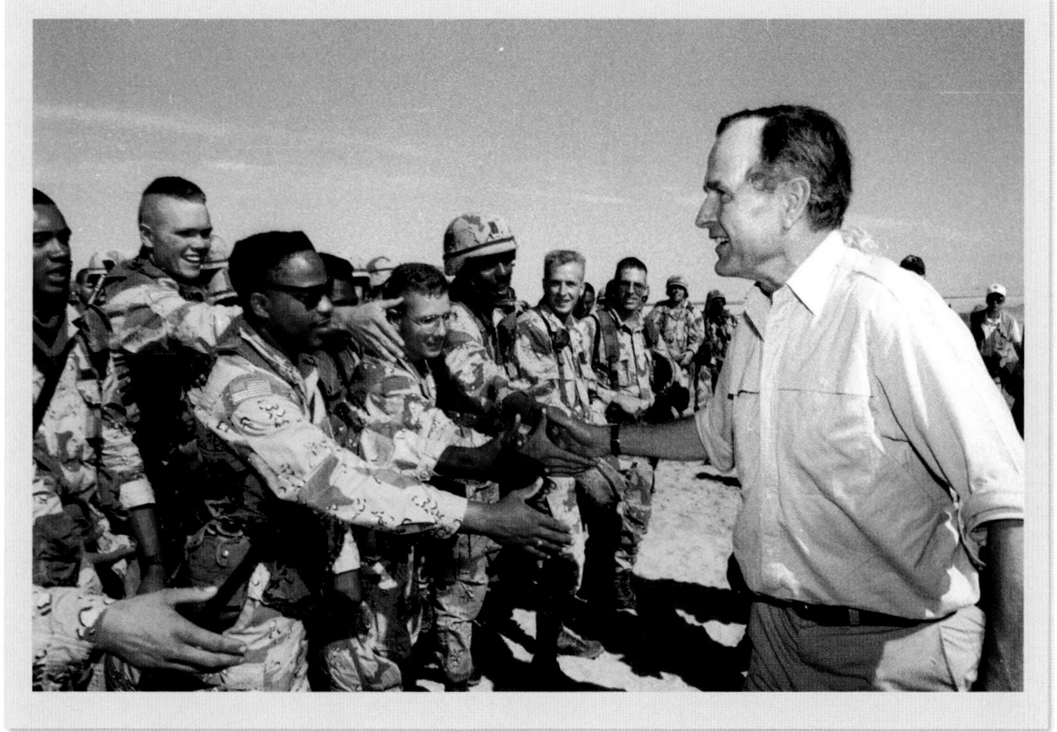

OPPOSITE: *Patricia Elvin follows her conscience even though her President "may never even know of my letter."*
ABOVE: *George H.W. Bush greets soldiers dispatched to the Persian Gulf in Operation Desert Storm.*

a civilian on the home front are replaced by the calm self-assurance of a U.S. Marine on the battlefront. Writing from a base in Saudi Arabia, Lance Cpl. Eric Colton doesn't question why he's there. After a cheerful "Howdy!" he tells President Bush that his unit is "ready to accomplish any mission we are assigned to do" and closes with words to gladden the heart of any Commander in Chief: "I promise you and the rest of the country we will win this one." Eric Colton came home safe and sound. Almost 300 other Americans died in the Gulf War.

I am writing to you out of a sense of conscience, aware that you may never even know of my letter, to urge you none the less, to share with the American people your understanding and rationale for drawing on us to make war with Iraq. A pointed and difficult question, perhaps, and one which you may think you have been answering. However, Mr. President, the answer still is not clear and there is growing concern that we are periously close to being at war and losing some of those whom we love for an uncertain purpose.

We are the people who elected you because we had more confidence in you than in the others who sought your office. We now want your confidence in us, not simply to follow your lead blindly, but to proceed in a direction because it is justifiably right.

I've often heard that although our justice system is flawed, or even wrought with error that the jury, largely ignorant of the law in general and of the intricacies of the system, is usually accurate in deciding the truth of a case. This must be so because the American people in general, are a reasonable lot. They are capable of weighing the facts--even complex ones, setting aside their emotions, and coming to the right conclusion.

We are your jury, Mr. President, and we need to hear your full case against Iraq. We must know the facts in order to come to a reasonable conclusion regarding your position in the situation.

You ask for our confidence in you by asking for our willingness to use force against another people. We ask for your confidence in us by allowing us the opportunity to understand the reasons why.

Sincerely and respectufully yours,
Patricia Elvin

. . . When we first arrived in this country we felt it could possibly be another Vietnam. During the six months of Operation Desert Shield we knew the United States will not approach Iraq lightly. We respect all of your decisions.

We will not let the American people down. As a United States Marine, Mr. President I promise you and the rest of the country we will win this one.

Semper Fidelis,
Eric Colton
Lcpl USMC

OPPOSITE: *Marine Lance Cpl. Eric Colton expresses confidence in his leader and his mission.*

p.53

12 Feb

Mr. President,

Howdy!

My name is Eric Colton. I am a 20 year old Marine Serving in Saudi Arabia. I grew up on a Cattle Operation in the Mountains of Oregon. I am Stationed out of 29 Palms, California.

The reason I am writing to you is to tell you that me and my Comrades feel you are doing an outstanding job concerning the Gulf War.

My Unit is positioned near the Kuwaiti border ready to accomplish any mission we are assigned to do. Morale is high, and everybody believes in what we are fighting for.

When we first arrived in this Country we felt it Could

Congrat re Moon Walk
auto photo

EXECUTIVE
PR 5-1/Z*
OS 3

THADDEUS A. ZAGOREWICZ
774 - 33RD AVENUE
SAN FRANCISCO, CALIF. 94121

July 20,1969

Mr.President
of the United States of America
White House,
Washington, DC

Dear Mr.President.

A few minutes ago my family and I were watching the astronauts walking on the moon and heard your short conversation with our national heroes on the moon.

Mr.President, I am a naturalized citizen of this wonderful country and I am proud to be one of You. When we looked at our flag waving on the surface of the moon - my wife and myself had tears in our eyes.

Mr.President, please accept our deepest congratulations and sincere thanks to you and our three astronauts for their efforts and echievements.

We are very proud to be American citizens.

Very truly yours,

Thaddeus A Zagorewicz

Thaddeus A Zagorewicz

PS. I would appreciate very much a copy of your authographed picture.

11FE690258 inscribed, To Thaddeus A. Zagorewicz With best wishes, Richard Nixon

Thaddeus A. Zagorewicz to Richard Nixon
John Glenn to Bill Clinton

San Francisco, CA ★ *July 20, 1969*
Space Shuttle Discovery ★ *November 6, 1998*

Most of the time, most of us enjoy the lazy luxury of taking our American-ness for granted. But once in a while, something—a speech, a picture, a song, an event—triggers a moment when we are suddenly caught up in the proud realization of who we are and what it means.

One of those moments occurred on July 20, 1969, when millions of living rooms were lit by the bluish glow of TV screens showing the heart-stopping image of an American man stepping onto the surface of the moon. Among those watching was a naturalized citizen named Thaddeus Zagorewicz, who found the experience so moving that he sent a letter to President Nixon that very evening. Zagorewicz writes that the "efforts and achievements" of the astronauts have made him "proud to be one of You." We know what he means, of course, but his choice of pronoun isn't quite right: On that July evening 36 years ago, the me's and you's disappeared for a while, and we all became—simply, proudly, gloriously—Us.

After the triumph of the moon landing, America's space program settled into a sequence of missions—most of them successful, a few harrowing, one tragic—that stretched over three decades. Then, in 1998, there was a satisfying sense that the program had come full circle when John Glenn, who in 1962 had become the first American to orbit the earth, returned to space on the shuttle Discovery.

Near the end of the nine-day mission, Glenn sent an E-mail to President Clinton. It may be, as Glenn notes, the first E-mail ever sent to the President from an orbiting spacecraft—but except for the fact that it is prefaced by the long chains of letters and numbers that constitute the DNA of cyberspace, the message suggests a postcard from a happy vacationer to the folks back home: Thanks for seeing us off, we're having a good time, regards to the missus, see you soon.

Glenn's laconic statement that his craft has "gone almost a third of the way around the world in the time it has taken me to write this" is a telling indicator of the profound changes—social and political as well as technological—that have shaped and transformed American life since John Langdon sent his handwritten letter to George Washington in 1789.

The long epistolary affair between Americans and their Chief Executive certainly doesn't end here. Right now, someone somewhere is picking up a pen or sitting down at a keyboard—and the White House is about to get another message from the real voice of America.

A few minutes ago my family and I were watching the astronauts walking on the moon and heard your short conversation with our national heroes on the moon.

Mr. President, I am a naturalized citizen of this wonderful country and I am proud to be one of You. When we looked at our flag waving on the surface of the moon--my wife and myself had tears in our eyes.

We are very proud to be American citizens.

OPPOSITE: *Seeing the Stars and Stripes on the moon electrified – and unified – Americans of every stripe.*

Dear Mr. President,

This is certainly a first for me, writing to a President from space, and it may be a first for you in receiving an E mail direct from an orbiting spacecraft.

In any event, I want to personally thank you and Mrs. Clinton for coming to the Cape to see the launch. I hope you enjoyed it just half as much as we did on board.. It is truly an awesome experience from a personal standpoint, and of even greater importance for all of the great research projects we have on Discovery. The whole crew was impressed that you would be the first President to personally see a shuttle launch and asked me to include their best regards to you and Hillary. She has discussed her interest in the space program with Annie on several occasions, and I know she would like to be on a flight just like this.

We have gone almost a third of the way around the world in the time it has taken me to write this letter, and the rest of the crew is waiting. Again, our thanks and best regards. Will try to give you a personal briefing after we return next Saturday.

Sincerely,
John Glenn

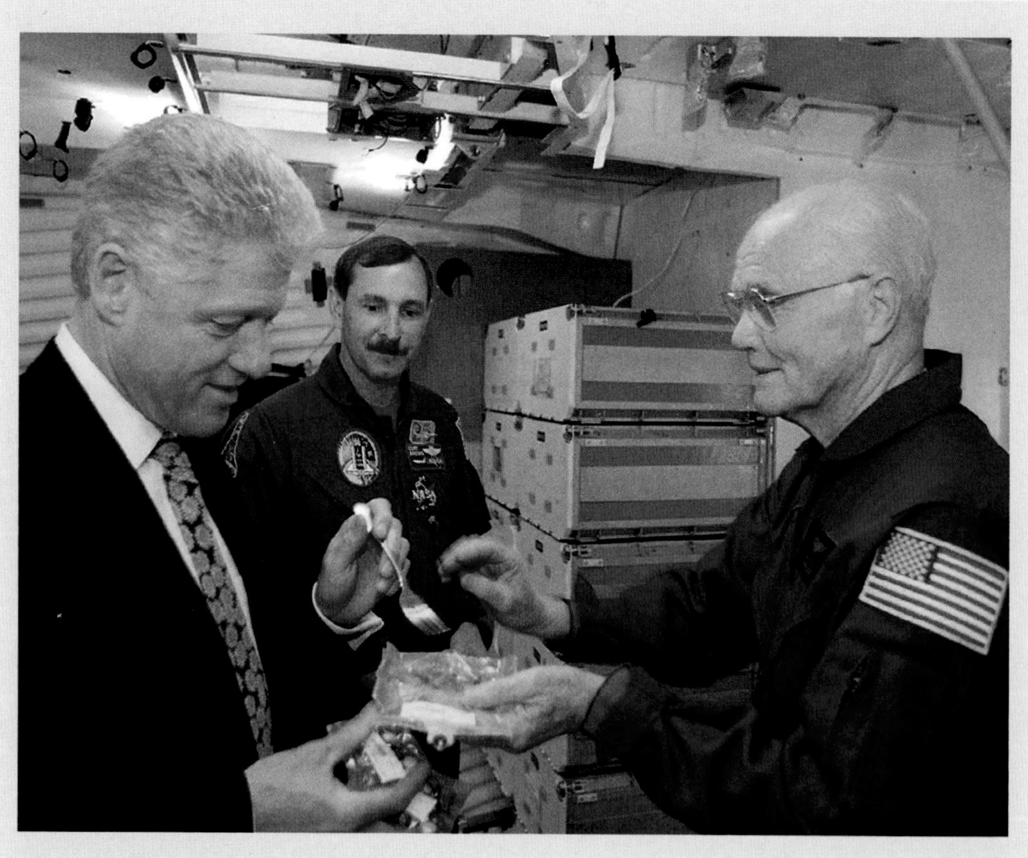

ABOVE: *Old space hand John Glenn (right) gives Bill Clinton a taste of NASA cuisine, as mission commander Curtis Brown looks on.* OPPOSITE: *Even a seasoned second-term President likely thrills to an E-mail from space.*

RECORD TYPE: PRESIDENTIAL (NOTES MAIL)

CREATOR: Phillip Caplan (CN=Phillip Caplan/OU=WHO/O=EOP [WHO])

CREATION DATE/TIME: 6-NOV-1998 17:55:33.00

SUBJECT: Senator Glenn's message from space

TO: Kevin J. Cosgriff (CN=Kevin J. Cosgriff/OU=NSC/O=EOP @ EOP [NSC])
READ:UNKNOWN

TEXT:
For transfer to Air Force 1
---------------------- Forwarded by Phillip Caplan/WHO/EOP on 11/06/98
05:55 PM ---------------------------

Stephen K. Horn
11/06/98 05:28:38 PM
Record Type: Record

To: Phillip Caplan/WHO/EOP
cc: Daniel W. Burkhardt/WHO/EOP
Subject: Senator Glenn's message from space

Here is the message:

==================== ATTACHMENT 1 ====================
ATT CREATION TIME/DATE: 0 00:00:00.00

TEXT:
From margie.s.keller1@jsc.nasa.gov Fri Nov 6 15:44:27 1998
Received: (from uucp@localhost) by WhiteHouse.gov (8.7.1/uucp-relay) id PAA1941
5 for ; Fri, 6 Nov 1998 15:44:27 -0500 (EST)
Received: from storm.eop.gov/198.137.241.51 via smap
Return-receipt-to: "KELLER, MARGIE S. (JSC-CB)"

Received: from DIRECTORY-DAEMON by STORM.EOP.GOV (PMDF V5.1-12 #29131)
id <01J3UX518GIO000XPO@STORM.EOP.GOV> for President@WhiteHouse.GOV; Fri,
6 Nov 1998 15:43:11 EST
Received: from SCAN-DAEMON by STORM.EOP.GOV (PMDF V5.1-12 #29131)
id <01J3UX4ZT0OC000OX6@STORM.EOP.GOV> for president@Whitehouse.GOV; Fri,
06 Nov 1998 15:43:09 -0500 (EST)
Received: from jsc-ems-gws03.jsc.nasa.gov ([139.169.39.19])
by STORM.EOP.GOV (PMDF V5.1-12 #29131)
with ESMTP id <01J3UX4R0VHW000XUJ@STORM.EOP.GOV> for president@Whitehouse.GOV;

Fri, 06 Nov 1998 15:43:01 -0500 (EST)
Received: by jsc-ems-gws03.jsc.nasa.gov with Internet Mail Service (5.5.2232.9)

id ; Fri, 06 Nov 1998 14:43:06 -0600
Content-return: allowed
Date: Fri, 06 Nov 1998 14:42:56 -0600
From: "KELLER, MARGIE S. (JSC-CB)"
Subject: STS-95 Downlink Mail
To: "'president@whitehouse.gov'"
Message-id:
<81F639B56628D011A32D0020AFFC01900231E72D@jsc-ems-mbs07.jsc.nasa.gov>
MIME-version: 1.0
X-Mailer: Internet Mail Service (5.5.2232.9)
Content-type: MULTIPART/MIXED; BOUNDARY="Boundary_(ID_4wKF5vI8SCrlrTB4D1H6vg)"

Importance: high
Comments: This message scanned by SCAN version 0.1 jms/960226
X-Priority: 1

--Boundary_(ID_4wKF5vI8SCrlrTB4D1H6vg)
Content-type: TEXT/PLAIN; CHARSET=US-ASCII
Content-transfer-encoding: 7BIT

President Bill Clinton, The White House, Washington, D. C.

Dear Mr. President,
This is certainly a first for me, writing to a President from space, and it may be a first for you in receiving an E mail direct from an orbiting spacecraft.

In any event, I want to personally thank you and Mrs. Clinton for coming to the Cape to see the launch. I hope you enjoyed it just half as much as we did on board.. It is truly an awesome experience from a personal standpoint, and of even greater importance for all of the great research projects we have on Discovery. The whole crew was impressed that you would be the first President to personally see a shuttle launch and asked me to include their best regards to you and Hillary. She has discussed her interest in the space program with Annie on several occasions, and I know she would like to be on a flight just like this.

We have gone almost a third of the way around the world in the time it has taken me to write this letter, and the rest of the crew is waiting. Again, our thanks and best regards. Will try to give you a personal briefing after we return next Saturday.

Sincerely,

John Glenn

Margie S. Keller
Admin Officer
Astronaut Office
281-244-8991

--Boundary_(ID_4wKF5vI8SCrlrTB4D1H6vg)--

================== END ATTACHMENT 1 ==================

About the Presidential Records Act and the Freedom of Information Act

The Presidential Records Act (PRA) of 1978, 44 U.S.C. Sections 2201-2207, governs the official records of Presidents and Vice Presidents created or received after January 20, 1981. The PRA changed the legal ownership of the official records of the President from being private papers of the President to public ownership under the stewardship of the Archivist of the United States once an administration ends. The PRA also established a process for restriction and public access to these records. Specifically, the PRA allows for public access to Presidential records, including through the Freedom of Information Act (FOIA) beginning five years after the end of the administration, but allows the President to invoke as many as six specific restrictions to public access for up to 12 years. At the end of the 12-year period following the end of the administration, these PRA restrictions no longer apply but certain FOIA restrictions continue to apply.

The records of former Presidents are voluminous and most of the records are processed upon the receipt of a FOIA request. Once the records are reviewed by archivists at the Presidential Library, a notice of intent to open is sent to representatives of the former President and to the incumbent President for their review and opportunity to raise any concerns of executive privilege. Following the review and resolution of any concerns, the records are open to the requestor and are available to any other researcher.

About the Authors

Brian Williams became the anchor of *NBC Nightly News* in 2004, taking over for Tom Brokaw, the first such announced change in the major network news anchors in two decades. He was the *NBC News* Chief White House correspondent, and was the anchor and managing editor of the Saturday edition of *NBC Nightly News* for six years. Williams has been awarded three Emmys, and in over 20 years of broadcasting, Williams has reported from 23 countries on countless stories of national and international importance.

Dwight Young has been actively involved in historic preservation for almost 30 years. He joined the staff of the National Trust for Historic Preservation in 1977, and moved to Trust headquarters in Washington in 1992. He is the author of *Alternatives to Sprawl,* and *Saving America's Treasures.* He is best known as author of the "Back Page" feature in Preservation magazine. In 2003, the National Trust published a collection of these essays titled *Road Trips Through History.*

ABOUT THE FOUNDATION FOR THE NATIONAL ARCHIVES

The Foundation for the National Archives is a 501(c)(3) organization di-rected by men and women from the private sector who are dedicated to bringing America's records to the public in exciting new ways. The Foundation was created to support the Archivist of the United States in developing programs, technology, projects and materials that will introduce and interpret the holdings of the National Archives and Records Administration (NARA) to the American people and to people around the world.

Within the National Archives building in Washington, D.C., as well as its many branches and Presidential Libraries, and in outreach through traveling exhibitions and national media, the Foundation's goal is to assist in presenting the historical records that reveal the ideals and values of the nation's Founders, point to the meaning of the records and accomplishments of previous generations, and establish the significance of these records as proof that individual citizenship is vital to our lives. In this public/private partnership the role of the Foundation is to generate financial and creative support from individuals and corporations to provide this extensive outreach, which has not been mandated by Congress.

As part of these efforts to create public awareness of the importance of the nation's records, the Foundation for the National Archives is proud to partner with NARA to create a new National Archives Experience. One component of this multi-media experience is the Dear Uncle Sam unit of the Public Vaults exhibit, in which visitors to the National Archives building in Washington, D.C., can view some of the letters included in this book as well as many others written to the U.S. government.

Foundation for the National Archives
700 Pennsylvania Avenue, NW, Room G12
Washington, DC 20408-0001
202-357-5312
Email: foundationmembers@nara.gov
Website: http://www.archives.gov

National Archives and Records Administration I
700 Pennsylvania Avenue, NW
Washington, DC 20408-0001
202-501-5400 or

National Archives and Records Administration II
8601 Adelphi Road
College Park, Maryland 20740-6001
301-837-2000

Email: inquire@nara.gov
Website: http://www.archives.gov

About the Presidential Library System

Part of the National Archives

The Presidential Library system is made up of eleven Presidential Libraries. This nationwide network of libraries is administered by the Office of Presidential Libraries, which is part of the National Archives and Records Administration (NARA), located in College Park, MD. These are not traditional libraries, but rather repositories for preserving and making available the papers, records, and other historical materials of U.S. Presidents since Herbert Hoover. Each Presidential Library contains a museum and provides an active series of education and public programs. When a President leaves office, NARA establishes a Presidential project until a new Presidential library is built and transferred to the Government.

The Presidential Library system formally began in 1939, when President Franklin Roosevelt donated his personal and Presidential papers to the Federal Government. At the same time, Roosevelt pledged part of his estate at Hyde Park to the United States, and friends of the President formed a nonprofit corporation to raise funds for the construction of the library and museum building. Roosevelt's decision stemmed from a firm belief that Presidential papers are an important part of the national heritage and should be accessible to the public. He asked the National Archives to take custody of his papers and other historical materials and to administer his library. At the dedication of his library on June 30, 1941, Franklin Roosevelt observed:

"To bring together the records of the past and to house them in buildings where they will be preserved for the use of men and women in the future, a Nation must believe in three things.

It must believe in the past.

It must believe in the future.

It must, above all, believe in the capacity of its own people so to learn from the past that they can gain in judgement in creating their own future."

Office of Presidential Libraries
Sharon K. Fawcett
Assistant Archivist for Presidential Libraries
National Archives at College Park
8601 Adelphi Road
College Park, MD 20740-6001
Telephone: 301-837-3250
Fax: 301-837-3199

Herbert Hoover Library
Timothy G. Walch, Director
210 Parkside Drive, P. O. Box 488
West Branch, IA 52358-0488
Telephone: 319-643-5301
Fax: 319-643-6045
Email: hoover.library@nara.gov
Website: http://hoover.archives.gov

Franklin D. Roosevelt Library
Cynthia M. Koch, Director
4079 Albany Post Road
Hyde Park, NY 12538-1999
Telephone: 1-800-FDR-VISIT
or 845-486-7770
Fax: 845-486-1147
Email: roosevelt.library@nara.gov
Website: http://www.fdrlibrary.marist.edu

Harry S. Truman Library
Michael Devine, Director
500 West U.S. Highway 24
Independence, MO 64050-1798
Telephone: 816-268-8200
Fax: 816-268-8295
Email: truman.library@nara.gov
Website: http://www.trumanlibrary.org

Dwight D. Eisenhower Library
Daniel D. Holt, Director
200 SE 4th Street
Abilene, KS 67410-2900
Telephone: 785-263-4751
Fax: 785-263-6718
Email: eisenhower.library@nara.gov
Website: http://www.eisenhower.archives.gov

John Fitzgerald Kennedy Library
Deborah Leff, Director
Columbia Point
Boston, MA 02125-3398
Telephone: 877-616-4599 (toll free)
or 617-514-1600
Fax: 617-514-1652
Email: kennedy.library@nara.gov
Website: http://www.jfklibrary.org

Lyndon Baines Johnson Library
Betty Sue Flowers, Director
2313 Red River Street
Austin, TX 78705-5702
Telephone: 512-721-0200
Fax: 512-721-0170
Email: johnson.library@nara.gov
Website: http://www.lbjlib.utexas.edu/

Nixon Presidential Materials Staff
Vacant, Director
National Archives at College Park
8601 Adelphi Road, Room 1320
College Park, MD 20740-6001
Telephone: 301-837-3290
Fax: 301-837-3202
Email: nixon@nara.gov
Website: http://nixon.archives.gov/index.php

Gerald R. Ford Library and Museum
Elaine K. Didier, Director

Gerald R. Ford Library
1000 Beal Avenue
Ann Arbor, MI 48109-2114
Telephone: 734-205-0555
Fax: 734-205-0571
Email: ford.library@nara.gov
Website: http://www.fordlibrarymuseum.gov

Gerald R. Ford Museum
303 Pearl Street, NW
Grand Rapids, MI 49504-5353
Telephone: 616-254-0400
Fax: 616-254-0386
Email: ford.museum@nara.gov
Website: http://www.fordlibrarymuseum.gov

Jimmy Carter Library
Jay E. Hakes, Director
441 Freedom Parkway
Atlanta, GA 30307-1498
Telephone: 404-865-7100
Fax: 404-865-7102
Email: carter.library@nara.gov
Website: http://www.jimmycarterlibrary.gov

Ronald Reagan Library
R. Duke Blackwood, Director
40 Presidential Drive
Simi Valley, CA 93065-0699
Telephone: 800-410-8354
or 805-577-4000
Fax: 805-577-4074
Email: reagan.library@nara.gov
Website: http://www.reagan.utexas.edu

George H.W. Bush Library
Warren Finch, Director
1000 George Bush Drive, West
College Station, TX 77845
Telephone: 979-691-4000
Fax: 979-691-4050
Email: bush.library@nara.gov
Website: http://bushlibrary.tamu.edu

William J. Clinton Library
David E. Alsobrook, Director
1200 President Clinton Avenue
Little Rock, AR 72201
Telephone: 501-244-2887
Fax: 501-244-2883
Email: clinton.library@nara.gov
Website: http://clinton.library.gov

Presidential Materials Staff
Nancy Kegan Smith, Director
National Archives and
Records Administration
700 Pennsylvania Avenue, NW
Washington, DC 20408-0001
Telephone: 202-501-5705
Fax: 202-501-5709

Acknowledgments

Presidential Libraries:

Claudia Anderson
Jason Bigelow
Bonnie Burlbaw
Debbie Carter
Joshua Cochran
Barbara Constable
Stacy Davis
Jim Detlefsen
Susan Donius
Mike Duggan
Jennifer Evans
Sharon Fawcett
Gary Foulk
Allan Goodrich
Maryrose Grossman
Kenneth Hafeli
Laura Harmon
William Harris
Ben Irwin
Shelly Jacobs
Sharon Kelly
Tammy Kelly
Deanna Kolling
Michelle Kopfer
Jim Leyerzapf
Ben Pezzillo
Stephen Plotkin
Emily Robison
Sam Rushay
Sara Saunders
Matt Schaefer
Nancy Smith
Randy Sowell
Richard Stalcup
David Stanhope
Martin Teasley
Alycia Vivona
Timothy Walch
Ronald Whealan,
Amy Williams

Foundation for the National Archives:

Thora Colot
Franck Cordes
Christina Gehring
Ted Segal
Lisa Trovato

National Archives and Records Administration, D.C.:

Stacey Bredhoff
Bruce Bustard
Kahlil Chism
Thomas Hart
Miriam Kleiman
Jessica Kratz
Darlene McClurkin
Mary Frances Morrow
Richard Peuser
Marvin Pinkert
Lee Ann Potter
Rodney Ross
Chris Rudy-Smith
Daniel Rulli

National Archives and Records Administration, MD:

John Davenport
Michael Hussey
Tab Lewis
Wilbert Mahoney
Gene Morris
Catherine Nicholson
David Pheiffer
Steve Puglia
Jeffrey Reed
Erin Rhodes
Fred Romanski
Chris Runkel
Joseph Schwarz
John Taylor
Jim Zeender

A very special acknowledgment to Christina Gehring of the Foundation for the National Archives, and especially to Margaret Johnson and her keen pursuit of the most interesting letters and the people who wrote them.

Letter Citations and Permissions

National Archives and Records Administration
Washington D.C.

Page 18: John Langdon to George Washington, April 6,1789: Sen 1A-J3, Records of the U.S. Senate, RG 46

Page 24: James H. Gooding to President Lincoln, Sept. 28, 1863: Colored Troops Division, Letters Received, 1863-1865, Records of Adjutant General's Office 1780s-1917, RG 94

Page 26: Annie Davis to President Lincoln, Aug. 28, 1864: Colored Troops Division, Letters Received, 1863-1865, D-304.1864, Records of Adjutant General's Office 1780s-1917, RG 94

Page 30: Wolf Chief to President Garfield, Dec. 1881: File 18388 (Enclosure to Kaufman-Price, dated 1881), Letters Received, (1881-1907), Records of the Bureau of Indian Affairs, RG 75

Page 33: Gov. Edmund Ross et al to President Cleveland, Aug. 14, 1886: M 689, Letters Received by the Office of the Adjutant General (Main Series), File 5024 AGO 1886, (Filed w/ 1066 AGO 1883), Records of the Adjutant General's Office, 1780s –1917, RG 94

Page 34: Annie Oakley to President McKinley, April 5, 1898: Oversized Document File, 1805-1917, File 33879 (2441), Records of the Adjutant General's Office, 1780s-1917, RG 94

National Archives and Records Administration
College Park, Maryland

Page 20: King Mongkut of Siam to President Lincoln, February 14, 1861: Ceremonial letters, Siam (Entry A-1, Entry 32); General Records of the Department of State, RG 59

Page 28: Lincoln's Cabinet to President A. Johnson, April 15, 1865: Vol. 419; Miscellaneous Letters 1789-1906 (Entry A1-113); General Records of the Department of State, RG 59

Page 36: Upton Sinclair to President T. Roosevelt, March 10, 1906: Letters received by the Secretary of Agriculture 1893-106 (Entry 8); Records of the Office of the Secretary of Agriculture, RG 16.
Copyright © 2005 by John and Jeffrey Weidman. Reprinted with the permission of McIntosh and Otis, Inc.

Page 38: Charles D. Levy to President Coolidge, June 24, 1924: File 198589, sub 560-619(5); Straight Numerical Files, General Records of the Department of Justice, RG 60

Page 40: Women of the KKK to President Coolidge, May 15, 1924: File 164/14; Chief Clerk's Files; General Records of the Department of Labor, 1907-1942, RG 174

Page 42: Alva P. Jones/Cigarette Law Enforcement League to President Hoover, May 25, 1929: Folder: "J"; Letters from the Public; Office of the Secretary, Records of the National Commission on Law, Observance, and Enforcement, RG 10
Published with permission of James F.A. Jones and Marianne Jones Sullivan

Page 46: Citizens of South Dakota to President Hoover, April 26, 1932: File 109-1. Section 5; Classified Files; General Records of the Department of Justice, RG 60

Page 48: Henry Johnson to President McKinley, June 5, 1899: File 1899 - 17743, Folder 1; Year Files, 1884-1903; General Records of the Department of Justice, RG 60

Page 50: Ara Lee Settle to President Harding, June 18, 1922: File 158260, Sections 1-3, Sub 141-232; Straight Numerical Files; General Records of the Department of Justice, RG 60

Page 53: Horace Robinson to President Hoover, November 20, 1929: File 158260, Sections 4-7, Sub 233; Straight Numerical Files, General Records of the Department of Justice, RG 60

Page 56: Gisella (Lacher) Loeffler to Eleanor Roosevelt, July 27, 1939: File 651.3159, State Series - New Mexico; Records of the Works Projects Administration, RG 69. Published with permission of Undine L. Gutierrez

Page 64: Fidel Castro to President F. Roosevelt, November 6, 1940: File 8811001 Roosevelt 6757, Havana Post Files; Records of the Foreign Service Posts of the Department of State, RG 84

Page 66: C Dearman to President Taft, July 18, 1912: File 150719-62, Folder: "Section 2. Item 62"; Straight Numerical Files (Entry 112); General Records of the Department of Justice, RG 60

Page 69: George A. Murray to President Wilson, February 14, 1920: File P-19-3; General File of Director General 1918-27, Subject-Classified; Records of the U.S. Railroad Administration, RG 14

Page 74: French R. Massey to President F. Roosevelt, November 12, 1943: Folder: "Nov.11-20, 1943"; 1940, Fan mail (unclassified); Records of the Selective Service System, RG 147
Published with permission of James Barnett Massey

Page 76: Anna Rush to President F. Roosevelt, November 18, 1943: Folder: "Nov.11-20, 1943"; 1940, Fan mail (unclassified); Records of the Selective Service System, RG 147.
Published with permission of Ruth Guthrie Ballard

Page 77: Carolyn Weatherhogg to President F. Roosevelt, October 14, 1943: Folder: "Oct.10-15, 1943"; 940, Fan mail (unclassified); Records of the Selective Service System, RG 147
Published with permission of Carolyn Weatherhogg Wassung

Page 83: Harold Ickes to President F. Roosevelt, June 1, 1944: Office Files of Undersecretary Abe Fortas (Entry 772); Records of the Office of the Secretary of the Interior, RG 48

Page 87: Scientists to President Truman, July 17, 1945: File 76; General Correspondence, 1942-1946; Harrison Bundy File; Manhattan Project; Frank Report 76-86; Records of the Office of the Chief of Engineers, RG 77

Page 88: Guy von Dardel to President Truman, March 27, 1947: File 701.5864/3-254; Central Decimal Files 1945-49; General Records of the Department of State, RG 59
Published with permission of Guy von Dardel

Page 116: Ho Chi Minh to President Truman, February 28, 1946: Kunming-SI-INT-32-33, Washington/ Pacific Coast Field Station Files,1942 –1946 (Entry 140); Records of the Office of Strategic Services, 1919-1948, RG 226

Page 128: Gladys McPherson to President Kennedy, March 14, 1963: Folder: "McM – McZ 1963"; President's Council on Physical Fitness Correspondence and Reports, 1956-1968; General Records of the Department of Health, Education and Welfare, RG 235

Page 131: Richard Millington to President Kennedy, February 11, 1963: Folder: "Mie – Mill 1963"; President's Council on Physical Fitness Correspondence and Reports, 1956-1968; General Records of the Department of Health, Education and Welfare, RG 235
Published with permission of Richard John Millington

Herbert Hoover
Presidential Library

Page 44: Womans Home Missionary Society to President Hoover, June 15, 1932: Presidential Subject File, Prohibition, Folder 'Correspondence, June 15, 1932.'

Page 45: Mr. and Mrs. William E. Wilson to President Hoover, June 15, 1932: Presidential Subject File, Prohibition, Folder 'Correspondence, June 15, 1932.'

Franklin D. Roosevelt
Presidential Library

Page 54: Amelia Earhart to President F. Roosevelt, November 10, 1936: President's Personal File 960 (Putnam, Mr. and Mrs. George Palmer [Amelia Earhart]) TM 2005 Amelia Earhart by CMG Worldwide, Inc. / www.AmeliaEarhart.com

Page 62: Petra Engebretson Harthun to Eleanor Roosevelt, August 7, 1941: Eleanor Roosevelt Papers, Series 75, Old Age Pensions, 1945, A-K

Page 70: Stephen Wise/American Jewish Congress to President F. Roosevelt, December 2, 1942: Official File 76c (Jewish matters), October-December 1942
Published with permission from American Jewish Congress

Page 72: J B Manual to President F. Roosevelt, February 24, 1942: President's Personal File 200b (Public reaction letters), Radio addresses of the President, February 23, 1942, Pro I-O.

Page 78: Winston Churchill to President F. Roosevelt, May 1, 1944: President's Personal File 7683 (Churchill, Winston S).
Reproduced with permission of Curtis Brown Ltd, London on behalf of the Estate of Sir Winston Churchill

Page 80: Wilma Lindsay to President F. Roosevelt, February 9, 1944: President's Official File 4675 (World War II), Japanese treatment of prisoners at Baatan and Philippines.

Page 84: Albert Einstein to President F. Roosevelt, August 2, 1939: President's Secretary's Files, Safe file: Sachs, Alexander.

Harry S. Truman
Presidential Library

Page 90: Ella Leber to President Truman, 1948: Museum Collection (Accession No. 3025)

Page 92: Phyllis Bamberger to President Truman, 1948: PPF 67: President's Personal File: White House Central Files: Harry S. Truman Papers.
Published with permission of Phyllis B. Katz

Page 98: Ray Fadden to President Truman, September 3, 1951: OF 471-B—Burial of Sgt. John Rice "A": Official File: White House Central Files: Harry S. Truman Papers.
Published with permission of John Fadden

Page 100: Ralph Ziegler to President Truman, January 31, 1949: PPF 1824-A: President's Personal File: White House Central Files: Harry S. Truman Papers.

Page 138: Herbert Hoover to President Truman, December 19, 1962: Hoover, Herbert C.: Secretary's Office File: Post-Presidential Papers: Harry S. Truman Papers.
Reprinted with permission of The Herbert Hoover Presidential Library Association.

Dwight D. Eisenhower
Presidential Library

Page 97: John Nabors to President Eisenhower, April 3, 1955: Dwight D. Eisenhower Records as President, White House Central Files, President's Personal File, Box 726 B, Folder: PPF 28-B Letters to Children – Heart Interest N"
Published with permission of Mrs. John C. Nabors

Page 102: Mrs. Edmund (Margaret M.) Powers to President Eisenhower, April 18, 1955: Dwight D. Eisenhower Records as President, General File, Box 1026, Folder: GF 131-D-2 Dr. Jonas Salk (1)
Published with permission of Margaret M. Powers

Page 103: Douw Fonda to President Eisenhower, August 8, 1955: Dwight D. Eisenhower Records as President, President's Personal File, Box 694, Folder: 27-B-3 Infantile Paralysis
Published with permission of Sue Fonda

Page 104: Linda Kelly, Sherry Bane and Mickie Mattson to President Eisenhower, 1958: Dwight D. Eisenhower Records as President, White House Central Files 1953-1961 (alpha file) Box 2496. Folder: President (2).

Page 106: Queen Elizabeth II to President Eisenhower, June 24, 1960: Museum Manuscripts Transferred to the Library FY70
Given with the permission of Her Royal Majesty Queen Elizabeth II

Page 108: Jackie Robinson to President Eisenhower, May 13, 1958: Dwight D. Eisenhower Records as President, Official File, Box 731, Folder: OF 142 – Negro Matters-Colored Question (6)
TM 2005 Rachel Robinson by CMG Worldwide, Inc./ www.JackieRobinson.com

Page 110: Woodrow W. Mann, Mayor of Little Rock, to President Eisenhower, September 23, 1957: Dwight D. Eisenhower Records as President, White House Central Files, Official File, Box 732, Folder: "OF 142 A-5-A (2)"

Page 113: Leah Russell to President Eisenhower, September 25, 1957: Dwight D. Eisenhower Records as President, Official File, Box 733 Folder: OF 142- A-5-A Negro Matters Colored Question Integrated Program for Public Schools...(13)

John F. Kennedy
Presidential Library

Page 112: Dr. Martin Luther King, Jr. to President Kennedy, September 15, 1963: White House Central Subject Files, Box 367, Folder: HU2/ST1 7-1-63.
Reprinted by arrangement with the Estate of Martin Luther King Jr., c/o Writers House as agent for the proprietor, New York, NY Copyright ©1963 Martin Luther King, Jr., copyright renewed ©1991 Coretta Scott King

Page 119: Ngo Dinh Diem to President Kennedy, February 23, 1963: JFK Library, Papers of John F. Kennedy; President's Office Files 1/20/1961-11/22/1963; File Unit: Papers of President Kennedy: President's Office Files: Vietnam, General 1963 2/23/1963

Page 120: Bobbie Lou Pendergrass to President Kennedy, February 18, 1963; *Page 123:* President Kennedy's response to Bobbie Lou Pendergrass, March 6, 1963: White House Central Subject Files, Box 604, Folder: "M"

Page 132, 135: Leonard Lyons to President Kennedy, October 2, 1961 and October 16, 1961; *Page 134:* President Kennedy's response to Leonard Lyons, October 11, 1961: White House Central Subject Files Box 754, Folder: Autographs, Photographs – Holographs, April 21, 1961 – Nov. 21, 1961. *Published with permission from the Estate of Leonard Lyons*

Page 136: Harry Truman to President Kennedy, June 28, 1962: President's Office Files, Box 33, Folder: Truman, Harry S. 1/15/62 – 12/5/62
Published with permission of Margaret Truman Daniel

Lyndon B. Johnson
Presidential Library

Page 14: Brian Williams to President L. Johnson, November 25, 1966: White House Central Files, Name File, "Williams, Br," Box 324.
Published with permission of Brian Williams

Page 94: Edwin Burtis, Texas Humane Federation, Inc. to President L. Johnson, April 30, 1964: White House Central

Files, Subject File, "General PP 15-10, 11/22/63-5/26/64," Box 119. *Published with permission of Eloise Burtis Crow*

Page 96: John Starnes to President L. Johnson, received June 20, 1966: White House Central Files, Subject File, General PP 15-10, "6/28/66," Box 120. *Published with permission of John P. Starnes*

Page 114: Roy Wilkins, National Association for the Advancement of Colored People to President L. Johnson, November 5, 1964: White House Central Files, Subject File, "General PP 2-2/ST 32, 11/11/63-11/25/64," Box 49. *The National Geographic Society wishes to thank The National Association for the Advancement of Colored People for authorizing the use of this work.*

Page 124: John Steinbeck to President L. Johnson, May 28, 1966: White House Central Files, Subject File, "Executive PR 8-1/STE-STRHZ," Box 245. *"05/28/1966 to Mr. President (Lyndon B. Johnson) by John Steinbeck, from STEINBECK: A LIFE IN LETTERS by Elaine Steinbeck and Robert Wallsten, editors, copyright ©1952 by John Steinbeck, ©1969 by The Estate of John Steinbeck, ©1975 by Elaine A. Steinbeck and Robert Wallsten. Used by permission of Viking Penguin, a division of Penguin Group (USA) Inc.*

Page 125: Tom Smothers and Dick Smothers, The Smothers Brother Comedy Hour, to President L. Johnson, October 31, 1968: White House Central Files, Subject File, "Executive SP 3-274/Pro," Box 254. *Published with permission of Knave Productions, Inc.*

Page 127: President Johnson's response to the Smothers Brothers, November 9, 1968, provided by Knave Productions.

Page 142: Lady Bird Johnson to President L. Johnson, August 1964: Personal Papers of Mrs. Johnson, Box 3, Folder "August 1964, President's Decision to Run in 1964"

Nixon Presidential Materials

Page 144: Elvis Presley to President Nixon, December 21, 1970: Folder [EX] HE 5-1, 1/1/72-1/31/72, Box 19; White House Central Files, Subject Files

Page 148: Mrs. John Shields to President Nixon, July 16, 1971: Folder [China Trip – Comments on Announcement], Box 7; White House Special Files: Staff Member and Office Files: President's Personal Files

Page 148: Mary Ann Grelinger to President Nixon, July 16, 1971: Folder [China Trip – Comments on Announcement], Box 7; White House Special Files: Staff Member and Office Files: President's Personal Files. Published with permission of Mary Ann Grelinger

Page 172: Thaddeus Zagorewicz to President Nixon, July 20, 1969: Folder Zagor; White House Central Files, Alphabetical Name File *Published with permission of Sophie Zagorewicz*

Gerald R. Ford Presidential Library

Page 139: Barry Goldwater to President Ford, May 7, 1976: Folder: "PL, 06/01/1976-06/30/1976 Executive;" Box 3; White House Central Files, Subject File

Page 150: Jackie Anne Lucas to President Ford, circa November 1974: Folder: "JL 1/Nixon 12/1-15/1974 (1), General;" Box 12; White House Central Files, Subject Files

Page 152: Robert Lind to President Ford, circa September 1974: Folder: "JL 1/Nixon 10/31/1974 (2): GRF to Blazer, General;" Box 11; White House Central Files, Subject Files

Page 153: Anthony Ferreira to President Ford, September 11, 1974: Folder: "JL 1/Nixon 10/31/1974 (1): GRF to Wertheim, General;" Box 11; White House Central Files

Page 154: Tyson Garrison to Betty Ford, August 13, 1975: Folder: "Betty Ford's '60 Minutes' Interview, Con, Box 459, #3;" Box 17; White House Social Files, Bulk Mail File Samples *Published with permission from Rev. Deron S. Cobb on behalf of Mt. Olive Baptist Church, Inc.*

Page 157: Dorothy Tabata to Betty Ford, August 18, 1975: Folder: "Betty Ford's '60 Minutes' Interview, Pro, Box 439, #1;" Box 14; White House Social Files, Bulk Mail File Samples

Jimmy Carter Presidential Library

Page 158: Mother Teresa to President Carter, November 17, 1979: Box MA-0, "MA 36 Executive 4/1/79-1/20/80", White House Central Files *Letter from Mother Teresa to U.S. President Jimmy Carter, November 17, 1979, © 2005 Missionaries of Charity Sisters c/o Mother Teresa of Calcutta Center, 2498 Roll Drive, PMB 733, San Diego, CA 92154, www.motherteresa.org. All rights reserved. Used with permission. No portion of this text may be reproduced by any means without the permission of the copyright owner.*

Page 160: Roy Klober to President Carter, 1980: Museum Collection, 88.21 *Published with permission of Roy L. Klober*

Page 160: L.W. McKenzie Jr. to President Carter, 1980: Museum Collection, 88.18 *Published with permission of L.W. McKenzie*

Page 162: Cy Vance to President Carter, April 21, 1980: Box 183, "4/28/80", Staff Secretary Files

Ronald Reagan Presidential Library

Page 140: Richard Nixon to President Reagan, August 13, 1987: White House Office of Records Management, Subject File, ID #533859, SP1169

Page 164: Andy Smith to President Reagan, April 18, 1984;

Page 167: President Reagan's response to Andy Smith, May 11, 1984: White House Office of Records Management, Subject File, ID # 226267, PRO 14-10 *Published with permission of Andrew J. Smith*

George H.W. Bush Presidential Library

Page 168: Patricia Elvin to President Bush, November 27, 1990: Folder "Letters Concerning the Persian Gulf War Situation SMG163 [1] [1/9/90-100 letters] [1]", OA/ID 03471, Shirley Green Files, Correspondence Office, Bush Presidential Records *Published with permission of Patricia J (Elvin) Bickel*

Page 171: Eric Colton to President Bush, February 12, 1991: Folder "Colton, A-H", OA/ID 15709, White House Office of Records Management: Alpha File, Bush Presidential Records *Published with permission of Eric E. Colton*

William J. Clinton Presidential Library

Page 175: John Glenn to President Clinton, November 6, 1998: White House Office of Records Management, FG 001.284

PHOTO CREDITS

Cover image and design: Melissa Farris Pages 2, 10-11, 21, 47, 73, 81, 91, 95, 99, 105, 118, 129, 133, 156, 161, 165: © Bettmann /CORBIS. Pages 4-5, 13, 31: © CORBIS. Pages 9, 115: LBJ Library photo by Yoichi Okamoto. Page 15: Brian Williams. Page 16: LBJ Library photo by Jack Kightlinger. Page 27: Library of Congress LC-B8171-7929. Page 39: Library of Congress LC-USZ62-131570. Pages 41, 68, 79: © Hulton-Deutsch Collection/CORBIS. Page 145: National Archives, Richard Nixon Presidential Papers. Page 149: © Wally McNamee/CORBIS. Page 151: Gerald R. Ford Library. Page 169: George Bush Presidential Library. Page 174: © F. Carter Smith/CORBIS Sygma.

Selected Transcriptions

Full transcriptions of selected letters that appear in abridged form within the body of the book

PAGE 20: KING MONGKUT OF SIAM TO ABRAHAM LINCOLN, FEBRUARY 14, 1861:

The true translation of the proceeding Siamese Royal letter into English

Sendeth friendly Greeting!

Respected and Distinguished Sir,

At this time we are very glad in having embraced an excellent opportunity to forward our Royal letter under separate envelope together with complimentary presents—Viz

A sword with a photographic likeness of ourselves accompanying herewith, directly to Washington as being a much better way of forwarding it than the way we had intended, by delivering it to the Consul of the United States of America here to be forwarded on, sometimes by a steamer, sometimes by a sailing vessel from one port to another till It should reach Washington. This sending where there are many changes from one vessel to another is not a trustworthy way. There is danger of delay and indeed that the articles may be damaged and never reach their destination.

On this one occasion, occurred in February Christian Era 1861 corresponding to the Lunar time being in connection of the Siamese months of Magh and Phagun, the 3rd & 4th month from the commencement of the cold season in the year of Monkey, second decade Siamese astronomical era 1222. A ship of war, a sailing vessel of the United States Navy, the "John Adams" arrived and anchored outside the Bar, off the mouth of the River "Chaw Phya", Captain Berrien with the officers of the ship of war came up to pay a friendly visit to the country and has had an interview with (illegible) hence to him we have entrusted our Royal Letter in separate envelope which accompanies this and the presents specified in that letter.

We are assured that Captain Berrien will deliver them in safety to you who are President of the United States when our letter would reach Washington. During the interview in reply from Captain Berrien to our enquiries of various particulars relating to America he stated that on that continent there are no elephants. Elephants are regarded as the most remarkable of the large quadripeds by the Americans so that if any one has an elephant's tusk of large size, and will deposit it in any public place, people come by thousands crowding to see it, saying, it is a wonderful thing. Also, though formerly there were no camels on the continent the Americans have sought for and purchased (illegible) some from Arabia, some from Europe and now camels propagate their race and are serviceable and of benefit to the country, and are already numerous in America.

Having heard this it has occurred to us that, if on the continent of America there should be several pairs of young male and female elephants turned loose in forests where there was abundance of water and grass in any region under the sun's declination both North and South, call by the English, the Torrid Zone, and all were forbidden to molest them, to attempt to raise them would be well and if the climate there should prove favorable to elephants, we are of opinion that after a while they will increase till there be large herds as there are here on the continent of Asia until the inhabitants of America will be able to catch them and tame and use them as beasts of burden making them of benefit to the country. Since elephants being animals of great size and strength can bear burdens and travel through uncleared woods and matted jungles where no carriage and cart roads have yet been made.

Examples we have coming down from ancient times of this business of transplanting Elephants from the main land of Asia to various islands. Four hundred years ago when the island of Ceylon was governed by its native princes an Embassy was sent to beg of the King of (illegible) or Pegu to purchase young elephants in several pairs to turn loose in the jungle of Ceylon and now by natural increase they are many large herds of elephants in that island.

We have heard also a tradition that a long time ago the natives of Achen in the island of Sumatra and the natives of Java came to the Malayan Peninsula to obtain young elephants to turn loose in the jungles of Sumatra and Java, and, in consequence of this elephants are numerous in both those islands.

On this accounts the desire to procure and send elephants to be let loose in increase and multiply in the continent of America. But we are as yet uninformed what forests and what regions of that country are suitable for elephants to thrive and prosper. Besides we have no means nor are we able to convey elephants to America, the distance being too great.

The islands of Ceylon & Sumatra & Java are near to this continent of Asia and those who thought of this plan in former days could transport their elephants with ease and without difficulty.

In reference to this opinion of ours if the President of the United States and Congress who conjointly with him rule the country see fit to approve let them provide a large vessel loaded with hay and other food suitable for elephants on the voyage, with tanks holding a sufficiency of fresh water and arranged with stalls so that the elephant can both stand & lie down on the ship—and send it to receive them.

We on our part will procure young male and female

elephants and forward them one or two pairs at a time.

When elephants are on board, the ship let a steamer take it in tow that it may reach America as rapidly as possible before they become wasted and diseased by the voyage.

When they arrive in America do not let them be taken to a cold climate out of the regions under the Sun's declinations or Torrid Zone—but let them with all haste be turned out to run wild in some jungle suitable for them not confining them any length of time.

If these means can be done, we trust that the elephants will propagate their species, hereafter in the continent of America.

It is desirable that the President of the United States and Congress give us their views in reference to this matter at as early a day as possible.

In Siam it is the custom of the season to take elephants from the herds in the jungles in the months of Shagun & Chetre—4th & 5th generally corresponding to March and April.

If the President and Congress approve of this matter and should provide a vessel to come for the elephants, if that vessel should arrive in Siam on any month of any year after March and April as above mentioned, let notice be sent on two or three months previous to those months of that year in order that the elephants may be caught and tamed. Whereas the elephants that have been long captured & tamed and domesticated here are large—and difficult to transport—and there would be danger they might never reach America.

At this time we have much pleasure in sending a pair of large elephant's tusks, one of the tusks weighing 52 cents of a piced, the other weighing 48 cents of a piced—and both tusks from the same animal—as an addition to our former present to be deposited with them for public inspection. That thereby the glory and renown of Siam may be promoted.

We hope that the President and Congress who administer the government of the United States of America will gladly receive them as a token of friendly regard.

★★★

PAGE 24: JAMES H. GOODING TO ABRAHAM LINCOLN, SEPTEMBER 25, 1863

Camp of 54th Mass Colored Regt
Morris Island Dept of the South, Sept 25th 1863

Your Excelency, Abraham Lincoln:

Your Excelency will pardon the presumtion of an humble individual like myself, in addressing you, but the earnest Solicitation of my Comrades in Arms, besides the genuine interest felt by myself in the matter is my excuse for placing before the Executive head of the Nation our Common Grievance: On the 6th of the last month, the Paymaster of the department informed us that if we would decide to receive the sum of $10 (ten dollars) per month, he would come and pay us that sum, but, that on the sitting of Congress, the Regt would, in his opinion, be allowed the other 3 (three.) He did not give us any guarantee that this would be, as he hoped, certainly he had no authority for making any such guarantee, and we can not supose him acting in any way interested. Now the main question is. Are we Soldiers or are we Labourers. We are fully armed, and equipped, have done all the various Duties, pertaining to a Soldiers life, have conducted ourselves, to the complete satisfaction of General Officers, who, were if any, prejudiced against us, but who now accord us all the encouragement, and honour due us: have shared the perils, and Labour, of Reducing the first stronghold, that flaunted a Traitor Flag: and more, Mr President. Today, the Anglo Saxon Mother, Wife, or Sister, are not alone in tears for departed Sons, Husbands, and Brothers.

The patient Trusting Decendants of Africs Clime, have dyed the ground with blood, in defense of the Union, and Democracy. Men too your Excellency, who know in a measure, the cruelties of the Iron heel of oppression, which in years gone by, the very Power, their blood is now being spilled to maintain, ever ground them to the dust. But When the war trumpet sounded o'er the land, when men knew not the Friend from the Traitor, the Black man laid his life at the Altar of the Nation,—and he was refused. When the arms of the Union, were beaten, in the first year of the War, And the Executive called more food. for its ravaging maw, again the black man begged, the privelege of Aiding his Country in her need, to be again refused, And now, he is in the War: and how has he conducted himself? Let their dusky forms, rise up, out the mires of James Island, and give the answer. Let the rich mould around Wagners parapets be upturned, and there will be found an Eloquent answer. Obedient and patient, and Solid as a wall are they. all we lack, is a paler hue, and a better acquaintance with the Alphabet. Now Your Excellency, We have done a Soldiers Duty. Why cant we have a Soldiers pay? You caution the Rebel Chieftain, that the United States, knows, no distinction, in her Soldiers: She insists on having all her Soldiers, of whatever, creed or Color, to be treated, according to the usages of War. Now if the United States exacts uniformity of treatment of her Soldiers, from the Insurgents, would it not be well, and consistent, to set the example herself, by paying all her Soldiers alike? We of this Regt. were not enlisted under any "contraband" act. But we do not wish to be understood, as rating our Service, of more Value to the Government, than the service of the exslave, Their Service is undoubtedly worth much to the Nation, but Congress made express, provision touching their case, as slaves freed by military necessity, and assuming the Government, to be their temporary Gaurdian:—Not so with us—Freemen by birth, and consequently, having the advantage of thinking, and acting for ourselves, so far as the Laws would allow us. We do not consider ourselves fit subjects for the Contraband act. We appeal to You, Sir: as the Executive of the Nation, to have us Justly Dealt with. The Regt, do pray, that they be assured their service will be fairly appreciated, by paying them as american SOLDIERS, not as menial hierlings. Black men You may well know, are poor, three dollars per month, for a year, will suply their needy Wives, and little ones, with fuel. If you, as chief Magistrate of the Nation, will assure us, of our whole pay. We are content, our Patriotism, our enthusiasm will have a new impetus, to exert our energy more and more to aid Our Country. Not that our hearts ever flagged, in Devotion, spite the evident apathy displayed in our behalf, but We feel as though, our Country spurned us, now we are sworn to serve her.

Please give this a moments attention.
Corporal James Henry Gooding
Co. C. 54th Mass. Regt.
Morris Island S.C.

★★★

PAGE 33: GOV. EDMUND ROSS TO GROVER CLEVELAND, AUGUST 14, 1886

President, Sir,
We are much surprised to learn that opposition is being made to the proposition of Gen. Miles to remove portions of the Apache Indians from their present reservation in Arizona.

It does not seem possible that such opposition could originate with persons who comprehend the situation here and the need of radical measures for the pacification of our Indian troubles, or that it could be inspired by a desire to promote the civilization and welfare of these Indians, or the peace and successful development of these territories.

Many of us have resided here for years, have seen this country the victim of Indian raids year after year, and have a right to be credited with intelligent and practical views on this subject. We are firmly convinced that no permanent cessation of these raids, or enduring safety to the isolated camps of miners and ranchmen, can be secured so long as the Chiricahua and Warm Springs bands of these Apaches are permitted to remain in any part of these territories. For two hundred years they have been traditional enemies and at constant war with the white race. It is true there are but few of them, less than five hundred all told, but there are enough, owing to the generally rugged and inaccessible character of the country they infest and raid, and the isolated nature of the settlements, to keep a very large scope of country in a state of ferment, and thereby to retard the development of valuable mining, ranching and grazing properties upon which this country largely depends for its prosperity.

Generations of hostility show them to be implacable, and that nothing short of extermination will stop their raids so long as they remain here in proximity to their traditional enemies. So long as they are here, that process of extermination will go on, but at a fearful cost of life and property to our people and of treasure to the government. For every warrior killed some boy is now growing up to take his place.

The boys of today are the outlaws and bandits—the Jus, the Nanes and the Geronimos—of tomorrow. It has been so for generations and will continue so, if they remain here, till they are exterminated; all the interests of these territories, in the meantime languishing and their development paralyzed, by the presence of an element that momentarily threatens destruction to our most important industries.

The other bands of the Apaches are peaceful, and in the main, self-sustaining. There is no special occasion or desire for their removal, but the removal of the others named we deem imperative to the restoration of confidence and tranquility to these territories. The lives and property of large numbers of people, and the development of the extraordinary sources of wealth to the country found here are at stake in this matter, and we sincerely hope and pray that the suggestions of Gen. Miles, in the premises, may be adopted.

Gen. Miles has so far since he has been placed in command here, by the wisdom of his plans and the vigor of their execution, kept the actively hostile portion of these bands out of New Mexico and finally driven them out of Arizona. They are practically conquered and are understood as being desirous to return to the reservation. To permit them to do so would be simply to tempt fate, and a repetition of the folly of two years ago—another drunken debauch and a murder of some of their number at the first opportunity, and a return to the warpath of pillage and murder to escape punishment. That will be the inevitable result if they are permitted to return. Of this we repeat that we are firmly convinced, and that no permanent peace can come to New Mexico or Arizona till these bands are removed to distant and isolated localities.

Very respectfully,
Edmund G. Ross, Governor, Et al

★★★

PAGE 36: UPTON SINCLAIR TO THEODORE ROOSEVELT, MARCH 10, 1906

My dear President Roosevelt:
I have just returned from some exploring in the Jersey glass factories and find your kind note. I am glad to learn that the Department of Agriculture has taken up the matter of inspection, or lack of it, but I am exceedingly dubious as

to what they will discover. I have seen so many people go out there and be put off with smooth pretences. A man has to be something of a detective, or else intimate with the working-men, as I was, before he can really see what is going on. And it is becoming a great deal more difficult since the publication of "The Jungle." I have received to-day a letter from an employe of Armour & Company, in response to my request to him to take Ray Stannard Baker in hand and show him what he showed me a year and a half ago. He says: "He will have to be well disguised, for 'the lid is on' in Packingtown; he will find two detectives in places where before there was only one." You must understand that the thing which I have called the "condemned meat industry," is a matter of hundreds of thousands of dollars a month. I see in to-day's "Saturday Evening Post" that Mr. Armour declares in his article (which I happen to know is written by George Horace Lorimer) that "In Armour and Company's business not one atom of any condemned animal or carcass, finds its way, directly or indirectly, from any source, into any food product or food ingredient." Now, compare with that the following extract from a formal statement transmitted to Doubleday, Page & Company by Mr. Thomas H. McKee, attorney at law, (111 Broadway, New York) who is a personal friend of Mr. Walter H. Page, and was sent out to Chicago by that firm to investigate the situation:

"With a special conductor, Mr. B. J. Mullaney, provided for me by Mr. Urich, attorney for Armour interests, I went through the Armour plant again. Mullaney introduced me to T. J. Conners, manager, who called Mr. Hull, Superintendent of beef plant and said to him: 'I have just told Mr. McKee that we have nothing here to conceal and that he can see anything he wants and can stay as long as he likes. Please see that my promise is made good.' I expressed my desire to investigate two points, 1st, the system of inspection; 2nd, the by-product industry..."

"I saw six hogs hung in line which had been condemned. A truck loaded with chopped up condemned hogs was in my presence (I followed it) placed in one of the tanks from which lard comes. I asked particularly about this and the inspector together with Mr. Hull stated that lard and fertilizer would be the product from that tank. The tanks are in a long room. The East side is lined with tanks for manufacture of lard and fertilizer; the West side with tanks whose product is grease and feritlizer. The grease is for soap, lubricator, etc. Here is a clear infraction of the law, because it requires that such condemned meat be mixed with sufficient offal to destroy it as food. This seems ot be done on the 'Grease' line of tanks; it is not done at the 'Lard' line of tanks. See Department of Agriculture Rules, June 27, 1904, Article IX. The excuse probably is that the inspector has not found the animal unfit for one kind of human food, to wit—lard."

"Of the six condemned hogs referred to two were afflicted with cholers, the skin being red as blood and the legs scabbed; three were marked 'tubercular,' though they appeared normal to a layman, the sixth had an ulcer in its side which was apparent. Two men were engaged in chopping up hogs from this line. The truck load prepared while I stood there was deposited in a lard tank. I asked particularly about the line of demarcation between the carcasses used for lard and carcasses used for grease. No explanation was given by either the insprector or my conductor. 'It all depends on how bad he is,' was the answer. I gathered the impression, however, that not very many carcasses were placed in the Grease tanks."

So much for Mr. McKee. For myself, I was escorted through Packingtown by a young lawyer who was brought up in the district, had worked as a boy in Armour's plant, and knew more or less intimately every foreman, "spotter," and watchman about the place. I saw with my own eyes hams, which had spoiled in pickle, being pumped full of chemicals to destroy the odor. I saw waste ends of smoked beef stored in barrels in a cellar, in a condition of filth which I could not describe in a letter. I saw rooms in which sausage meat was stored with poisoned rats lying about, and the dung of rats covering them. I saw hogs which had died of cholera in shipment, being loaded into box cars to be taken to a place called Globe, in Indiana, to be rendered into lard. Finally, I found a physician, Dr. William K. Jaques, 4316 Woodland avenue, Chicago, who holds the chair of bacteriology in the Illinoic State University, and was in charge of the city inspection of meat during 1902-3, who told me he had seen beef carcasses, bearing the inspectors' tags of contamination, left upon open platforms and carted away at night, to be sold in the city. I quote a few words from Dr. Jaques' statement, furnished to Mr. McKee, and would add that he has written an article which will appear in the "World's Work" for May, and of which a proof could possibly be furnished you, if you cared to see it.

"My education as a physician teaches me that disease follows the same law whether in animals or human beings. An accurate post mortem requires close inspection of all the internal organs together with the use of the microscope before a physician can say there is no disease present. How many post mortems could the most exert physician make in a day? Ten would be a big day's work; fifty would take the endurance of the most strenuous. It is reported that one hundred and fifty thousand animals have been received at Union Stockyards in a single day. How many animal pathologists are employed by the government who are capable of making a reliable post mortem and saying that an animal is not diseased? In round numbers, say there are are fifty—a few more or less, for the sake of illustration, are not material. Say there are only fifty thousand animals killed a day at the stock yards. This would be a thousand to each inspector, a hundred an hour, nearly two a minute. What is such an inspection worth? It is true, there is some inspection that is well done; it is that which is done for the sharp eyes of the foreigner."

"Inspection to be effective should include the entire twenty-four hours. Federal inspection is probably effective in day light. City inspectors work during city hall hours. The railroads and express companies bring animals into the city every hour in the day. When John Dyson has access to every room in the packing houses and knows what is done there every hour in the twenty-four; when his army of inspectors know the disposition of the meat brought into the city by more that thirty railroads; when he knows the destination and use of the refuse which the meat and liver wagons gather after nightfall from Fulton market, south Water street and other markets; when he knows the meat that comes to the city by wagon and other ways, then, in my estimation, he can give something like an accurate estimation of the amount of diseased, putrid meat that is converted into meat in Chicago. Until he has this information, he must confess to the ignorance of which he accuses others. No one has this information. There are a hundred streets and avenues by which diseased meat can enter the city and be put on sale in the markets. The public has made no effort to find out and it is left to the men who deal in this merchandise to dump what they please into the stomachs of the blissfully ignorant public. Neither do any of us know how much disease and suffering this food causes. The diagnosis of the best physicians is so often turned down at the post mortem table that the actual results of diseased food are difficult to ascertain."

Finally, I might add that I have a long affidavit from a man named Thomas F. Dolan, now at the head of the Boston & Maine News Bureau, who was for many years a superintendent in Armour's plant, and has letters to show that he was considered by Armour as the best man he ever employed. He makes oath to Armour's custom of taking condemned meat out of the bottoms of tanks, into which they have been dropped with the idea of rendering them into fertilizer. It seems that the tanks are or were then built with a false bottom, which lets down on a hinge; and that when you stand at the top and see the meat dropped in, you are flooded by blinding clouds of steam which pour up from a pipe down in the tank. When this affidavit was published, Dolan was paid $5,000 by Armour to make another one contradicting himself. He took the $5,000 and went on to give away the whole story, which was published in the "Evening Journal." March 16, 1899. The fact that it is a Hearst story would tend to discredit it; but having investigated the whole thing, and met every man who was concerned in the exposé, I am convinced that the affidavit is worth attention.

Baker knows intimately a man who is high in the counsels of Armour and Company, and was present at a conference in which Odgen Armour personally gave the decision to bribe Dolan.

This is a very long letter, but I feel the importance of the subject excuses it. It would give me great pleasure to come down to Washington to see you at any time, but I would rather it was after you had read "The Jungle," because I have put a good deal of myself into that.

You ask—"Is there anything further, say in the Department of Agriculture, which you would suggest my doing" I would suggest the following: That you do as Doubleday, Page & Company did; find a man concerning whose intelligence and integrity you are absolutely sure; send him up here, or let me meet him in Washington, and tell him all that I saw, and how I saw it, and give him the names and addresses of the people who will enable him to see it. Then let him go to Packingtown as I did, as a working-man; live with the men, get a job in the yards, and use his eyes and ears; and see if he does not come out at the end of a few weeks feeling, as did the special correspondent of the London "Lancet," whom I met in Chicago, that the conditions in the packing-houses constitute a "menace to the health of the civilized world." *(The Lancet for Jan 8, 15, 22, 29—1905.)*

Thanking you for your kind interest,
Very sincerely,
Upton Sinclair

P.S. I might add that when I was in Chicago I learned a good deal about the connections which the packers have in Washington, so that I think it most likely that before the Department of Agriculture get anybody started for the purpose of investigating Packingtown, word has been sent there to the packing-houses that things should be cleaned up. I know positively that this was done in the case of Major Seaman, who went out there for "Collier's Weekly".

PAGE 54: AMELIA EARHART TO FRANKLIN D. ROOSEVELT, NOVEMBER 10, 1936

Dear Mr. President:
Some time ago I told you and Mrs. Roosevelt a little about my confidential plans for a world flight. As perhaps you know, through the cooperation of Purdue University I now have a magnificent twin-motor, all-metal plane, especially equipped for long distance flying.

For some months Mr. Putnam and I have been preparing for a flight which I hope to attempt probably in March. The route, compared with previous flights, will be unique. It is east to west, and approximates the equator. Roughly it is from San Francisco to Honolulu; from Honolulu to Tokio—or Honolulu to Brisbane; the regular Australia-England route as far west as Karachi to Aden; Aden via Kartoon across

Central Africa to Dakar; Dakar to Natal, and thence to New York on the regular Pan American route.

Special survey work and map preparation is already underway on the less familiar portion of the route as, for instance, that in Africa.

The chief problem is the jump westward from Honolulu. The distance thence to Tokio is 3900 miles. I want to reduce as much as possible the hazard of the take-off at Honolulu with the excessive over-load. With that in view, I am discussing with the Navy a possible refueling in the air over Midway Island. If this can be arranged, I need to take much less gas from Honolulu, and with the Midway refueling will have ample gasoline to reach Tokio. As mine is a land plane, the seaplane facilities at Wake, Guam, etc., are useless.

This matter has been discussed in detail by Mr. Putnam with Admiral Cook, who was most interested and friendly. Subsequently a detailed description of the project, and request for this assistance, was prepared. It is now on the desk of Admiral Standley, by whom it is being considered.

Some new seaplanes are being completed at San Diego for the Navy. They will be ferried in January or February to Honolulu. It is my desire to practice actual refueling operations in the air over San Diego with one of these planes. That plane subsequently from Honolulu would be available for the Midway operation. I gather from Admiral Cook that technically there are no extraordinary difficulties. It is primarily a matter of policy and precedent.

In the past the Navy has been so progressive in its pioneering, and so broad-minded in what we might call its "public relations", that I think a project such as this (even involving a mere woman!) may appeal to Navy personnel. Its successful attainment might, I think, win for the Service further popular friendship.

I should add the matter of international permissions etc. is being handled very helpfully by the State Department. The flight, by the way, has no commercial implications. The operation of my "Flying Laboratory" is under auspices of Purdue University. Like previous flights, I am undertaking this one solely because I want to, and because I feel that women now and then have to do things to show what women can do.

Forgive the great length of this letter. I am just leaving for the west on a lecture tour and wanted to place my problem before you.

Knowing your own enthusiasm for voyaging, and your affectionate interest in Navy Matters, I am asking you to help me secure Navy cooperation—that is, if you think well of the project. If any information is wanted as to the purpose, plane, equipment, etc., Mr. Putnam can meet anyone you designate any time any where.

Very sincerely yours,
Amelia Earhart

P.S.—My plans are for the moment entirely confidential—no announcement has been made.

PAGE 83: HAROLD ICKES TO FRANKLIN D. ROOSEVELT, JUNE 1, 1944

My dear Mr. President:

I again call your attention to the urgent necessity of arriving at a determination with respect to revocation of the orders excluding Japanese Americans from the West Coast. It is my understanding that Secretary Stimson believes that there is no longer any military necessity for excluding these persons from the State of California and portions of the States of Washington, Oregon and Arizona. Accordingly, there is no basis in law or in equity for the perpetuation of the ban.

The reasons for revoking the exclusion orders may be briefly stated as follows:

1. I have been informally advised by officials of the War Department who are in charge of this problem that there is no substantial justification for continuation of the ban from the standpoint of military security.

2. The continued exclusion of American citizens of Japanese ancestry from the affected areas is clearly unconstitutional in the present circumstances. I expect that a case squarely raising this issue will reach the Supreme Court at its next term. I believe that the Department of Justice will agree that there is little doubt as to the decision which the Supreme Court will reach in a case squarely presenting the issue.

3. The continuation of the exclusion orders in the West Coast areas is adversely affecting our efforts to relocate Japanese Americans elsewhere in the country. State and local officials are saying, with some justification, that if these people are too dangerous for the West Coast, they do not want them to resettle in their localities.

4. The psychology of the Japanese Americans in the relocation centers becomes progressively worse. The difficulty which will confront these people in readjusting to ordinary life becomes greater as they spend more time in the centers.

5. The children in the centers are exposed solely to the influence of persons of Japanese ancestry. They are becoming a hopelessly maladjusted generation, surrounded by apprehension about the outside world and divorced from the possibility of associating—or even seeing to any considerable extent—Americans of other races.

6. The retention of Japanese Americans in the relocation centers impairs the efforts which are being made to secure better treatment for American prisoners-of-war and civilians who are held by the Japanese. It is a fact, for example, that in many localities American nationals were not interned by

the Japanese government until after the West Coast evacuation; and the Japanese government has recently responded to the State Department complaints concerning treatment of American nationals by citing, among other things, the circumstances of the evacuation and detention of the West Coast Japanese Americans.

I will not comment at this time on the justification or lack thereof for the original evacuation order. But I do say that the continued retention of these innocent people in the relocation centers would be a blot upon the history of this country. *(Please note that the following passage is marked through on the original draft letter. It was not included in the final version sent to Roosevelt.):* It is inconsistent with the fundamental ideas of fairness and decency upon which civilization is based. What has been done cannot be repaired, but I hope that you will see to it that history will not recite that these people were incarcerated and detained long after even the feeblest pretense could be made that there existed any military or security reason for this treatment; and that they were released only after the Supreme Court had branded their continued detention as lawless and unconstitutional.

Sincerely yours, Secretary of the Interior.

★★★

PAGE 88: GUY VON DARDEL TO HARRY S. TRUMAN, MARCH 27, 1947

Dear Mr. President:
I write to you concerning the whereabouts of my brother, Raoul Wallenberg, a Swedish citizen who went to Hungary in July, 1944 as the representative of President Roosevelt's War Refugee Board and who has been missing since the Soviet Foreign Office early in 1946 declared him to be under Russian protection.

I appeal to you because I believe that his fate, apart from being a source of continuous anguish to his family, also touches the conscience of this great democracy. I ask your aid because my brother's mercy mission—which included the rescue of 20,000 Hungarian Jews—was carried out under American auspices, and because two years of effort through regular diplomatic channels have failed.

The success of Raoul Wallenberg's humanitarian mission from July, 1944 until his disappearance on January 17, 1945 is a matter of public record. The War Refugee Board officially credits him with saving 20,000 lives; his former American associates in Stockholm as well as the people of Budapest estimate that perhaps 100,000 men, women and children owe their survival to him.

The manner in which he carried out his singular assignment has been described as unparalleled in both courage and resourcefulness. In the midst of furious battle and barbarous persecution, he literally snatched thousands of human beings from freight trains bound for Himmler's extermination camps. He furnished many thousands of otherwise doomed Hungarian Jews and anti-Nazis with documents of Swedish protective citizenship. He established an extraterritorial compound in the heart of Nazi-occupied Budapest and fought off German and Hungarian fascist marauders who tried to violate this sanctuary.

He set up hospitals, nurseries, schools and public soup kitchens to care for the hunted and fear-ridden of Budapest. And when Fascist Premier Szalasi decreed in October 1945 that Swedish protective channels would no longer be honored—an edict which spelled death to the surviving Jews of Budapest—Raoul Wallenberg still found a way. With ingenuity and daring, he managed to forestall this cruel decree long enough to save many thousands from the final fires of Ausschwitz, Oswiecim and Dachau.

When the Germans were being driven from Budapest, Raoul remained at his post. On January 17, 1945 he went out to meet Marshal Malinovsky, the Soviet commander, in order to place his charges—thousands of men, women and children—under the protection of the Red Army.

Since leaving Budapest under Russian escort for Soviet headquarters, my brother has been missing. Rumors were circulated more than two years ago that he had been killed by Hungarian fascists. But while these rumors have never been supported by a shred of proof, a large body of evidence has come to the attention of the Swedish government which indicates that Raoul Wallenberg has been a Soviet prisoner since January, 1945.

The Soviet government has never retracted the admission by the Russian Foreign Office that Wallenberg was taken under Soviet protection more than two years ago. Nor has Moscow submitted any evidence to support the inspired rumors of his death at fascist hands.

Quite the contrary, the evidence that my brother established contact with the Russian command just before his disappearance has recently been corroborated by Iver Olsen, the former War Refugee Board representative in Stockholm who sent Raoul on his mission to Budapest, and by other reputable witnesses, including members of the Swedish Legation in Budapest. Some of the latter, who were interrogated by Soviet NKVD officers nearly a month after Raoul's disappearance, are firmly convinced that my brother was arrested on the preposterous charge of espionage. This belief is shared by officials of the U.S. State Department and the Swedish Foreign Office.

It is significant, however, that the Soviet government has never admitted holding Wallenberg as a prisoner. On the contrary, Mme. Kollontai, wartime minister to Stockholm, gave our family assurance that Raoul was alive and safe.

Later, the Soviet military authorities permitted the city of Budapest to hold memorial services for Raoul and to name a street in his honor. With this convenient ceremony, the curtain of oblivion was to be dropped on the actual fate of my brother.

Since that time, however, an ever-larger body of evidence has reached the Swedish government to indicate that Raoul was arrested by the Soviet secret police in January 1945 and is still alive in a Soviet internment camp. The latest report, transmitted to Stockholm only a few weeks ago, places him in Estonia. Earlier testimony by neutral diplomats and journalists as well as other persons held for some time in Soviet custody, indicates that Raoul was sent to a Soviet internment camp in Czechoslovakia in April 1945; that he was later transferred to Bessarabia and was subsequently sent to a camp in the Ukraine.

The Swedish government has, on a number of occasions, requested the Soviet government for definite information regarding my brother's whereabouts. But since the Soviet Foreign Office announced in January, 1945 that Wallenberg was under Russian protection, Moscow has remained noncommittal.

In view of the manifest inability of ordinary diplomacy to cut through the tangle of red tape and misunderstanding that may still be holding my brother a prisoner—more than two years after the completion of his American-inspired humanitarian mission—I ask your assistance, Mr. President, in obtaining the true facts.

Respectfully yours, Guy von Dardel

★★★

PAGE 102: MARGARET M. POWERS TO DWIGHT D. EISENHOWER, APRIL 18, 1955

Dear Mr. President,
Enclosed you will find a picture of a one year old child receiving an injection of the limited supply of the Salk antipoliomyelitis vaccine.

As the mother of two children, (two years old and the other three and a half years old) I should like very much to have them immunized against this disease, but I am willing that they should forego their injections in order not to deprive other more susceptible children of their injections.

I consider the administration of the vaccine to other than the most susceptible age group to be a gross abuse, while the vaccine is in such limited supply.

I know that you are burdened with great and important tasks, but I feel that it is the responsibility of the President's office to see that no favored treatment is accorded to some at the expense of helpless children.

Very sincerely, Margaret M. Powers

HHH

PAGE 162: CYRUS VANCE TO JIMMY CARTER, APRIL 21, 1980

Dear Mr. President:
I have the greatest respect and admiration for you and it is with a heavy heart that I submit my resignation. It has been a privilege and a high honor to serve you and our nation. I look with pride and satisfaction at the many actions and new directions which have marked our foreign policy under your leadership. The Panama Canal Treaty, The Camp David Accords, The Egyptian—Israeli Peace Treaty, normalization of relations with the People's Republic of China, the strengthening of our military forces and our alliances, the negotiation of the Salt II Agreement, The Zimbabwe settlement, and the new thrust and direction given to our relations with the nations of the Third World are several of these major steps.

I know how deeply you have pondered your decision on Iran. I wish I could support you in it. But for the reasons we have discussed I cannot. You would not be well served in the coming weeks and months by a Secretary of State who could not offer you the public backing you need on an issue and decision of such extraordinary importance.... Such a situation would be untenable and our relationship, which I value so highly, would constantly suffer. I shall always be grateful to you for having had the opportunity to serve. I shall always have for you the deepest respect and affection, and you know you can count on my support for your continued leadership of our nation.

Respectfully yours, Cy

★★★

PAGE 171: ERIC COLTON TO GEORGE H.W. BUSH, FEBRUARY 12, 1991

Howdy!
My name is Eric Colton, I am a 20 year old Marine serving in Saudi Arabia.... I am stationed out of 29 Palms, California. The reason I am writing to you is to tell you that me and my comrades feel you are doing an outstanding job concerning the Gulf War. My unit is positioned near the Kuwaiti border ready to accomplish any mission we are assigned to do. Morale is high, and everybody believes in what we are fighting for. When we first arrived in this country we felt it could possibly be another Vietnam. During the six months of Operation Desert Shield we knew the United States will not approach Iraq lightly. We respect all of your decisions. We will not let the American people down. As a United States Marine, Mr. President I promise you and the rest of the country we will win this one.

Semper Fidelis,
Eric Colton
Lcpl USMC

Dear Mr. President

Published by the National Geographic Society

John M. Fahey, Jr.
President and Chief Executive Officer

Gilbert M. Grosvenor
Chairman of the Board

Nina D. Hoffman
Executive Vice President

Prepared by the Book Division

Kevin Mulroy
Senior Vice President and Publisher

Staff for this Book

Lisa Lytton
Senior Project Editor

Margaret Johnson
Illustrations Editor/Researcher

Melissa Farris
Art Director/Illustrations Editor

Margo Browning
Text Editor

Maggie Johnson Sliker
Illustrations Specialist

Gary Colbert
Production Director

Rick Wain
Production Project Manager

Manufacturing and Quality Control

Christopher A. Liedel
Chief Financial Officer

Phillip L. Schlosser
Managing Director

One of the world's largest nonprofit scientific and educational organizations, the National Geographic Society was founded in 1888 "for the increase and diffusion of geographic knowledge." Fulfilling this mission, the Society educates and inspires millions every day through its magazines, books, television programs, videos, maps and atlases, research grants, the National Geographic Bee, teacher workshops, and innovative classroom materials. The Society is supported through membership dues, charitable gifts, and income from the sale of its educational products. This support is vital to National Geographic's mission to increase global understanding and promote conservation of our planet through exploration, research, and education.

For more information, please call 1-800-NGS LINE (647-5463) or write to the following address:

National Geographic Society
1145 17th Street N.W.
Washington, D.C. 20036-4688 U.S.A.

Visit the Society's Web site at www.nationalgeographic.com.

This special edition published in 2008

ISBN 978-1-4262-0416-6

ISBN 978-1-4262-0417-3 (deluxe)

Printed in the U.S.A.